SPEAK UP FOR JUST WAR OR PACIFISM

A Critique of the United Methodist Bishops' Pastoral Letter "In Defense of Creation"

BOOKS BY PAUL RAMSEY

The Ethics of Fetal Research
The Patient as Person: Explorations in Medical Ethics
Fabricated Man: The Ethics of Genetic Control
The Just War: Force and Political Responsibility
Deeds and Rules in Christian Ethics
*Who Speaks for the Church? A Critique of the 1966 Geneva Conference on Church and
Society*
Nine Modern Moralists
Christian Ethics and the Sit-In
War and the Christian Conscience: How Shall Modern War Be Conducted Justly?
Basic Christian Ethics

EDITED BY PAUL RAMSEY

The Ethical Writings of Jonathan Edwards
(with John F. Wilson) *The Study of Religion in Colleges and Universities*
(with Gene H. Outka) *Norm and Context in Christian Ethics*
Religion: Humanistic Scholarship in America
Freedom of the Will (by Jonathan Edwards)
Faith and Ethics: The Theology of H. Richard Niebuhr

BOOKS BY STANLEY HAUERWAS

Vision and Virtue: Essays in Christian Ethical Reflection
Character and the Christian Life: A Study in Theological Ethics
Truthfulness and Tragedy: Further Investigations in Christian Ethics
A Community of Character: Toward a Constructive Christian Social Ethic
The Peaceable Kingdom:: A Primer in Christian Ethics
Against the Nations: War and Survival in a Liberal Society
*Suffering Presence: Theological Reflections on Medicine, the Mentally Handicapped, and the
Church*
Christian Existence Today: Essays on Church, World, and Living in Between

SPEAK UP FOR JUST WAR OR PACIFISM

A Critique of the United Methodist Bishops' Pastoral Letter "In Defense of Creation"

Paul Ramsey

Epilogue by
Stanley Hauerwas

THE PENNSYLVANIA STATE UNIVERSITY PRESS
University Park and London

Library of Congress Cataloging-in-Publication Data

Ramsey, Paul.
Speak up for just war or pacifism : a critique of the United
Methodist Bishops' pastoral letter "In defense of creation" / by
Paul Ramsey, with an epilogue by Stanley Hauerwas.
p. cm.
Includes index.
ISBN 0-271-00619-6
ISBN 0-271-00639-0 (pbk.)
1. United Methodist Church (U.S.) Council of Bishops. In defense
of creation.   2. Peace—Religious aspects—Methodist Church.
3. Nuclear warfare—Religious aspects—Methodist Church.
4. Methodist Church—Doctrines.   5. United Methodist Church (U.S.)—
Doctrines.   6. Just war doctrine.   7. Pacifism.   I. Hauerwas,
Stanley, 1940–   .   II. Title.
BX8349.P43R36   1988
241'.6242—dc 19   87-21295
                                                                              CIP

Contents

Editorial Note

The fine-print passages inserted into pages of text may at first puzzle the reader. These are, in effect, substantive footnotes. The text can be read with or without them. Since I hope they will be read, I judge that these notes should not be relegated to the back of the book, where they would be difficult to find. There are no notes at the back of this volume; the fine-print passages contain their own citations. I hope readers will agree that this is a convenient mode of publication today, when substantive notes at the bottom of the page are prohibitively costly.

Published in the year of my seventy-fifth birthday, this book is dedicated expectantly to our first great-grandchild.

Paul Ramsey
Center of Theological Inquiry
Princeton, New Jersey

Introduction

THE first duty of an author is to tell the reader what he holds in his hands. This book is a study in comparative Christian ethics. The *occasion* for my writing it, and for my collaboration with Stanley Hauerwas in doing so, was the United Methodist Bishops' initiative issuing their pastoral letter and related documents entitled *In Defense of Creation: The Nuclear Crisis and a Just Peace: Foundation Document* (FD).

Published by *Graded Press* (201 Eighth Avenue, South, P.O. Box 801, Nashville, Tennessee 37209), 1986. FD will be my reference throughout to the several documents published together in this one volume: Bishop C. Dale White's *Preface*; a *Foreword* recounting some of the history of the episcopal initiative; the *Overview*, intended to be an overall summary (FD, pp. 11–22); the *Foundation Document*, originally so called (pp. 23–90); and the *Pastoral Letter* itself, printed as an appendix (pp. 91–93). The final version of the *Pastoral Letter* is much shorter and therefore less useful than in the first draft. The *Overview* serves as the best introduction. My references will give page numbers only, usually without distinction among these several documents. I shall also refer to the *Guide for Study and Action*, distributed for use by pastors and teachers in local churches.

This publication was the occasion for deep disappointment Hauerwas and I shared over the theological, ethical, and political inadequacy of this first recent venture of our Bishops in exercising as a council the capacity of chief pastors and teachers of the church.

This was the beginning. Moreover, I should say here at the outset that the Methodist Bishops' episcopal initiative is never left behind in the much larger purpose of the later chapters of the present volume. Their text is analyzed with exact and exacting detail: No higher respect can be accorded any document. Throughout (and especially in the final chapter) I have also been assiduously searching for those conditions and procedures that might enable the church to gain its authentic voice in instruction and in moral exhortation directed to its own members and to our fellow citizens on urgent public questions all of us face in the late twentieth century. If there is a tone of passion whenever I touch *In Defense of Creation*, I ask the reader to believe this is because it is *my* church we're talking about. If there is fault to be found, it is systemic; and besides, I'd rather criticize the seminary faculties that train future bishops than anyone individually.

So the Methodist pastoral letter was the occasion. This explains why I dare to begin with theological criticism in the first chapter, "Biblical and Theological Foundations," postponing specific ethical analysis until the third. Indeed, both the first and second chapters are biblical and theological, since, in the second, I select a single theme from the U.S. Catholic Bishops' pastoral letter, *The Challenge of Peace: God's Promise and Man's Response* (May 3, 1983), for comparison with the Methodist letter. This theme is the error of too closely identifying Christ's kingdom with world peace. From this small beginning in chapter 2, called "An Ecumenical Interlude," the volume offers, in the whole of it, a study in "comparative pastorals" on war and peace issues in the nuclear age.

The third chapter, "Thinking about Just Peace in the Nuclear Age," fulfills the title of the volume: *Speak Up for Just War or Pacifism*, or be sure you know what you're saying. This is the longest chapter so far and may be the first really to engage some readers. But deep flaws in the Bishops' moral reasoning about war and peace, and their failure to understand fully either Christian just-war teaching or Christian pacifism, follow from the operational absence of great relevant themes of a Christian theological context. Our bishops' "writers" seriously failed them in work on the foundations. As a result, the superstructure of moral-political argument won't hold together.

In the fourth chapter, "An Ecumenical Consultation," a comparison of ecclesial positions on war and deterrence in a nuclear age is the promised task, now fully articulated. I do not invent this "consultation," or carry it out in my own mind or sole authorship. Instead, the pastoral letters of two great churches are set beside one another. I analyze the explanations of selected just-war criteria in the Methodist and the U.S. Catholic pastoral letters for comparison and contrast—and in the light of this, give my own renewed reflection on the meaning of these norms. Then I enlarge the ecumenical character of the discussion by including a text of Christian pacifism. This third "participant" is John Howard Yoder, widely recognized as an able, fresh, and articulate spokesman for Christian pacifism, whose own writings are more ecumenically directed than those of other pacifists, with the possible exception of Stanley Hauerwas.

In the fifth and final chapter, I turn to the desperate problem—for which there may be only least bad solutions—of how in substance and procedurally the church (whether through bishops, boards, councils, or committees) can speak with authenticity, from Christian warrants, for itself to itself and to the world of today on any of the complex, particular, and fateful choices we face in our common life. It may be that in the very formulation of my question—"*for* the church, *to* the church, and *to* the world"—I already uncover an area of disagreement between myself and Hauerwas: He may wish to say that, especially on war and peace, the church's moral insight and message should primarily be directed *to* the church, not minimized or made double-minded by attempting at the same time to speak to the nation, or to ourselves *as* citizens *as such.*

The following are some of the questions that will be raised in the course of these pages. To answer them should be of interest not only to church people but also to anyone outside the churches who is concerned enough about war and peace to want to know what Christians may be saying and teaching.

****What do people—and various parties or positions—mean by "non-violence" in a Christian context?*

****What is the bottom-line assumption of Christian pacifism and of Christian just-war teaching? What does each recognize as "that than which nothing can be more evident" about the Christian moral life?*

****Are there different interpretations of the person and work of Jesus Christ in Christian pacifism and in Christian just-war participation?*

****Are Christian pacifism and just-war statecraft irreducibly different but equally valid options for disciples of Jesus Christ? How can this be so?*

****Do the tests of discrimination and proportion lead to the same moral prohibitions on war and in war in the nuclear age?*

I should also say at least something in this introduction about the "justifiable war" tradition I have espoused for many years as a Christian ethicist, and which I have sought to apply to modern warfare. An indication of his own viewpoint is a second thing readers are owed by an author, if for no other reason than to enable them to begin to correct for bias (which no one can accomplish alone).

In military policy there are two principles that are rightly used to divide the "truth to be done" or never done: discrimination and proportion. The former—don't tie babies to bumpers in order to get safely to a journey's end or in order to control the traffic along the way—tells us, in war, always to aim at lethal machines and their operators, never deliberately enlarge the target to include the civil society of an adversary. During the "peace" obtainable by deterrence, it tells us never to enter into a bargain with a potential adversary in which we both make ourselves "conditionally will-ing" to murder each other's babies provided the other does so first, or to prevent each other from doing so. The latter—economy of force—tells us always to choose the least destructive, least lethal, force necessary. We use "proportionable reason" also when we judge that violent resistance of evil must be used instead of nonviolent resistance (neither of which can be equated with Christ's reconciling, nonresisting love).

The nuclear crisis presently upon us consists in a possible or actual systemic violation of either or both of these principles. By these measures, Mutual Assured Destruction and Mutual Assured Defense are both MAD policies.

To move toward defense, and the moral reformation of deterrence, is the mini-mum responsibility of states in the protection of the people they govern. That must be the manifold work of political intelligence and action. If the only alternative is "the arcane logic of the nuclear age" (that peace can be preserved only by *not* defending people), then the great powers are (in President Eisenhower's words) "doomed malevolently to eye each other across a trembling world." Nuclear weap-ons are not going to be un-invented. Still, Mutual *Assured* Defense is a pipe dream, in this or any other age. To seek such assurance—survivability by any means—disposes us as a people to wickedness in thought and action. If the churches address questions of military policy, and their members as citizens, they should be unceas-ing in quest of a moral deterrent, nuclear or non-nuclear—that is, one that neither gives up defense nor targets populations as such.

How did we come to these stark alternatives of total war or total deter-rence by shared threat of total war? Not from fear alone, but from too much hope—or hope misplaced. When John Foster Dulles, Eisenhower's Secre-tary of State, headed the National Council of Churches' Commission on the Church and International Affairs, a report was issued bearing his stamp of authorship and entitled "A Just and Durable Peace." Our Bishops share this hope for a "just and durable" world peace. *At the time*, H. Richard Niebuhr, my teacher at Yale, observed that a "just endurable" peace was all we had reason to hope for or aim at. I have sometimes used that expression without quotation marks in articles, only to have it "corrected" by some editor to "just and durable."

Drunk from too many nips from the flask of the Enlightenment, states-men and churchmen alike are condemned to dreaming either unearthly military schemes or impossible political dreams. The former are tempted to believe that military technology provides the fix seemingly sustaining those dreams; so Total Peace/Total Defense and Total War are machine-built to embrace each other. The latter are tempted to believe that, over time, the reform of international institutions will produce a "world order changing orderly"; church people are urged to engage in peacekeeping and peace-making by institutional-work-righteousness in hope of success at the end of the line. These are nice illustrations, I'd say, and a fitting outcome of the identification of world peace (always just endurable, sometimes unendurable) with the peace that passes understanding, since the eighteenth-century Enlightenment brought the Heavenly City down to the level of historical possibility.

Just above I used the words "condemned *to* dreaming." This expression of mine has also been "corrected" by the insertion of "(*sic*)" after the word "to," suggesting that I meant "condemned *for* dreaming"! Perhaps I should have used the verb "condemned *to dream* impossible dreams" instead of a gerund. I use the gerund again here in order to stress how pervasive utopianism is in our culture. Right-wingers, Centrists, and Left-leaners in national politics, or running for high office, must do obeisance to hopes that have no operative effect on their decisions concerning practices or policies between which there is *real* choice. Likely also they *believe* those hopes; this only shows that placing hope in earthly peace is an *archetypal* cultural dream.

In their analysis of the morality of the use of nuclear weapons in war or to deter it, the U.S. Catholic Bishops rightly used the two principles, discrimination and proportion. No pastoral letter should be without these principles. No pastoral letter should abuse their meaning. As we will see, our Methodist Bishops used these principles, and other just-war tests, *in passing*. As we proceed, the reader should not suppose that "just war" criteria are the peculiar property of Roman Catholics in their address to states. Our Methodist Bishops do not. After all, before the Reformation there was only the common Christian tradition; and the celebrated "rule of double effect" can be found in the Puritan divine William Ames's *Cases of Conscience*. I have not the time or space here to demonstrate again that these two principles, especially discrimination, devolve from a *charitable* quest for justice in our conflict-prone world. This will be the task of chapters to come.

See William Ames, *Conscience with the Power and Cases Thereof* (1639), Bk. V, p. 187. The passage is in answer to Question 6: *Whether in no case it bee lawfull to kill ones self*. Answers 2 and 4 are worth quoting in full:

A.2. It doth not excuse this sinne, though it bee done for the avoydance of any great evils whatsoever, or for the getting any great good whatsoever: or for revenge upon our selves for our sinnes past. For no man is a competent Judge to decree such a thing upon himself: Nor is evill to bee done, that good may come thereof, or that other evils may not follow; and therefore in vaine is the fact of *Saul* by some excused, who fell upon his sword, lest hee should have been mocked by God and his enemies; I Sam. 31.4.

A.4. It is lawfull too sometimes to expose ones self to such a danger, by which death must necessarily though indirectly follow. So a souldier may keepe his Station, or obey any command of his Leader though hee know hee shall therein bee killed. So *Sampson* (out of singular instinct) did *directly* intend to kill the Philistins and not himself, although hee foresaw that his owne death must follow. Judg. 16.30. And somewhat like is the case of those, who with gun-powder blow up the ship they are in, lest the Enemy should possess her. For they do not directly intend to kill themselves, but disadvantage the Enemy.

In the next question, Ames defines an action "done by chance," including "the casuall killing of a man," as that "which is done beside the scope and intention of the Doer." In current U.S. constitutional law the wavering line between church and state is determined according to whether the action or policy of a public entity has the promotion of religion as its immediate *objective* and *primary* effect. Nothing shows the bankruptcy of contemporary moral philosophy more than the common talk about morality without distinguishing among actions according to whether they are *beside* or *within* the scope of the intention of the Doer.

I believe also that only by taking the two principles in "lexical" order can we keep quite clear the *distinction* between and separate application of judgments of discrimination and judgments of proportion. Beyond question these two sorts of prohibitions do converge in a possible outbreak of all-out use of massive strategic weapons and in peacekeeping by mutual "horrifying" seriously intended. By "lexical" order I mean that discrimination is logically prior to proportion in reasoning about what to do in conflict cases, even when the two modes of analysis do converge in the same verdict; and when they do not, no good sought or evil to be prevented, however great, can justify deliberately aiming at populations as such, as direct targets in war or for deterrence's sake. One should never do evil, or intend to do evil, that good may come.

This means that counter-people war and hostage-people deterrence are indiscriminate; they also exhibit a disproportion between arms and political purpose. Here the criteria do converge in utterly condemning any war policy that uses or seriously threatens to use strategic nuclear weapons directly against population centers. By these measures, we also should not hesitate to condemn any peacekeeping by means of the shared deterrent effect of a Faustian bargain to use nuclear weapons so.

Enough for now, in brief outline of the point of view the principal author of this volume brings to the discussion, which the reader is invited to join. I venture to reprint, in the Appendix, a revision of part of an article I submitted to the Bishops' drafting committee. This will be in further explication of what I call "graduated deterrence."

A third and final point is needed to introduce the reader to the present volume, namely, some account of how the United Methodist Church came to adopt into its statement of Social Principles, without much thought about what this would mean in practice, a pacifism that floats above questions of the responsible use of power. Some time ago it ceased to be a Methodist virtue to mean what we say politically by limiting ourselves to saying only what *can* be meant, and by spelling out how we mean whatever we say to mean.

In their account of the United Methodist heritage in witness for peace and world order, the Bishops cite the following passage from our Social Principles, first adopted by General Conference, meeting in Atlanta in 1972:

> We believe war is incompatible with the teachings and example of Christ. We therefore reject war as an instrument of national foreign policy and insist that the first moral duty of all nations is to resolve by peaceful means every dispute that arises between or among them. (FD, p. 20)

My notes on how this paragraph emerged in the Study Commission (chaired by Bishop James Thomas), which formulated the new statement of social principles for consideration and adoption by General Conference, may be of some interest to readers of the analysis of *In Defense of Creation* that Hauerwas and I offer here. Members of the Study Commission had before us the following paragraph from our new "writer" (the first having been discharged after two years' work with us)—along with a multitude of other proposed social principles—for revision and adoption by the Commission at a single, final meeting:

> International armed conflict has characterized our world for as long as anyone can remember. We reject all war as destructive of human persons and their societies and press for the day when nations shall forego war and the threat of war as instruments of policy. Toward that end, we support efforts at arms control and disarmament and the elimination of the military dominance of the economies of the world.

The explanation given of this paragraph was the trivially obvious one that, of course, war is "destructive." In the discussion that ensued, it was pointed out in reply that war may be justified if there are no other options for the correction of a *more* destructive evil. It was pointed out that the statement condemns the war that brought Hitler down, and all Christians who served in it as in error; and that it likewise would condemn the then-recent action of the Indian government (and any Indian Christians who participated in it) in East Bengal to stop an internal violent turmoil far more destructive to persons and to their society than the armed action itself.

It was the Commission's procedure, after we had generally discussed the writer's penultimate draft of the Social Principles in its entirety, to appoint subgroups to meet, discuss further, and revise main sections of the Principles. "Working parties," for example, went to work on the draft on such topics as Civil Disobedience, Crime and Rehabilitation, and Military Service (Pt. V. The Political Community), and on War and Peace and (International) Justice and Law (Pt. VI. The World Community). The Social Principles are printed and reprinted as revised every four years by General Conference in the Book of Discipline of the United Methodist Church. Naturally, there is a continuing struggle for the heart and soul of the church temporal. Among Methodists this takes the form of passion for victory over *particulars*, on which we yield to none despite the animus at home and irrelevance abroad to which we are led. This is also why neither the Board of Church and Society, nor General Conference, nor the Council of Bishops can be expected to do better *without some major reformation of their procedures.*

The paragraph our Bishops quote from the Social Principles would, if or when taken seriously, mean that Methodist men and women should come out of the armed services and related industries. It, too, is an example—Hauerwas and I would agree—of "be sure you know what you're saying," or "Speak Up for Just War or Pacifism." The working party responsible for the topic War and Peace brought back to the Commission as a whole two proposals—the first, half in jest. But only half in jest.

> A. We reject all war.
> B. We believe that war is incompatible with the teachings and example of Christ. We therefore must reject war as an instrument of national policy, and insist that the first moral duty of all nations is to resolve by peaceful means all disputes that arise among or between them; that human values must out-weigh military claims as governments determine their priorities; that the militarization of society

must be challenged and stopped; and that the manufacture, sale, and deployment of arms must be limited and controlled.

I pointed out that if there is any war that is justified it is "an instrument of national policy" and that the war we should really worry about is a war that is not and cannot be an instrument of national policy (i.e., nuclear war)—which is only made more likely by sweeping pacifist statements such as both A and B. I also pointed out that "military claims" should not be set over against "human values," that if they are warranted military claims it is because weighty human values are at stake (just as property is not a right if it is not one among the human rights). Then I proposed, in effect, three amendments. First, I proposed that the first line read: "We believe that war is *ultimately* incompatible with the teachings and example of Christ." That would be like inserting "*ultimately* contrary" or "contrary to the *perfect* will of God" in a statement to the effect that "war is contrary to the will of God." This was defeated 5 to 4. (A commissioner with me in the airport limousine twenty minutes later observed that we hadn't had a quorum for the last hour! I myself didn't know whether we were under that parliamentary requirement or not.) Second, I proposed that the second sentence read: "We insist that the first moral duty of all nations is to resolve by peaceful means all disputes that arise among or between them"—striking out the words "therefore must reject war as an instrument of national policy." This was defeated 6 to 4. (I might add here that for lack of better thought the working group and the Commission reached back into ecumenical ethics to get this stock expression—which I had subjected to at least weighty criticism in *Who Speaks for the Church?*) Third, I proposed that the words "and stopped" be stricken out—because it could be understood to presume a question of fact that is arguably false, that is, that our nation was militarized.

Since none of these mitigating amendments was accepted, I do not see how the verdict voiced by Professor Douglas Jackson, a commissioner who teaches social ethics at Perkins School of Theology, could be denied: If adopted by the General Conference, the paragraph would commit our church to a pacifist position for all its sons and daughters, and to a pacifist position for the nation—unilaterally. No significant change was made, and the Final Report forwarded to the 1972 General Conference read:

> *War and Peace.* We believe war is incompatible with the teaching and example of Christ. We therefore reject war as an instrument of national policy and insist that the first moral duty of all nations is to resolve by peaceful means every dispute that arises between or

among them; that human values must outweigh military claims as
governments determine their priorities; that the militarization of
society must be challenged and stopped; and that the manufacture,
sale, and deployment of arms must be reduced and controlled.

The Bishops quote from this paragraph in their pastoral.

For consistency, the Commission should have gone back and revised the
last line of its statement on Military Service to read: "We also support those
persons who choose *in erring conscience* to serve in the armed forces, while
urging them to go only so far as to accept alternate service." The words "in
good conscience" were in identical sentences (on decisions to participate in
military service) in both alternative paragraphs brought to the Commission
as a whole by the working group; and they were, I believe, in the final
revision the Commission adopted. Our statement read in any draft I ever
saw, "We also support those who choose *in good conscience* to serve in the
armed forces or to accept alternative service." Did redactors drop "in good
conscience" from the report that went to General Conference? If so, was the
change made in order to shorten the sentence, because the words seemed
unnecessary; or because the redactors felt there was some contradiction
between *renouncing war* as an instrument of national policy and supporting
the *good* conscience of those who serve in military forces? If the latter, a
more forthright change would have been to mention the *error* of their
subjectively conscientious decision to serve in the military, and to urge
them to accept alternative service instead. Or else, the section on War and
Peace was the one that needed revision.

On the specific matter of military service, the Commission began with
our writer's paragraph:

> Enforced military service, including conscription of civilian labor, is
> not only an affront to free men; it is contrary to the Gospel, *which
> asserts each person's right to live his own life so long as he does not
> endanger the welfare of his fellows.* We support the individual who
> conscientiously is opposed to all war or to any particular war and
> therefore refuses to serve in the armed forces. We also support those
> who choose in good conscience to serve in the armed forces or to
> accept alternate service.

The Commission in general, and the working group of which I was a
member, agreed that the draft before us was entirely unacceptable in its
identification of the Gospel with doing one's own thing so long as one does

not endanger anyone else. So the words I italicized above were stricken. But we were not agreed on coercion as appropriate to government action; for example, in a broad system of national service and in maintaining adequate military forces. Because of severe lack of time to probe further, two proposals were brought back to the Commission as a whole, the first drawn up by Bishop Ward, the second by Ramsey.

(A) In as much as governments of free people rest upon the support of conscientious citizens, we believe that involuntary military service is not only an affront to free men but in conflict with the Gospel. We must hold in fellowship in the church all who hold sincerely differing points of view as Christians regarding military service. We support the individual who conscientiously is opposed to all war or to any particular war and therefore refuses to serve in the armed forces. We also support those who choose in good conscience to serve in the armed forces or to accept alternate service.

(B) We support the individual who conscientiously is opposed to all war or to any particular war and therefore refuses to serve in the armed forces. We also support those who choose in good conscience to serve in the armed forces or to accept alternate service. To relieve this agony of conscience of our youth, we urge serious consideration of the feasibility of a system of voluntary military services. Such a system should be adopted if it can be seen to meet the needs of national security, if it would not bear with great injustice upon the classes of young men who would be induced to serve, and if it would not produce professional military services more alienated from the common life.

I attempted to state objective conditions under which it might on balance be right to abolish the peacetime draft and move instead to voluntary military service. I confess that I could not then, nor can I now, understand why sober and informed church people can ignore the possibly countervailing three tests, set down in (B) above, for evaluating whether voluntary armed services would actually work out to the good of a nation and with fairness to poor or black inductees. Was it that to say something affirmative about making and keeping service in the military a more *just* system was too much complicity in the war system, like commending those who in good conscience serve in the military? Like saying there may be justified war? In any case, the paragraph submitted to General Conference read:

Military Service. Though coercion, violence, and war are presently the ultimate sanctions in international relations, we reject them as incompatible with the Gospel and Spirit of Christ. We therefore reject national policies of enforced military service as likewise incompatible with the Gospel. Nevertheless, we acknowledge the agonizing tension created by the demand for military service by national governments. Thus, we support those individuals who conscientiously oppose all war or any particular war and therefore refuse to serve in the armed forces. We also support those persons who choose to serve in the armed forces or to accept alternate service.

Observe that opposition to all war or to particular wars was described as at least subjectively "conscientious," while even that word was omitted from support of persons who choose to serve. (That imbalance has subsequently been corrected.) Earlier, in the paragraph on Civil Obedience and Civil Disobedience, the Commission had refused to include the following statement proposed by the working subgroup at our final session: "In accord with the principles of the New Testament we affirm our respect for properly constituted civil authority. We affirm both *love of country* and love of all men" (my italics).

My notes on the coming into existence of the part of our Social Principles relevant to *In Defense of Creation* are, I am confident, accurate in all important respects. Since I did not believe the report sent to General Conference would greatly assist the Holy Spirit to work his will in Atlanta, I was with a minority varying from four to six as we approved the document paragraph by paragraph.

I hope that those who continue to read these pages will believe my good faith in saying that the system, the procedures, fail the people (i.e., the Bishops) involved in them. (To mention only one thing: Methodist Bishops are busy administrators who lack both time and theological advisors on their staffs.) I respect, for example, both "writers" who served the Social Principles Commission; the first continues on his way rejoicing in good works at church ethics, while the second now feels freed from the constant pressure to hew to the line of current ecclesial "orthodox" social teaching (e.g., the gaff he received upon publishing an article of mine!). I have not the contentment of the former with the direction in which our church is being led, nor can I break free from it as did the second. Hence, my renewed search for a better way of speaking *for* the church *to* the church, *to* one another *as citizens* of this nation, and *to* the world of today an authentic Christian word, if, perchance, it may be heard. Theologians and Christian ethicists do not speak for the United Methodist Church. General Conference alone does. I have sometimes wondered, however, what sort of report would have been sent to General Conference, for its debate and action, if the members of the Social Principles Commission had been Methodist scholars and teachers of Christian ethics in colleges and seminaries of our church—instead of the extraordinary mixture of classes of people that actually composed our group. To be sure, there would have been no less a variety of clashing opinions, but maybe the issues latent in many things said would have been better understood and deliberated. Maybe General Conference would have been better served to work its will. Was there not a better way, I have asked myself, to assist the Holy Spirit?

There is a story yet to be told about the origins of the section on abortion in the Social Principles (Pt. II. The Nurturing Community), its revision on the floor of the 1972 conference (a sentence inserted at the wrong place), and subsequent revision joining that sentence with the previous one and *restricting* what the church declares it believes about abortion and the law. The sentence now reads: "In continuity with past Christian teaching, we recognize tragic conflict of life with life that may [morally] justify abortion, and *in such cases* support the legal option of abortion under proper medical procedures" (1984 *Book of Discipline*; my italics). I am assured by persons in a position to know that this limitation was a deliberate action, not an inadvertent consequence of "Revising papers line by line / Diverts the mind from Things Divine" (Boulding, below).

An earlier episode in this continuing story involved stopping the Religious Coalition for Abortion Rights from using the name of the United Methodist Church in full-page advertisements in the Sunday editions of the *New York Times* and the *Washington Post* in December 1981. Readers of this volume need to know more about this episode in order to be minimally informed concerning the "polity"—the governance—of the United Methodist Church. For I mean to address anyone who (1) is concerned about a rudderless church, his own or mine, or who (2) hoped and prayed that our Bishops could devise procedures enabling them to resume leadership as chief pastors and teachers of the church. Our highest authority—General Conference, meeting for ten days or two weeks every four years—may not be the wisest or best deliberative body that could be imagined. But sometimes wondrous things can happen. Instruction in church administration (or the lack of it) need not be utterly bereft of amusement. So I will continue the story about those abortion ads by printing here a letter of mine that was published in the New Jersey *Methodist Relay*, December 1981–January 1982:

To the Editor:
  Who speaks for the United Methodist Church? Only *the General Conference.*
  Doesn't the Discipline *say that? The* Discipline *is a book few laypeople ever see. But every Methodist minister has one. And the rules of our church plainly reserves to General Conference, in session every four years, and to these conferences alone, the rightful power to speak for Methodists in "the U.S. of A." (as we Southerners say). To speak for me, that is. And for you.*

And what happens when General Conference speaks for the United Methodist Church? For you and me? There is a Book of Resolutions in which are recorded what General Conference says when speaking for our church.

I've never seen that Book (or any of the Resolutions), but I understand there is one. There one goes—and only there—to find out what stands have been taken on public and moral issues in our name.

Be patient with me; I'm only trying to understand: just a few more questions. . . . Could it be the case, I ask myself, that one of those Resolutions delegates to somebody else the rightful power to speak for Methodists, to speak for you and me? Somebody's been doing precisely that; so there must be some explanation. How came it about that another group claims to speak for the Methodist Church when only General Conference can do that? Could that be merely because of one of those Resolutions—delegating what's reserved to General Conference to one group or another not the General Conference?

I should say not. If there is such a "resolution" written somewhere, it is null and void— a contradiction of the Discipline of the United Methodist Church. No single session of General Conference could by resolution alienate itself of the rightful power—exclusive of all other groups—to speak for Methodists. Nor could such a resolution—passed repeatedly by a dozen General Conferences, meeting every four years over a period of half a century—gather the strength to throw away speaking in our name, or convey it into the hands of some other body or group.

The only way that could be done would be by changing the Methodist "rule book"—the Discipline—which plainly states that General Conference alone speaks for United Methodists. Since this has not been done, you and I should know who's responsible, and by what procedures, for what's said in the name of Methodists. Disagree we may. But if we disagree, by the constitution of our church we have the right to know where to locate the decision-maker and the decision-making we question when things are said and done in our name.

Good point, you may say, but why all the questions? What's the trouble? Just this enormity:

On two Sunday mornings within the past month I have opened my New York Times and found facing me full-page ads placed by something called the Religious Coalition for Abortion Rights. Listed among the sponsors was the United Methodist Church.

No ifs, ands, or buts. It did not say these five Bishops by name or for that matter fifty. It did not say such and such conference or Methodist body in N.Y. State. It did not say the Washington Office, or for that matter the whole Board of Church and Society. I could easily distance from any such group within our church. I could say they didn't speak for me nor did they claim to do so. The ad said—plain as day—the United Methodist Church! That's the problem.

For, you see, I don't want to have to take out ads saying that the Religious Coalition for Abortion Rights doesn't speak for the Methodist Church, and so not for me—and not, perhaps, for you. Besides, that organization isn't supposed to observe the Discipline. Methodists are, and all our boards and agencies.

One ad was scandalous in its equation of the freedom of elective abortion (now a holocaust of 1,400,000 a year, afflicting as a main group teens and pre-teens) with First Amendment religious liberty. It was stupidly ill-informed about the variety of bills and amendments now before Congress. There were no nuances for difference of specific opinion as to the least worst solution of this terrible problem.

Not to be drawn into discussing the substantive issue of abortion and public policy, I had to say that much about the ads in order to say this: mere consistency with some General Conference resolution, or one line in our Social Creed, is not enough to warrant using the name of the United Methodist Church—my name, your name—on those ads. Mere consistency is not enough, since the ad said it spoke for, among others, our church.

If one day I decide to cease to be a member of the Methodist Church, I just want to know that it is not necessary for me also to withdraw my (implied) membership in the Religious Coalition for Abortion Rights. And on that day I would need to know that it was my church that departed too far from me, and from what seem to me to be Christian principles, and not the RCAR claiming to speak in her name, in my name—and perhaps in yours.

Paul Ramsey
Department of Religion
Princeton, New Jersey

An abbreviated version of this letter was published in the *Circuit Rider*, February 1982. (A copy was sent also to *Good News*.) Some time later I received a telephone call from one of our Bishops—I suppose, but do not know, a Bishop connected with the operations of our Board of Church and Society in the Methodist Building in Washington, D.C., where space was (and still is?) rented to the Religious Coalition for Abortion Rights. He wanted to know the dates of those ads. I didn't remember but said it must have been in November/December of 1981. I received the impression that the Bishop thought something should be done about the abuse of our church's name. I had forgotten all this until quite some time later, when I received a letter from someone in Church and Society saying the RCAR would no longer be allowed to use our church's name "until they got their theology straight." Theology? I thought that funny; but I rejoiced over the good one individual soul can do sometimes. Then I felt sad, thinking of quite a number of women over the years— prominent Methodist women, if that matters—who have spoken or written to me with desperation/exasperation, asking if anything could be done about the *Women's Division* of the United Methodist Church—which presumes to speak *for them* in ways they as Christians do not understand. On those ads, for example!

At the Southeastern Jurisdictional Convocation (Junaluska) I had several conversations with an able worker in the vineyards of one of the Methodist offices in Nashville. From him I learned more about many fine things our church is accomplishing in social action. On the problem of a rudderless church, however, he was in agreement with me. He said our policy once was tripartite, legislative, executive, judiciary: General Conference was the legislature; the Bishops, the executive. I knew there was a judicial system, from a section in my father's *Discipline* entitled "The Trial of a Deaconess," which fascinated me as a lad because I read that to be the *trials* of a deaconess! I asked him, "You mean that someone could have brought charges against ——— for ordaining ——— contrary to the plain statement on homosexual *practice* in our Social Principles? That Methodist women could have some recourse against the *Women's Division*?" He, hesitating, said Yes. He was mistaken, and I misled—to a degree. Our Social Principles do not have *juridical* status; requirements for ordination to the ministry do. Among these requirements is "responsible self-control," which includes "fidelity in marriage and celibacy in singleness" (*Discipline*, par. 404.4). This states one of the grounds for which a minister may be suspended. Having for many years defended the proposition that there are binding moral *principles* (which is one reason I think we should not have so many of them), I forgot for a moment that, even so, there need not be a *law* for every unexceptionable principle. Not even all of Moses' Law can be legislated.

I myself do not know the reform needed in administration. Still, anyone can see that without specific locus of moral and spiritual leadership, structured as a continuing deliberative body, furnished with the resources needed to lead, there must be a constant political struggle over the mind and heart of the church—which then is hardly worth winning except as backing for using the Methodist Building to launch lobbying the Congress. Which would not be so bad, if one could be sure the church was being truly *represented*, and that the church spoke only as the church for the church (and not for partisan causes) at General Conference.

One has to cultivate a sense of humor, and/or irony, in these matters. So I dug out of my files a mimeographed publication of "Verses inspired by attendance at various meetings of the National Council of Churches Department of the Church and Economic Life, 1950–1959," by Kenneth Boulding, entitled *A Decade of Unofficial Minutes*. Kenneth Boulding, member of the Society of Friends and distinguished economist and author, penned these verses instead of doodling while he and other members (including myself) tried to express the voice of the church on questions of national and world economy. We served together, years ago, in my first participation in ecumenical ethics, when "Church and Economic Life" was still the bastion of the "social gospel" movement. He has given me permission to publish here a selection of "stanzas" from different poems that struck me, again, as especially delightful—and pertinent to the pages to come.

> Revising papers, page by page,
> Can try the patience of a sage.
> Revising papers, line by line,
> Diverts the mind from Things Divine.
> Revising papers, word by word,
> Borders on the patently Absurd.
> This all comes from our predilection
> For unattainable perfection.

> Although not everybody buys
> The law of Christian compromise
> We cannot comfortably sit
> With bigot, or with hypocrite
> So let us all get in and fight
> For what we are not sure is right.

Introduction

We all agree we have been led
To think that something should be said.
One difficulty bars the way—
We don't agree on what to say.
We question if we have the gall
To issue anything at all.

So let us sprinkle with theology
This vast explosion of technology
With one conclusion in the lead—
The Christian Life is hard indeed.

We all believe in conservation
And nobody denounces Mother
But sad dilemmas face the nation
When one good contradicts another.

Niebuhr
How can we come to terms with Justice
When pure equality would best us?
And can we (short of Heaven above)
Deal with the troubling thought of Love?

And finally—to be pondered especially today, when *at least* every Christian
believes he or she knows what should be done about injustice in Africa or
South and Central America—this late-afternoon meditation:

4:30 p.m.
So lastly we should mention
In ringing down the curtain
We favor intervention
Provided it's uncertain.

    I wish to thank Professor Joseph L. Allen of Perkins School of Theology,
Southern Methodist University, Professor Theodore R. Weber of Chandler
School of Theology, Emory University, Professor Timothy P. Jackson of
Department of Religious Studies, Stanford University, J. Bryan Hehir, Secre-
tary, Department of Social Development and World Peace at the United
States Catholic Conference and Senior Research Scholar at the Kennedy
Institute of Ethics, Georgetown University, James T. Johnson, Professor of
Religion and Director of International Programs, Rutgers University, Cath-

leen Kaveny, graduate student in Religious Ethics at Yale University, and, of course, Professor Stanley Hauerwas, Duke University Divinity School, for reading my manuscript at one stage or another and for giving me the benefit of their comments. Cindy Masterson did the typing.

This volume is sent forth as a contribution to the discussion that my bishops invited in *In Defense of Creation*. To revert once more to intra-church talk—and a bit of special pleading—I add that any Methodist pastor or current graduate student reading the pastoral letter who was not assigned lengthy readings from Ramsey, together with John Howard Yoder and Stanley Hauerwas, during his or her seminary education may want to catch up. Perhaps the catch-up can start with *Speak Up for Just War or Pacifism*.

1

Biblical and Theological Foundations

WE live in an age when *the world as we know it* could come to an end at any moment. In that night there will be two men in one silo; one shall be taken and the other shall be left. There shall be two women holding hands in a human chain nonviolently resisting the launching of a Trident submarine in Groton, Connecticut; a native American, a black, and a Hispanic will be linked together in "Hands Across America" for aid for the hungry; Bishop C. Dale White of New York and Governor Mario Cuomo with their "parishioners" will be protesting the opening of the Shoreham Nuclear Power Plant on Long Island; Pat Robertson, Jerry Falwell, and Andrea Dworkin will be picketing a pornographic bookstore: One shall be taken and the other shall be left. Let him that is aloft on air-force alert, or at work in the Upper Room Publishing House, not come down to take out things that are in his house. And let them that are in the field with the Witness for Peace along the Nicaraguan border not return back for their cloaks. Let them that are in Judea flee unto the mountains. Woe unto them that are with child and to them that give suck in those days! And pray that your flight be not in the nuclear winter, neither on the sabbath: for then shall be great tribulation, such as hath not been from the beginning of the world. For as the lightning cometh forth from the east, and is seen even unto the west, so shall be the coming of the Son of Man.

So the nuclear crisis can be no more than the *second* most urgent crisis confronting humankind in the present aeon that stretches from the First to the Second Advent. That said, the prevention of nuclear war is the great overhanging challenge to Christian discernment and Christian social action during this time of God's patience. In all we do, however, we should remember that, when the Lord comes to put principalities and powers under his feet, he will ask not whether there is peace but whether there is any faith in the earth.

I wish to thank the sacred Scriptures for first suggesting these opening paragraphs to me. Any errors of interpretation are, of course, strictly my own.

The Council of Bishops of the United Methodist Church proposes to the churches a *new* theology for a just peace (FD, pp. 23, 35). Now, in theology the truth is not new, nor is the new apt to be true—especially not if a *new language* has to be invented in which to say it (i.e., "primal" and "consequent" issues, and an *ethics* of reciprocity where an *invitation* to reciprocity is the meaning).

I am bound to say first of all that our Bishops' address to the question of a just peace in the nuclear age is seriously flawed theologically: seriously flawed (1) in its understanding of Creation, (2) in its understanding of the responsibilities of citizens in the bent and broken political communities through which the church is on pilgrimage during the "meanwhile" of this aeon, and (3) in its doctrine of Last Things toward which God's Creation, Providence, and Redemption move from the Fall of Man to the End of the World. Simply put, no profound doctrine of Creation, of Sin, or of Last Things is the source of our Bishops' address to the nuclear crisis. By "Last Things" I also mean, of course, "Ultimate Things." Any lack in these sources is bound to result in a corresponding lack in political wisdom brought to any problem in any age.

1. "[T]he Creation itself is under attack," we are told (FD, pp. 6, 11, 92); and the title of our Bishops' address to the churches is *In Defense of Creation*. The word "creation" is, of course, a theological term for a theological concept. "Creator" and "creation" go together. "Creation" is not a term from geology, or any other science. If our Bishops mean mainly something ecological (as in the prominent identical paragraphs of both their Letter and the Foundation Document), they should say so without using "creation" alternatively with "earth." The fact that the Bishops were thinking more about ecocatastrophe than about God and his creation may, more subtly, be indicated by the fact that both "creation" and "earth" were capitalized in the first and final draft; lowercase for both words was the work of a copy editor. Rather to be regretted, in my opinion, is the printed version's use of lowercase when speaking of the exposure of "earthlings" to possible ozone depletion (FD, p. 38)! That may have been ecological outreach to other

living species, or it may have been overreaching for "inclusive" language; it is certainly not the language of theology—old or new.

Bishop White's account of the genesis of the Bishops' initiative makes quite clear that their concern was ecological: "We were startled by new scientific data that shows a nuclear exchange may have even more grave consequences for the human family than we knew. . . . [F]rom a meeting of some one hundred physicists, biologists, and atmospheric scientists in Washington, D.C., came even more distressing news" (FD, p. 7). The meeting to which Bishop White refers, on the topic "The World after Nuclear War," was held quite some time ago, in Washington, D.C., Oct. 31–Nov. 1, 1983 (see "Nuclear Winter: Global Consequences of Multiple Nuclear Explosions," *Science*, Dec. 23, 1983). Reports of this meeting of atmospheric and other scientists triggered and largely shaped the Methodist Bishops' response in the beginning of their initiative a year later (Nov. 1984). The two-day hearing at which theologians and biblical scholars were among key witnesses asked to testify was held the following year (July 16–17, 1985).

The definitive impact of "nuclear winter," especially on Bishop White, will be prolonged in the churches by the first session of the six or thirteen planned for the educational program now launched. This, we are told, will present "the testimony of the expert witnesses in the order in which they appeared." That means *on the videotape* to be used in teaching that first lesson, *not* in the order of our appearance at the hearing. Hence it is not without significance that Carl Sagan is shown first, "describing the current situation in a nutshell" (*Guide for Study and Action*, p. 3).

I can understand the dread of secular humanists over the alleged possible destruction of all human life on "planet earth," since for them that would be the end of all known *purpose* in the universe. We who believe in God, however, should not suggest by thought, word, or deed that the end of planet earth would be the end of *the world*, the end of God's *purpose* for his creatures, the end of his *creation*. The Prologue of St. John's Gospel is the Christian story of creation, our chief creation story, primary over Genesis, as John 1:3 states. This is good news forevermore, the ground of all hope or of "patient endurance" in face of the Four Horsemen of the end-time. The pastoral should contain no suggestion that "the creation itself" could be under attack—with the more than faint implication throughout that such "attack" might be successful unless we Christians work harder at preventing it. The sense of "futurelessness" in preteens today and the agony of young parents over "bringing children into such a world" (which the Bishops observe in FD, pp. 16, 61) will, I fear, only be aggravated by an address to the nuclear crisis that does not bring fully to bear on it a profound Christian understanding of Creation and Last Things (Ultimate Things)—in short, of trust only in God, who holds the future in his hands. Perspectives that

Christians hold or should hold in common—on creation, species survival, and the future—are, indeed, more basic than any perils and anxieties we share with others in this age.

Since this criticism of the first and only public draft was sent to the Bishops' committee by more than one person, I can only suppose it to be included among "some suggestions [that] actually called for a repudiation of the thrust or substance of the entire document or one of its main sections. While these were carefully read, the Committee [it said] was not prepared to make a 180-degree turn on basic issues." What the Committee called "substantive additions or changes" (*ten* were listed, on a two-page summary provided the Council of Bishops meeting in Morristown to approve revisions and adopt the final draft) are "substantive" only in contrast to minor corrections, such as improvements in grammar. It is somewhat disingenuous for Bishop White to write in his Preface that "in November 1985, a first draft was made available for public scrutiny, eliciting an extraordinary amount of thoughtful and expert response from across the country" (FD, p. 8)—when no substantial change was made in the final draft. Anyone concerned with *the process* will ask, Did all the Bishops receive copies of every one of these responses before they met as a Council to approve the final documents to be published? Also, why not two public drafts, with a year between them for criticism and improvement?

I want to drive home this point in the following way. Years ago I wrote: "God means to kill us all in the end, and in the end he is going to succeed." Though we might quibble about the sense in which "God means" the future of his creatures, and you may dislike the seeming harshness of my rhetoric, still that statement is undeniably true. It is undeniable from what we know within the limits of reason alone. It is undeniable from what we know, beyond reason, or revealed biblical truth.

That quotation of mine was first used in *Fabricated Man* (New Haven: Yale University Press, 1970), directed against "survivalists" who plan *genetic* alterations to produce beings quite *unlike* us to come after us, to insure that we Earthlings have descendants. People who sing "Our hope is placed in nothing less than Jesus' blood and righteousness" should hope not those hopes, nor fear our Bishops' fear. What is called "hope" today is largely "anticipatory disposition" of the future; and that is the opposite of hope in God. This means, in ethics, that calculating the consequences, predicting either benefits or disaster to come, is not the paramount way to distinguish right and wrong actions. We tend the garden of the future we see, but we do not *depend on* outcomes or take charge of God's ruling and overruling providence.

In *Fabricated Man* I took for granted the most extreme view of the genetic cul-de-sac—the genetic Apocalypse—into which humankind is heading, namely, the predictions of H. J. Müller, and wrote:

His fellow geneticists can correct, if they must, the extremism of his vision. For the purpose of making clear, however, how one intends the world as a

Christian, even in the face of such an apocalyptic account of the end toward which we are proceeding, it is best to leave the vision unaltered and assume it to be a true account of the scientific facts. (p. 23)

For the same reason, I now assume something like "nuclear winter" may be a plausible prediction, as may be the expectations of Jonathan Schell in *The Fate of the Earth* or of Dr. Helen Caldicott and other contributors to *The Final Epidemic*. What's incredible is that Christians should premise their responsibilities upon the outcome of technical disputes. So I not only begin with *theology* but also ask the reader to join me in assuming some somber predictions, whether realistic or as "thought experiments," in order to concentrate attention on the relevant faith-warrants. This is rather heavy going.

Whether our earth ends from a collision of planets, or from the running down of the universe according to the law of entropy, whether in a fiery furnace or stark condensation in a "black hole," no science teaches us that our Earth mother, her progenitors, or her children are immortal. Suppose no nuclear weapons existed. Still, only lack of powers of imagination prevents us right now from conceiving of the plight of a last, "futureless" generation. So, at the Washington "hearing"—seeing that a psychologist was scheduled for the afternoon (who testified about children growing up mentally "numbed" and "nuclearized")—I suggested to the panel that the Bishops might inquire why John of Patmos omitted that topic from *his* pastoral letters to the churches.

Since ours is not the Last Judgment, on what do we stand to call in question God's righteousness or wisdom if the way it is to be is that his mercy over his creatures continues to thousands of generations of Australian aborigines, or new life-lines, or none at all on this earth? Moreover, species survival in itself is no great value; and we have it on good authority that in the Kingdom of Heaven there will be neither marrying nor giving in marriage.

But, you say, there is today an utterly different overhanging peril, namely, that *by our own actions* all human creatures could be destroyed. That's not the same as cosmic "accidents," however certain to come, or the musings of astrophysicists. A first level of response is to say that such a situation may not be unique as we suppose, fixated as we are by the thought of nuclear self-destruction.

In retrospect, 1776 may have settled the question of planetary survival. Symbolically, that was the year *homo faber*—man the inventor—became potential destroyer of the earth that nourishes and sustains us. In 1776 Isaac Watts invented the steam engine, on the same campus where in that same year Adam Smith published *The Wealth of Nations*, the book that freed human economic energies from bondage to governmental regulation of trade, enterprise, and quest for riches. That same year also symbolizes the genius of America, where was devised a constitution capable of governing a brawling continental empire of entrepreneurs (pioneers, we call them) and capable of spreading industrialization and modernization over the entire globe. All the world's America, only more so; or yearning to be, in respects that almost certainly will overload this planet. The industrial revolution may just as certainly, even if a little later, be the process by which human-kind perishes from this earth by human hands. At the World Council of Churches' Church and Society Conference at the Massachusetts Institute of Technology several years ago, some third-world people did not want such things as this to be said, *even if true*, so important is modernization to their impoverished people. As I write this page, the United Nations is meeting on development in Africa. The paradox is that success in justly and fairly raising standards of life the world over will most likely burden the planet more and deplete its resources more quickly. It seems an unreasonable hope for us to expect the finite but restless human spirit certainly to continue itself on a much more finite planet, unreasonable to believe that we can prosper world without end without ecocatastrophe. At least, no morality should *depend on it*.

Zero population growth, someone may reply. To reduce present pollution from electric power generated from burning sulphur-containing coal and oil to the level of the year 1940, the present population of the United States would have to be cut back to 20 million souls. The amount of nitrogen fertilizer used would not have increased since 1940 if all but 17 million Americans had returned to the homes of their ancestors. See Roger Revelle, "Paul Ehrlich: New High Priest of Ecocatastrophe," *Family Perspectives*, 3 (April 1971), 68, quoted by Arthur J. Dyck, *On Human Care: An Introduction to Ethics* (Nashville, Tenn.: Abingdon Press, 1977), p. 41 and n. 21.

Speaking still within the limits of reason alone, I'd have to *know* that ecocatastrophe is *not* this world's destiny before I'd invoke "futurelessness" as particularly relevant in discussing the nuclear politics of nations. Our responsibility is compelling enough without that thought. After all, death is every individual's atom bomb. There's something especially eerie about death by cancer and something especially eerie in the thought of the death of the species by nuclear evaporation or vaporization. But the first is by no means the major cause of individual death, and the latter may not be the only reason there may be none like us to come after us. The spook of "futurelessness" cannot be exorcised by talk about assault upon planet earth, meaning or even suggesting that by this we mean assault upon the creation. In fact, *such* futurelessness may be the plain, unvarnished truth. It is not likely that a worldwide industrial, chemical, and technological society can long endure.

The foregoing speculation has about as much evidence to support it as speculation that nuclear weapons will kill us all. Alongside "nuclear winter," the Methodist Bishops themselves list the "greenhouse effect": "Possible ozone depletion, exposing earthlings to increasingly lethal ultraviolet rays from the sun" (FD, p. 38). Why, then, pick on winter, and not human activities that are steadily depleting the species' protection from the sun?

The newspapers have recently been filled with reports of concern over a hole in the ozone over the South Pole that is now as large as the United States. First noticed by British scientists in 1985, the hole has been growing rapidly. As the *Times* reported on July 29, 1986, "the depletion of ozone was so severe that the computer analyzing the data had been suppressing it, having been programmed to assume that deviations so extreme must be errors. The scientists had to go back and reprocess the data going back to 1979" in order to calculate the "ozone summer," or greenhouse effect. Among human activities that, I understand, may be contributing to this is turning on your automobile engine, in addition to our general worldwide use of chlorofluorocarbons.

More recently, Worldwatch Institute reported ozone depletion among three "threshold crossings," likely already passed. (The other two thresholds are world population growth and the loss of biological diversity.) The most frustrating paradox emerging is that global efforts to achieve economic growth and improve living standards in the southern hemisphere are themselves producing these intolerable consequences and overwhelming the capacity of governments to deal with the results of pursuing justice. A "just and sustainable society" may be out of reach. (*New York Times*, Feb. 15, 1987.)

Readers may want to think back to these threats to an inhabitable earth when we come to what the Bishops say about the "*consequent*" social injustices of war, and the great good they suppose must flow from channeling the resources the world now wastes on arms into "development." Here, indeed, may be a palpable paradox.

In fact, *In Defense of Creation* was overtaken by events within weeks of its publication, its foundational appeal to Carl Sagan and "nuclear winter" shaken mightily if not destroyed. The *New York Times*, in a front-page story on June 26, 1986, reported new conclusions concerning the after-effects of nuclear war drawn from computer studies by scientists at the National Center for Atmospheric Research, the Los Alamos National Laboratory, and the Lawrence Livermore National Laboratory. The headline read: "Less Drastic Theory Emerges on Freezing after a Nuclear War."

I don't want to make too much of this, but I *do* want to take the *right point* from it. The scientists cautioned that they were signaling "no general retreat from the idea that indirect aftereffects of nuclear war would cause human misery on a scale without precedent." Still they drew a quite different picture than that first publicized in *Science* in December 1983. One of the scientists at the atmospheric center compared the more recent study with the discussion set afloat by the earlier one: "It's quite different from what people were talking about." They had "in their minds the image of frozen lakes and frozen cornfields and having to dig through frozen ground to bury the dead, and those images are too extreme. It was an excellent attention grabber, but those deep-freeze images are an exaggeration." By the original estimates, temperatures would plunge 45 degrees and stay below freezing for months; the new estimates suggest initial drops of 25 degrees and a return to within 10 to 15 degrees of normal in the first month, with only a few degrees of cooling lasting for several years. Still sufficient reason, of course, to prevent nuclear war and get rid of nuclear weapons if we can; but not Apocalypse.

Responses to these findings varied. For our purpose, it is sufficient to quote Carl Sagan. "I don't think nuclear winter implies subfreezing temperatures, not necessarily," Dr. Sagan said, according to the *Times*. "You can have winters in which the temperatures are not below freezing. You do not need temperature declines of 15 to 20 degrees to produce a kind of global horror. A single day in which the temperature dips below zero can destroy a rice crop. A local temperature decline of three or four degrees is enough to destroy all the wheat and barley growth in Canada."

Another scientist, who shared Carl Sagan's predictions of ecocatastrophe, made the best response: "I think they may have jumped the gun a bit. It's one calculation. Things could change again." I deem that to be the best response because it makes quite clear *the sole point* I want to draw from these calculations, and what I mean when I say that our Bishops were overtaken by events. They were overtaken by contingent events; indeed, by *contingency* itself, which is the nature of all events we know or shall ever know (not to speak of computer studies that could change again). Now, Carl Sagan adores Contingency and rejoices in it forever. Contingency is the Ruler whose works are manifest in the popular and instructive TV series *Cosmos*, used widely in high-school education (and there—I am bold to say—corrupting Methodist youth to believe in a Fortuity who is not our God). When the Bishops lighted upon the Concerned Scientists as their chosen experts, and made foundational these scientists' plausible or implausible predictions of futurelessness and the self-destruction of the human species, they built their house upon shifting sands. Not only are computer models mutable; commonly experienced events or supposed future events are also mutable. Among them the rock of our salvation is not to be found. An adequate Christian outlook or onlook upon the future cannot be drawn from common events; right and wrong do not depend upon eventualities for foundation. It would be strange beyond belief if the Christian church began to rest its opposition to modern warfare upon "findings" so complex that only computer models can comprehend them, or scientific philosopher-kings debate them, when a chief objection to Strategic Defense (and other modern weapons and deterrence systems as well) is that *political* decisions and military command are given over to technology to calculate.

There is a further irony in the article. Even in the brief space of a news story, it seemed very, very clear that even by the old figures the computers did not leave a "rational decision maker" *no options*. Suppose there is a threshold of explosions *above* which nuclear weapons produce "nuclear winter." Firing weapons above that explosive power would be suicidal to the nation that dares to go above that threshold. Therefore, both super-powers are effectively deterred from all-out nuclear war. But one can still contemplate a surprise attack limited to nuclear explosions *below* that total magnitude in the confidence that *the targeted nation* would not retaliate because *its* retaliation would be suicide. Such retaliation alone would produce nuclear winter, etc. Nuclear blackmail or even a first strike remains a possibility. (More than once in human memory a conqueror has wanted to take over the whole known world.) Nuclear weapons as such are policy-neutral (albeit, within a narrow range); they are also morally neutral in the sense that the Bishops cannot succeed in founding their categorical "No" to nuclear deterrence upon a *contingent* event, the mutual suicide of Earth-lings. Nuclear deterrence (or any other action or policy) must be moral or immoral in its inception, not on account of outcomes. Either there is or there is not a radically reformed nuclear deterrent. If not, nuclear deterrence is a moral atrocity before ever, and if never, the system is used in war-fighting. Before ever, and if never, there is nuclear winter. *Begone, then, with the politics of fear.* And in any case, theologically speaking, I'd rather be an Evangelical preaching Hell torments unto the saving of souls than scarify people unto paralysis for an elusive survival never promised us.

The drafters of the Methodist document may experience some disappointment if they study the project weaponeer Carl Sagan has in mind to give *purpose* again to our nation (or to a consortium of nations) and to our space program following the Challenger disaster, one that will deflect us from Strategic Defense as well as from nuclear war. See his "It's Time to Go to Mars," *New York Times*, Op-Ed. page, Jan. 23, 1987. Without engaging in comparative cost analysis, that project for humankind does not comport well with the hope our Bishops pour into correcting the "consequent" injustices of the war system. In addition to the theological despair I detected among scientific predictors of a genetic Apocalypse, resulting in various schemes for going "to meet the planets" (*Fabricated Man*, pp. 138–60, sections on "Questionable Aspirations to Godhood" and "A Penchant for Species-Suicide"), another significant encounter for me was at the celebration of an anniversary of Boston University's School of Theology some years ago, in connection with a meeting in Boston of the American Association for the Advancement of Science. The justly famous author Isaac Asimov seriously proposed on that occasion that we colonize the moon as soon as possible; our descendants living in glass houses in that uninhabitable environment would be forced to learn that *war is suicidal*! Is there not something a bit unseemly for Christians to espouse the most apocalyptic visions of the near future in order to bestir themselves? I'd say, by contrast, that there is no temptation to find substitutes for the theological hope or driving to theological despair in Freeman Dyson's *Weapons and Hope*—hope only within the limits of reason alone.

But suppose my illustration of other possible species-suicides is mistaken—suppose that in fact there is within reason *only one* human venture that, by human contrivance, fallibility, or wickedness, *could* destroy our own kind—such a supposition does not much change *the future no Christian should believe in*. For the same conclusion is undeniable from what we know, beyond reason, of biblical truth—that is, if the Revelation of St. John is still in your Bible.

2. The Bishops' address to the nuclear crisis is seriously flawed theologically in its doctrine of Last Things/Ultimate Things (eschatology). The "already" and the "not yet" of Christ our peace have been leveled into a possible continuity on planet earth. It matters not whether we say that this age in which we live has been *leveled up* to the Kingdom of Heaven, in which our ultimate hope is fixed (or leveled up to the Garden of Eden, whence we came), or whether we say that Kingdom of Heaven has been *leveled down* to the "heavenly city of the 18th century philosophers," that is, to some ideal historical time toward which human progress moves.

The "writer" chosen to do exegesis for the Bishops did not serve them well. The following is offered as a paraphrase of Revelation 7:

> The Revelation of John, in the darkest hour of despair, sings of a new earth, radiant with infinite love and compassion, in which all nations and peoples come together peaceably before the Lord God and in which hunger and hurt and sorrow are no more. (FD, p. 30)

Look for the Word of God in Revelation 7 and you will see not quite that. The chapter nowhere sings of a "new earth, radiant with infinite love and compassion." Not "all nations and peoples come together peaceably before the Lord God." Rather, "I looked, and behold, a great multitude which no man could number, from every nation, from all tribes and peoples and tongues, standing before the throne and before the Lamb, clothed in white robes, with palm branches in their hands . . . Then one of the elders addressed me, saying, 'Who are these, clothed in white robes, and whence have they come?' I said to him, 'Sir, you know.' And he said to me, 'These are they who have come out of great tribulation; they have washed their robes and made them white in the blood of the Lamb. . . . They shall hunger no more, neither thirst any more; the sun shall not strike them, nor any scorching heat.'" (Rev. 7:9–16; my italics). The final verse of the chapter tells us why: "For the Lamb, which is in the midst of the throne, shall feed them, and shall lead them unto living fountains of waters: and God shall wipe away all tears from their eyes."

It is Revelation 21:1 that speaks of "a new heaven and a new earth" and promptly states the obvious coordinate condition: "for the first heaven and the first earth had passed away, and the sea was no more." Individual or species death and futurelessness are no problem. God himself "will wipe away every tear from their eyes, and death shall be no more neither shall there be mourning nor crying nor pain any more, for the former things have passed away" (ver. 1–4; my italics).

Even apart from Revelation, I thought we Christians knew that death— even nuclear death—was the "last enemy" that shall be destroyed, that this death of death itself is not itself among Last Things, nor is there any disturbing "futurelessness" there. For the first heaven and the first earth—if there is ground for Christian hope and patient endurance in the between-times—have already effectively passed away. If God is with us, no future and no futurelessness can do us ultimate harm.

It is dismaying beyond measure that our Bishops chose ecocatastrophe to replace theology (and declined thereafter to change the thrust of their pastoral letter) as a strategy to awaken United Methodist people from their "nuclear numbness" and arouse them to speak and act for nuclear disarmament (FD, pp. 6–7). We Methodists should not be among those for whom "fear is a constant if unacknowledged presence because everyone had glimpsed the specter of the end of all things" (FD, p. 84). Indeed we have glimpsed the end of all things and seen there no "specter" but the face of Jesus Christ, whom "we now see through a glass darkly, but then face to face" (I Cor. 13:12).

A decade or so ago the distinguished political scientist Hans Morganthau under-stood that "nuclear numbness" needed explaining. His explanation was that (1) the modern world first became *secular*, "one-world" views prevailed over the religious ages, and the meaning of life came to rest in *some future time*; (2) then came the nuclear age, threatening that depository of the meaningfulness of present human existence; (3) *hence* we one-worlders can't allow ourselves to think seriously or for any length of time about the problem of nuclear weapons. See my "Morganthau and Nuclear War," *Commonweal*, vol. 78, no. 21 (Sept. 20, 1963), pp. 554–57. Put the Bomb together with living in one earthly city and you get benumbed Methodists and other Americans who need to be awakened by foundational appeal to the same benumbing prospect! I was reminded of Morganthau's diagnosis when, at the Southeastern Jurisdictional Convocation (Junaluska), one of our Bishops explained in private conversation why they had not allowed a year's time between *two* public drafts by saying they had to seize the moment *lest interest wane*. (This was coupled with the structural difficulties I am most interested in: cost, inadequate staff, and the time and energy demanded by church administration.) Whichever diagnosis of inattentiveness to nuclear *ethics* is correct, I thought we knew that "for tomorrow we die" was in all ages coupled with "eat, drink, and be merry."

Before coming to the third theological flaw in the Foundation Document, a question has quietly, insistently been forming in my mind. Am I not pounding away at the obvious? Should we not simply assume that the mistake—if there is one—is purely *verbal*? I fear not. An abbreviated version of the foregoing was published in September 1986 in the Methodist *Circuit Rider*, a journal that goes to every United Methodist minister in the United States. Of the letters the editor received in response—and chose to publish in the January 1987 issue—only one raised a solid theological point. This was that my theology is "more Augustinian than Hebraic"— which is true. My response (published June 1987), to the effect that the theology of these Methodist episcopal documents is more *Hebraic* than New Testament, would frame a proper discussion.

Other respondents seemed to prove my point about the critical difference between creation and planet earth. I (of all people) was supposed to believe that "God would have other purposes *somewhere* in the universe"; that "planet earth is an *insignificant part* of the creation"; that nuclear weapons cannot frustrate the creative and fulfilling purpose that God intends for the creation . . . *in a one-dimensional universe*; and to fail to understand that "nothing in the letter . . . denies God's having created *other 'worlds' than this planet*."

One-dimensional thinking about creation or about the consummation of Christ's kingdom is not mine. References to other "worlds" or to the earth as only a "part" of creation manifest the mortal sin of despair, not theological hope. And nothing I write implies that we are not to tend the garden, even the garden of God's fallen creation. To the latter we turn next—and to the need for obedience to God's preservative ordinances if we are properly to tend the garden of his fallen creation, and not to suppose our stewardship is the same as that our first parents once had.

3. We live in the between-times. So we need to note, thirdly, that the Bishops' statements are seriously flawed theologically in not taking adequately into account the deformation of human life from the Fall to the end of the world.

A modest beginning toward throwing light on the harsh constraints upon responsible government in a fallen world was contained in the quotation "No Bible-believing Wesley's-Standard-Sermons-packing Methodist preacher ever waited for the Twentieth Century to teach him the obduracy, the unfathomable wickedness and the dereliction of human hearts" (FD, pp. 24–25). That said I, in my written testimony to the drafting committee. A better starting point was the Bishops' quotation (FD, pp. 82–83) from John Wesley's *The Doctrine of Original Sin*. Like Shakespeare, Wesley was saying, "What a piece of work is man?"—meaning fallen man. Like James Madison's Federalist paper #51, he was saying, "What is government itself, but the greatest of all reflections on human nature?" Wesley said the same of war itself.

> What an amazing way of deciding controversies! *What must mankind be*, before such a thing as war could ever be known or thought of upon earth? How shocking, how inconceivable a want must there have been of . . . common humanity, before . . . any two nations in the universe, could once think of such a method of decision? [John Wesley, *The Doctrine of Original Sin: According to Scripture, Reason, and Experience*. Bristol, 1757, p. 58 (my italics). *Works*, IX (Zondervan, 1872, 1959), pp. 212–22.]

While our Bishops introduce those words with the statement "John Wesley counted war as the ultimate evidence of humanity's fallen, sinful state," nothing is made of the evidence.

Instead, the passage from Wesley is followed by quite another aspect of his "legacy": joining knowledge with vital piety. A second, brief reference to Wesley on war as "the prime example of human depravity" (FD, p. 31) is followed, in unbelievable sequence, by the statement "Many of the most prominent United Methodist leaders of the twentieth century have been pacifists." That may be correct, but why accent the *non sequitur*? A third reference to Wesley on war as "the ultimate evidence of humanity's fallen, sinful state" (FD, p. 20) is followed immediately by citation from our Social Principles renouncing "war as an instrument of national foreign policy." That is like saying "We renounce government" immediately after citing Madison's "What is government itself, but the greatest of all reflections on human nature?"

Wesley's words were, indeed, a splendid understanding of the *ultima ratio* of an arbitrament of arms in the course of government's rule in a fallen world. So I went to the library for a copy of this treatise by the founder of our church and read it for the first time. The quotation comes in a chapter in which Wesley undertakes to prove from reason and experience—and in tones of triumphant irony—that original sin is *a fact.* Fourteen pages later (73–74) he wrote: "We have now taken a cursory view of the present state of mankind in all parts of the habitable world, and seen in a general way, what is their real condition, both with regard to knowledge and virtue." A little later on (80–81): "This is the plain, glaring, apparent condition of humankind . . . the plain, naked fact, without any extenuation on the one hand or exaggeration on the other . . . [A] man may as modestly deny, that spring and summer, autumn and winter succeed each other, as deny one article of [this] account of the moral world." The next chapter, entitled "The Scriptural Method of Accounting for This Defended," begins (88): "The fact then being undeniable, I would ask, How is this to be accounted for?" In this chapter Wesley dismisses most of the answers many contemporary Methodists believe "resolve" the question: custom, institutional lag, bad example or habit, lack of education, rather than the scriptural account.

The documents our Bishops have addressed to the churches are *formally* correct in their description of this aeon from the Fall of man to the end of the world. Actually, however, the "peace" (*shalom*) of which they speak is the *perfect* peace that was pre-Fall and, we believe, shall be at the end of the story of Redemption. "*Shalom* means positive peace, joyous peace, just peace. *Shalom* is harmony between humanity and all of God's creation. In *shalom* there is no contradiction between justice and peace or between peace and security or between love and justice (Isaiah 32:16–18; Jeremiah 29:7)" (FD, p. 12; cf. p. 25). Jeremiah 29:7 is a strange verse to cite twice in support of the abolition of all those contradictions. The verse is Jeremiah's counsel to God's people in exile to "seek the peace of the city whither I have caused you to be carried away captives"—difficult as it may be to sing the Lord's song in a strange land—"for in the peace thereof shall be your peace." Isaiah 32:16–18 does express the messianic vision of the Hebrew prophets. The pastoral contains no suggestion that the coming of Christ significantly transformed those visions. The Bishops' writer failed them most of all in the New Testament exegesis.

So one way to understand *shalom* is as the perfect peace before the Fall. Thus the Bishops write: "*Shalom*, then, is the sum total of moral and spiritual qualities in a community whose life is in harmony with God's good creation. It indicates an alternative community . . ." (FD, p. 26).

Elsewhere (FD, p. 20) the church temporal is urged to *be* that alternative community, the sum total of those harmonious qualities! Surely that is not to be expected this side Resurrection. There is need for candor about the church's own life, and for some eschatological qualification of the claim that "there is neither Jew nor Greek, there is neither slave nor free, there is neither male nor female: for you are all one in Christ" (Gal. 3:28). The Bishops wrote, "It is Christ who has broken down the dividing walls of hostility, creating one new humanity (Ephesians 2:14–19)" (FD, p. 12), "overcoming enmity, so making peace" (FD, p. 28); we need to acknowledge that this does not describe the actuality of any church, let alone the international political system. The reference was to bringing near the Gentiles who were once far off and making them one with the household of Israel. The "not yet" of such an event was never "already" characteristic of the early church. The Treaty of Jerusalem (if I may so call Gal. 2:7–9) never really worked; it became obsolete with the passing of Jewish Christians from the scene; "the calling of the Jews" (Rom. 11:25–26) remained for St. Paul a messianic hope. As the Cambridge University historian Herbert Butterfield once wrote: "Take the animosity in your average church choir, extend it over the whole world, give it a history; and you have an adequate explanation of all the wars of human history."

The Bishops need to tell us whether they are addressing ideal expectations to the empirical church. And Hauerwas (who rejects any distinction between the visible and the invisible church) needs to spell out for the Bishops the message he believes they should have sent *to the church*. And since the Holy Spirit must be the subject of many of Hauerwas's sentences about "peaceableness" (if not a church within the church), he is bound to elaborate his understanding of eschatology, and not Christology only.

Shalom is "harmony, wholeness, health and wellbeing in all human relations. It is the natural state of humanity as birthed by God" (FD, p. 24). (I suppose "created by God" is meant.) It is the peace of the Garden of Paradise before the Fall, needing, therefore, no force of government.

Alternatively expressed, the church temporal is to preach to the conflict-ridden world of today this message coming to us from before the Fall and from the coming Restoration. The *consequent* nuclear issues "make the *wholeness* of the *shalom* vision most imperative for our time" (FD, p. 39). The letter itself speaks of "the biblical vision of a wholistic peace" (FD,

p. 91). That peace is eschatological. So *shalom*, in the Bishops' *description* of it, was before the Fall and shall be "after the Fall was over." "Creation" and "covenant," "covenant" and "end-time," go together.

Compare "A 'whole world of theology' in which there is no boundary between nature and grace, for God's presence is throughout all creation and revelation is everywhere" (FD, p. 68, among the spiritual gifts we may receive from Russian Christians).

Of course *meantime* we believe, as the Bishops say, that "It is Christ . . ." (or, as Colossians 2:15 says, it is *God*) who has "disarmed the principalities and powers and made a public example of them, triumphing over them in him," that is, in Christ (FD, pp. 12–13, 29). But we should not naturalize or socialize these powers. Two additional references in Scripture to "principalities and powers" are gerrymandered (by the exegesis the "writer" adopted) to direct the church's peacemaking to earthly powers or against subjective hostilities. "We have hardly begun to imagine what the church as a transnational community offers in proclaiming 'the unsearchable riches of Christ' to the principalities and powers (Ephesians 3:8, 10)" (FD, p. 82). Verse 10 continues: "in heavenly places." Without the complete verse and the words in between the clauses quoted, one is tempted to identify the "principalities and powers" with the "military-industrial-political-scientific-educational-recreational-media-religious complex" (FD, p. 56) against which United Methodists are urged to perform mighty acts of institutional good works. Again, our Bishops write that *prayer* is "the armor of the spirit 'against the principalities, against the powers, against the world rulers of this present darkness' (Ephesians 6:11–12)" (FD, p. 84). That *omits* verse 11 and truncates verse 12. The New Testament passage in its entirety tells us: "Put on the whole armor of God, that you may be able to stand against the wiles of the devil. For we are not contending against flesh and blood, but against the principalities . . . rulers of this present darkness, against the spiritual hosts of wickedness in heavenly places."

In the section entitled "Jesus Christ Is Our Peace," we read (FD, pp. 27–28): "There is a stark and sorrowful moment when Jesus, approaching Jerusalem from the neighboring heights, pauses to weep. And why does he weep? He foresees a terrible Day of Judgment when the Holy City itself will be totally leveled to rubble and dust without 'one stone upon another.' Why? Because the people there, even the most religious people in the supposedly sacred city, do not really know 'the things that make for peace' (Luke 19:41–44)." Rub not your eyes at the faint suggestion that Jesus deliberately "paused to weep" to teach political lessons on the day of his triumphal entry into Jerusalem. Rub your eyes rather over the lesson the Bishops (or their exegete) say he taught: "That moment is a powerful intimation of what false security policies based upon weapons of mass destruction can lead to." In all this, the church's peacemaking action in the present age is leveled up to final salvific importance even as Last Things/ Ultimate Things are leveled down.

Nothing in the foregoing need mean a literal belief in the Second Advent. But unless that means *something*, it means *nothing*; and one would have to conclude that our chief pastors meant to excise words from Scripture, to twist Jesus' sorrowful words over Jerusalem into a political sermon, and to reduce the Christian life to one-dimensional endlessness. I doubt that this was the case.

And nothing I have written about not looking ahead in a one-dimensional universe for the consummation of the peaceable kingdom of Christ entails that we need not actively seek for a better-ordered, more just, and longer-lasting peace on earth.

Some New Testament Christians prayed that the Lord come quickly (I Cor. 16:22); others counted on a time of his patience. "Why has the *parousia* been delayed?" I asked at the hearing in Washington; and replying to my own question, said: "So that you and I and our children may be included in so great a redemption, in God's end in creation itself."

In terms of *creation*, I recall from the work of the Social Principles Commission that the section drafted on Marriage moved swiftly from God's blessing upon marriage to his blessing (in our next sentence) upon *childless* marriages, with no mention (in common with Christians in all ages) of the child as among the goods of marriage. I moved the revision of that in our final report, which read: "We assert the sanctity of the marriage covenant. *The child is a blessing of marriage and a sign of hope.* Yet God also blesses childless marriages." (A minority of the commissioners wanted to say "the sanctity of marriage as a *lifelong* covenant" but were inexplicably outvoted.) One member of the Commission (a Bishop, as I recall) said, during the discussion of my amendment, that he did not see how in this day of *over-population* of the earth one could call a child a sign of hope! (Reference to the child as a sign of hope is not in the 1984 Discipline.)

No, I do not think it is at all obvious in churches today that "creation" means that the Creator is still with us and holds the future in his hands.

The Bishops know, of course, that "the *shalom* of God's good creation has been broken by the fallenness and violence of sinful human creatures." From this flows the second of two theological accounts of government: "The powers of government are not only legitimate expressions of the Creation's natural order of political community: they are necessary *constraints upon human sinfulness*" (FD, p. 12; my italics). "Defense against enemies" is listed among the imperatives of government in its function of restraining evil: "Human sinfulness is, according to scripture, a warrant for government, law enforcement, and defense against enemies—but also a warning against the iniquity of governors themselves" (FD, p. 25, following the "beaut" quoted from Ramsey). There is equivalent realism in nos. 6 and 9 of the "Guiding Principles for a Theology of a Just Peace" (FD, p. 36).

The *words* are there about the brokenness of mankind's fallen condition. But the matter and the melody are seldom the same. One wonders why Wesley was quoted if the Fall does not more radically determine the tasks and functions of government till the end-time. Why quote Wesley on human depravity if this has so little to do with where and how we are encouraged to expect and hope for the peace of God, toward which the church, individually and collectively, moves? If there is no great eschato-logical discontinuity along the way to, at long last, the peaceable kingdom of God, then no great discontinuity between Creation and Fall was meant.

Do the Bishops believe that *nations* shall stand before God, not multi-tudes *from out of* every nation and tongue? Do they believe that nations shall eventually be "born again"? Do they believe that all persons born again are entirely holy (that was called the "second blessing" by "holiness" people)? Do they believe (*contra* Wesley) that a revival of religion can be continuous, permanent? Do they believe that conversion goes onward and upward, so that it falls within the distant limits of credibility for us to believe that mankind's amazing way of deciding some of its insoluble controversies by arbitrament of arms need nevermore be conceivable, or needed?

Of course, among Methodist distinctives is our teaching concerning Christian perfection. But does this mean that *nations*—interrelated collec-tives—are to be urged always to be going on to perfection? That nations are the brands to be plucked from the burning? That statesmen and citizens in their political vocations should expect political holiness and perfect love to descend upon the system of collectives in which they live and work—any moment, any hour, any day now? Or for that matter, any *time*? It is God's redeemed people, individually and collectively, who are going on to perfec-tion and to a World of Love. That is the "progressive" element stressed in the Wesleyan heritage; that is the meaning of our legacy joining knowledge with vital piety, and of yearning for holiness. Whenever this is directed (without differentiation between church and world) toward secular prob-lems (however urgent), we swap our birthright for a "pot of message," while also sometimes speaking impossible dreams to states and instilling unearthly (i.e., misplaced) hope in laypeople. Like any church formed in the wake of the Reformation, we should have eyes to see darkness as well as light at the end of every man-made tunnel. Have not our Bishops *misplaced* the "roundedness," the wholeness, health, and harmony of *shalom*?

This does not mean that we are stuck with everything John Wesley said or believed; or for that matter with literally the account in Scripture that the *every* imagination of the thoughts of men's hearts was *only* evil *continually* (Gen. 6:5) when by God's covenant with Noah government was given its mandate to preserve the world. Still, radical departure from our Wesleyan heritage needs justification by going again to our deeper theological sources. If in the U.S. Catholic Bishops' pastoral letter there is too little tension between the "already" and the "not yet" of the gospel, in the Methodist pastoral there is still less. However difficult the task and long the journey, the peacemaking to which we are called by both pastorals assumes that this aeon and the next are more continuous than not. An inadequate eschatology may be excusable in the Roman Catholic tradition, with its natural-law optimism, its rumor that the Fall was not as serious as other Christians suppose. Thus the Catholic Bishops sent forth their call "conscious of God's continuing work among us, which will one day *issue forth* [!] in the beautiful final kingdom prophesied by the seer of the Book of Revelation"; then the Catholic pastoral ends by quoting (par. 339) the entirety of Revelation 21:1–5, ". . . Behold, I make all things new." That issuing forth of the new from the old, we saw, is also the Methodist interpretation of the "new creation." This smooths over the eschatology that is there in the Bible; and coordinated with that, its account of this world, this history, this earth, this aeon. No church of the Reformation, no church coming in the wake of the Reformation, *indeed no church before the Enlightenment*, NONE put its faith and hope or deeds of discipleship in context with such *elision* between this world and the next. There is more than a slash between the words "already/not yet." There is more than a *momentous* slash. The slash is *aeonic*.

Stanley Hauerwas has written a remarkable account of war as a moral institution woven into our history as a particular political people ("Should War Be Eliminated," in *Against the Nations*. Minneapolis: Winston Press, 1985, pp. 169–208). At least, the possibility of war is an essential part of the stories we tell ourselves of our eventful past, challenges and triumphs or failures, the heroes we honor, our monuments, institutions, laws, and national holidays. Yet he wishes to deny that this means that as the people of God we live also in an earthly city. There *are* two kingdoms, but we are citizens of one only. Hauerwas denies that between the first and second Advent we live in two cities. The aeonic mark across time made by Jesus' first coming means, rather, that our human history (outside of Christ) points backward; our life in Christ points forward. So our existence is not "constituted by two histories" (which would mean two cities, two citizenships): "There is only *one true history*—the history of God's peaceable kingdom." Only the qualifying word "true" prevents this from being a completely *realized eschatology*; indeed, Hauerwas argues against the "not yet" of the Catholic pastoral to which we next turn. So the question "Should war be eliminated?" turns out to be a false question; and Hauerwas's remarkable account of the secular history of political peoples turns out to be binding in no specifiable ways. ". . . It is a false question because war has been eliminated for those who participate in God's history. . . . in fact we do not live in such a history."

"We are a people who believe that God will have them exist through history without the necessity of war." Of course, war is not a "necessity," or a "fate"; nor is anything else historical. But Hauerwas goes so far as to announce that "we do not preclude that a *state* could exist for which war is not a possibility." Why is such not a proper characterization of states in the international system? Because to say so would be "the ultimate act of unbelief; for who are we to determine the power of God's providential care of the world?" A footnote confesses that "*theologically* we may not know how God can provide for the possibility of a nonviolent state, but neither can we act as if such were not a possibility." Are we then to *act as if* a *nonviolent* state *is* a possibility, maybe an actuality? Notably, the passage from Yoder quoted in this context (p. 195) does not use the expression "nonviolent." Instead, in the incarnation in Christ of Old Testament visions of peace, "the greatest novelty and the occasion of stumbling was His willingness to sacrifice, in the interest of *non-resistant* love, all forms of human solidarity, including the legitimate national interests of the chosen people" (my italics).

For Hauerwas, a company at the Lord's Supper is not threatened but enhanced by the "coming of the stranger" into its midst. The eucharist is a sort of training by which "we learn to make others' histories part of our own." So "the miracle of the church is God's sign that war is not part of God's providential care of the world." But if the church is such a "sign"—if indeed we are learning to make others' histories our own—then the peaceable kingdom of Christ is not yet. And, of course, there are churches that believe that God's "providential care of the world" specifically includes *the state* as a "preservative ordinance," and that the Lord's Supper is an eschatological meal in the sense that we show forth the Lord's presence till he comes. I do not wish here to cast any doubt upon Hauerwas's view on the issues my summary introduces. (After all, his book is dedicated to me and Yoder!) I do suggest that both pacifist and nonpacifist Christians take *the life and teachings of Jesus* with utmost seriousness. They do so in different fashions, such as that of St. Augustine, who said that it is precisely the *new* law of Christ that killeth; and Luther, who would not allow Christ the Pattern to come before his eyes except in moments of absolute assurance in Christ his Savior; and Reinhold Niebuhr, for whom the life, teachings, and crucifixion of Jesus were decisive for his elucidation of the *relevance* of an *impossible* ideal. Theological ethicists should simply cease charging one another with failure to take Jesus seriously. Here in Hauerwas's appropriation of Jesus Christ we can begin to see some of the things the chief pastors and teachers of the church should find ways of saying to the churches—if they mean or meant to speak up for pacifism.

We have come full circle. There is an *aeonic* discontinuity between the old and the new creation, which the Methodist Bishops level to a linear worldview. They write: "It is Christ who calls us to become ambassadors of a new creation, a new Kingdom, a new order of love and justice," citing 2 Corinthians 5:17–20 (FD, p. 12; cf. FD, pp. 28–29). Jonathan Edwards's interpretation of these verses was truer to the New Testament, and very likely quite Wesleyan as well. Verse 17 reads: "Therefore, if any one is in Christ, he is a new creation; the old has passed away, behold, the new has come." Edwards's comment on the new life in Christ is that the "new creation" is new in all its parts, only not perfectly so. If the new creature were not wholly new, if any particular of the old remained, that would be monstrous, just as, if any part was missing from the first creation, the "foetus" would be a monster. In this sense, the old has entirely passed away, only not perfectly so; the new has come, only not yet perfectly. (Sermon on I Cor. 13:7, entitled "Christian Graces Concatenated Together.") That was, for Edwards and Wesley, to be going on to perfection. By the "new creation" we mean the Kingdom Christ is building up in the soul, building up also in the history of Redemption. So the Corinthian passage ends, by specifying the un-*earthly* dimension of becoming "ambassadors of a new creation"; this means "ambassadors for Christ, God making his appeal through us. We beseech you on behalf of Christ, be reconciled to God" (ver. 20). *That* is not a message Bishops should address *to nations*, or teach Methodists to address to governments. The elision of this age with Last Things/Ultimate Things meant also an elision of the purposes of church and the purposes of government; and evangelists of *shalom* became ambassadors of a new order of worldly justice and peace—a considerable watering down of the gospel.

These serious theological flaws in our Bishops' initiative lead necessarily to their attempt to transcend or reach beyond past Christian political wisdom about the "just endurable" peace of this world, and also beyond a full account of justice in war if war-prevention/peace-keeping fails. Logically, then, when we examine the *moral argument* of *In Defense of Creation* in chapter 3, we should expect moral argument to be stretched thin— indeed, stretched until it snaps. Before coming to that, some perspective on what I have said so far may be provided by an analysis of the "already but not yet" theme in the U.S. Catholic Bishops' pastoral letter.

2

An Ecumenical Interlude

AMONG five points on which representatives of the U.S. Catholic Bishops received "guides and points of reference" from other national Bishops' conferences and the Holy See at the Vatican consultation (January 18–19, 1983), one point questioned the adequacy of the second draft's use of Scripture and its eschatology, particularly in the section on "Kingdom and History" and the final section on "Challenge and Hope."

See "A Vatican Synthesis," *Origins, NC Documentary Service,* vol. 12, no. 43 (April 7, 1983), pp. 691–95. A third criticism of general interest was formulated as follows: "The draft pastoral letter seems to presume that a certain *dualism* has existed in the whole tradition of the church with regard to the problem of war and peace: a tradition of non-violence *on the same level* as a tradition of acceptance of the just-war principles. Does this correspond to the historic reality?" (p. 692, col. 3). The discussion of this question reported that "several participants remarked that the draft pastoral letter in speaking about non-violence and just-war *seems to propose a double Catholic tradition*: a tradition of non-violence and a tradition along the lines of the just-war theory that existed throughout the history of the church. . . . Other participants indicated that non-violence has never been seen in the church as an alternative to the just-war theory. . . . *It was clearly affirmed that there is only one Catholic tradition: the just-war theory,* but that this tradition was subject to inner tensions coming from an ever present desire for peace. The relevant passage in the draft letter would therefore have to be re-elaborated. . . . *The U.S. Bishops denied* affirming in the pastoral *that a nation as such can adopt a pacifist stand*" (p. 694, col. 2 and 3; my italics). No significant changes were made in the pastoral in response to this fraternal criticism at the Vatican consultation. I judge that the U.S. Bishops' letter is a significant American "development of doctrine" in elevating pacifism as an alternative to participation in war for Catholic youths, but that the pacifism of "nonviolent resistance" was not made an alternative for responsible statecraft—except as a prudent choice of less lethal (i.e., nonlethal) means of resistance if deemed effective.

I propose in this chapter, as a kind of counterpoint to the Methodist Bishops' statement, to consider the "already/not yet" of the Catholic pastoral letter *The Challenge of Peace*. I apologize for the selectivity entailed in doing this: There is no space and this is not the time for a full and adequate comment on the Catholic document. Since, however, a chief theological criticism of our Methodist Bishops' document is its flawed account of Last Things/Ultimate Things, the reader may be instructed by a brief look at the same theme in the Catholic pastoral.

When transmitting the summary of discussion at the Vatican consultation to the *ad hoc* drafting committee, Archbishop John Roach and Cardinal Joseph Bernardin commented on the peace already and the peace to come. Concerning the first section singled out above, they wrote: "The question is one of emphasis—how we *express* the possibilities of realizing the 'peace of the kingdom' in history and whether we give too much significance to human effort in this explanation." Concerning hope and theology of Last Things in general, they reported that "the concerns expressed about eschatology can be met by *rephrasing about two paragraphs* of the pastoral letter" (my italics).

See "A Positive and Helpful Exchange of View," *Origins*, vol. 12, no. 43 (April 7, 1983), p. 696.

The two points the U.S. Bishops had no trouble accepting were summarized by the Vatican consultation:

> In the section on kingdom and history, the affirmation on "the kingdom to be achieved in history," especially with reference to Isaiah's promise, does not reflect correctly *the difference between the Old Testament and the New Testament*. It should also be made clear that "believing that peace is possible" expresses not a credal statement but *a mere conviction that respects the eschatological nature of the kingdom*. In the section on challenge and hope, it is said: "And we remind you that all of us have firm reasons for hoping that God is truly bringing about his kingdom of justice and peace, and that we can look to a future in which all God's people, even those who may be considered 'enemies' will live together in peace." Here again the

text should clearly *avoid mixing up two distinct levels and differing realities*: our faith that the kingdom of God will come and the realization that it is not certain if and when true peace will effectively exist in the world that is ours. ["A Vatican Synthesis," p. 694, col. 1 and 2; my italics.]

Notice the two-letter word "if": It is not certain if true peace will exist any "when" in our world; it *is* certain the kingdom of God is real in God's world and will come; his kingdom of justice and peace is the ground of our hope, but we do not "look to a future" for that. The Isaiah reference was the second draft's flat assertion that "Isaiah's promise of the reign of God (Is. 2:4), in which peace will be a primary characteristic, *must be achieved in history*" (my italics).

See the second draft of *The Challenge of Peace*, *Origins*, vol. 12, no. 20 (October 28, 1982), p. 310, col. 3. Isaiah 2:4 reads: "And he shall judge among the nations, and shall rebuke many people; and they shall beat their swords into pruning hooks; nations shall not lift up sword against nation, neither shall they learn war anymore."

That did not reflect correctly the difference between Old and New Testament expectations of a kingdom of peace and harmony.

Small changes these may have been, as Roach and Bernardin said, but they were changes that made considerable difference. The third and final draft of "Kingdom and History" simply omitted the references to Isaiah 2:4, with the assertion that has been questioned, and began instead with the *next* sentence: "The Christian understanding of history is hopeful and confident but also sober and realistic" (*The Challenge of Peace*, par. 56).

Nevertheless, merely to repeat "already but not yet" so many times is likely to continue to mislead readers to suppose that the "not yet" of the peaceable kingdom refers us once more, and again and yet again, to some future historical period. Indeed, the more one says "not yet" with only a slight difference between kingdom-expectation and real-world peace, the more liberal progressivism gains entrance. I know no way to express the needed correction *in propositions* except to say that Christ's Kingdom is now as fully present *in time* as it will ever be or that the coming consummation of the reign of his righteousness is trans-historical "history" (as was man's original life in innocence).

Now, no theological objection should be lodged against expressing the taut tension between the presence of the kingdom *behind* us and *with* us, on the one hand, and, on the other, the kingdom still *before* us, by using the shorthand "already but not yet." Indeed, there's much to be said for it. But if my point here is arguably merely verbal, it is a verbal matter that (like "discerning the signs of the times") tempts many persons to evacuate Christian meaning from their minds. If Bishops (Methodist or Catholic) haven't noticed this from splashes in the news of their pastorals or among the faithful they address, or even among episcopal minds, it may be appropriate for me to remind us all that we need to watch whether our language is still capable of conveying meanings it once had. If what is meant is something like Reinhold Niebuhr's "the *relevance* of an impossible ideal" (or block that word "ideal," the constant judgmental and redeeming *relevance* historically of an "impossible" world-transcending incarnational *reality*), then we'd better say so without the confusing "not yet . . . not yet . . . not yet"—which soon translates into "some day."

It is when the "already" and the "not yet" of the presence of the kingdom are spread out, as it were, over historical time in which we live toward the incoming kingdom that longing for the peace of God tends to blur with longing for world peace. The density and depth of Christology and Christian eschatology are stretched thin, into the wish that peace among the world's powers might be so. Only not yet. Not quite yet—ever. Now, who remembers that last little word? Or remembers that the Bishops just said that world peace can never be entirely obtained or long endure? The "*but not yet*" is flattened out into progress proposed by the Enlightenment.

Even if endless temporal progress lay before us, it would foster a rather unhealthy state of mind. A proper representation of human beings stretching *forward* in aspiration toward a future they fear to admit is unattainable is the account of Zeno's arrow that Tom Stoppard placed in the mouth of the philosopher G. E. Moore, in his play *Jumpers*: "It was precisely this notion of infinite series which . . . led . . . Zeno to conclude that since an arrow shot towards a target first had to cover half the distance, and then half the remainder, and then half the remainder of that, and so on *ad infinitum*, the result was, as I will now demonstrate, that though an arrow is always approaching its target, it never quite gets there, and Saint Sebastian died of fright."

Earlier than the revised section of Kingdom and History, the Catholic Bishops state, "We believe the religious vision [of peace] has an objective basis and is capable of *progressive realization*." That meliorist statement is followed by "Christ is our peace" and by Ephesians 2:14–16, about his creating "in himself one new man in place of the two, so making peace, and might reconcile us both to God." That, of course, called for the admission in the next sentence that we know that "this peace will be achieved fully only in the kingdom of God." Then follows a restatement of progressivism, in a "therefore" statement that plainly is a *non sequitur*: "The realization of the kingdom, *therefore*, is a continuing work *progressively accomplished*, precariously maintained and needing constant effort to preserve the peace achieved and expand its scope in personal and political life" (par. 20; my italics).

In the revised section itself, introducing the expression "already but not yet," we are told that because of sin "the realization of the peace of the kingdom [in history!] is never permanent or total," on the one hand, and, on the other, that "the kingdom of God will come in spite of sin, human weakness and failure" (par. 57). The big guns of the eschatological "already but not yet" thunder that "we already live in the grace of the kingdom, but it is not yet the completed kingdom" (par. 58).

That immediately translates into two tensed propositions: ". . . We are convinced that 'peace is possible.' At the same time experience convinces us that 'in this world a totally and permanently peaceful human society is unfortunately a utopia, and that ideologies that hold up that prospect as easily attainable are based on hopes that cannot be realized whatever the reason behind them'" (par. 59); such "deceptive hopes lead straight to the false peace of totalitarian regimes." These two opposed outlooks (both recent papal statements) are composed rather too smoothly into the expectation that "peace is possible but never assured and that its possibility must be continually protected and preserved in the face of obstacles and attacks upon it" (par. 60).

Why do I keep thinking of poor Saint Sebastian, and of Zeno's arrow endlessly striving toward its target but never reaching . . . ? Perhaps he died not of fright but from a coronary because of so much spiritual striving toward a goal that is *always* "always possible" *yet* always, always "not yet"!

Is it really necessary to use kingdom-expectation to fuel the fires of realistic and persistent worldly peacemaking and peacekeeping? Or to suppose there is one line on the heavenly railroad, with assuredly possible world peace as the next to last way station? That, however, is far, far better eschatology than some Protestants who, if I have been hearing rightly, fondly hope there will be a time when the conductor announces "World Peace and Justice, Last Stop"!

The section "Kingdom and History" is preceded by a section entitled "Peace and the Kingdom." We find there an account of the "already/not yet" that (for want of a better metaphor) we must call "vertical," or that contains greater stress on the "vertical." In contrast to the horizontal, future reference of the "not yet," these same words point to the transcendent presence of the peace of Christ now. Anyone comparing the two pastoral letters will find a foundational and transcendent *present* Presence of the peaceable kingdom that is sorely lacking in the Methodist document; at least this *primary* dimension does not have in *In Defense of Creation* the same density or solidity for the church to stand on.

The section on "Peace and the Kingdom" begins with four meanings of the word "peace": (1) "an individual's sense of well-being or security"; (2) "the cessation of armed hostility, producing an atmosphere in which nations can relate to each other and settle conflicts without resorting to the use of arms"; (3) "a right relationship with God, which entails forgiveness, reconciliation and union"; and (4) "eschatological peace, a final, full realization of God's salvation when all creation will be made whole." "Among these various meanings," the Catholic Bishops say, "the last two *predominate in the scriptures and provide direction to the first two*" (par. 27). This paragraph is introductory, of course. I suggest, in passing, a point the Catholic Bishops do not make concerning the relation of the last two points specifically to number 2. The "direction" provided by the distinctively theological meanings of peace insures that worldly "peace of a sort" may be more positive than is stated here. But if we adopt a *too expansive* notion of the peace possible on earth (no. 2), numbers 3 and 4 will to that degree be diminished in the heights and depths they have in Christian understanding.

For background, see two works by one of the "Fathers" of the Second Vatican Council: Yves M.-J. Congar's *Le Christ, Marie et L'Église*, Desclée De Brouwer, 1952 (English translation, *Christ, Our Lady and the Church: A Study in Eirenic Theology*, Longmans, Green and Co., New York, 1955); and his *Lay People in the Church: A Study for a Theology of Laity*, Bloomsbury Publishing Co., London, 1957. Citing the first, Bryan Hehir commented that because of our different theologies of nature/grace there is more room for human effort and "divine intervention in a collaborative mode" than in classical Protestantism. The second of Congar's books, he believes, stands behind the Kingdom and History section—together with *Gaudium et Spes*, Pt. I, ch. 1–4. Hehir does not believe that the quotation of Isaiah 2:4 was so integral to the pastoral that its deletion required substantive change. Indeed, I grant that the problem in a Christian theology of peace is striking a proper balance in expressing the proper tension between the "already" and the "not yet." In distinguishing and then seeking to relate the different meanings of peace, the Catholic pastoral was arguing that pursuit of peace is an authentic *work* of the Kingdom. Seeking "to build" peace (a regular modern papal refrain) has intrinsic significance in a Catholic vision.

We need now to notice how peace with God and eschatological peace— all creation "made whole"—are conceived to be "already" a present Presence. This is the upshot of a subsection, "Jesus and the Reign of God." So before coming to "Kingdom and History"—to the "not yet"—the Catholic pastoral begins with that kingdom present among us. It begins with Christology. "Jesus proclaimed the reign of God in his words and *made it present in his actions.* . . . the reign of God had begun" (par. 44; my italics). The Sermon on the Mount describes "a new reality in which God's power is manifested and the longing of the people is fulfilled" (par. 45). Jesus' words were also a depiction of "the conduct of one who lives under God's reign," for example, forgiveness and love as "an active, life-giving, inclusive force" (par. 46–47). These words would remain "an impossible, abstract ideal" were it not for two things: (1) ". . . [H]e made the tender mercy of God present in a world which knew violence, oppression and injustice" (par. 48). In particular, in the resurrection and "only in the light of this, the fullest demonstration of God's reign, can Jesus' gift of peace—a peace which the world cannot give (Jn. 14:27)—be understood." Peace he gives when "he greets them as their risen Lord in the fullness of salvation" (par. 51). And (2) Jesus gave his Spirit as a personal gift and a communal gift to the church (par. 52–54). In summary, "Jesus Christ, then, is our peace, and in his death-resurrection he gives God's peace to our world" (par. 54).

That's a good but by no means unusual account of the "already," that is, of the *first* term in taut tension with the "but not yet." The Catholic Bishops say as much: "The fullness of eschatological peace remains before us in hope and yet the gift of peace is already ours in the reconciliation effected in Jesus Christ" (par. 55). Why, then, do I introduce these themes?

I do so largely as background for a concluding brief comment on the present Presence of the peace now given and now ours in Catholic eucharistic piety. "Contemplative" prayer "rises, by divine grace, where there is total disarmament of the heart . . . This silent interior prayer bridges temporarily the 'already' and 'not yet,' this world and God's kingdom of peace" (par. 294). At the beginning of the rite of the Mass, "the community asks God, to 'grant us peace in our day,' not just at some time in the distant future." But this petition rises from human hearts in eucharistic encounter with the risen Lord who gave and gives us his peace. The priest continues the church's prayer for peace: "Lord Jesus Christ, you said to your apostles: I leave you peace, my peace I give you. Look not on our sins, but on the faith of your Church, and grant us the peace and unity of your kingdom" (par. 295).

In the eucharist, also and principally, the "already" and the "not yet" are bridged—even before participants are encouraged to make the sign of peace, or there is any sending forth of the people into the world. This is some guarantee that—at least among those who understand the faith of the church—the "not yet" of Christ's reign shall not be loosed from its moorings or the church set on pilgrimage to some distant future not the Kingdom of Heaven.

Ironically, a spirit of work-righteousness pervades *In Defense of Creation* more than it does *The Challenge of Peace*. This unexpected reversal is not a minor point, but it deserves mention only in footnote, because of my chosen abbreviation of the "interlude" you have been reading. There's a "natural law" optimism in the Roman Catholic ethos (and *since* the Second Vatican Council, a natural-law optimism more and more stripped of natural-law limits and prohibitions). Among Wesleyan distinctives none can be more fundamental than our teaching concerning Christian perfection. It sometimes seems that this emphasis in our understanding of the common Christian doctrines of *regeneration* and *sanctification* has begotten more optimism concerning *natural* "man and his communities" than that afforded (until lately) by the more inherently optimistic teaching based on "natural law." Nourished and formed by the Wesleyan tradition, the outlook and "on-look" of a pastoral letter on the pursuit of peace in the nuclear age should have a fundamental understanding of Christianity and politics *not unlike* the various versions of the "Two Cities" doctrine I cited and amplified in the first theological/biblical part of "A Political Ethics Context for Strategic Thinking," reprinted in part in the Appendix to this volume.

Readers of *In Defense of Creation* will find there also many of these themes common to Christian faith. On the present Presence of the peaceable kingdom in Scripture, however, our Bishops' (or their writer's) exegesis pales by comparison. But my main point is a constructive one. I venture to say that the Methodist Bishops—or anyone else—will not understand the Christian pacifism they pass over lightly until we recover the eucharistic piety and theology in the hymns of John and Charles Wesley. Witness to peace in the world unfolds and overflows from the *real presence* of the peace of Christ in Word and Sacrament, sealing together the "already/not yet." Out of this real presence in the community, hearts reach out to *signify* peace to the world—far, far more than they live future-related, seeking to bridge the gap between the here and now and some "not yet" kingdom on earth we were never promised.

I understand the Christian pacifism of Stanley Hauerwas, for example, to be eucharistic in nature; it is certainly not a result-oriented political strategy. To sum up, the "already" and the "not yet" are already bridged in the incarnation, cross, and resurrection, but the bridging is not yet complete in the whole life of God's redeemed people. Therefore, their different Christologies are crucial in understanding the fork in the road where Christian pacifists and Christian just-war participants part company and go on their incorrigibly different, perhaps *equally valid*, ways amid earthly kingdoms and empires.

A revival of Wesleyan eucharistic piety and practice may also be needed for Methodists to begin to understand again that the imperatives of government or the obligations of citizens simply cannot be the same as God's peace—whether we speak up for just war or for pacifism.

After this venture into comparative pastorals on theological foundations, we now turn to the moral and political reasoning of the Methodist statement.

3

Thinking about Just Peace
in the Nuclear Age

I AM bewildered overall, puzzled in detail, as to what to make of the Bishops' statements about pacifism and just-war traditions (and, for that matter, a one-sentence tribute to the "crusade" or holy war) among past Christian positions on participation in war. Our chief pastors claim to have used their "understanding of those insights of both pacifism and just-war theory which speak with relevance to the issues of the present nuclear crisis" (FD, p. 92). That "understanding" seems to be that the "common ground" between those two Christian outlooks is "their moral presumption against all war and violence" (FD, p. 13). Such an equivalent understanding is mistaken, although *after* a "just cause" has been determined there is in the secondary principle of "last resort" a presumption against violence *similar* to that of pacifism.

Here are grounds for my general bewilderment. The Bishops wish to "keep alive" in the churches both pacifism and just-war analysis, and at the same time they wish to "go beyond" or "transcend" them both. They claim to have devised a *new* theology for a just peace (FD, pp. 23, 35) based on consequent social-justice issues that neither pacifism nor just-war theory reaches, or decisively builds upon. In attempting the (quite impossible) transcendence of these two options for Christian conscience, the Bishops virtually recommend some sort of pacifism. Sticking close to the logic of what they *morally* justify, not only to what they say, this is clearly the upshot. Yet they continue to excuse (and "responsibly" support) military and deterrence policies for which any *ethical* justification has been denied. We are urged to tolerate the morally intolerable a while longer. This is all quite bewildering.

Hauerwas and I—and others of either likemindedness—are advised to make "fresh inquiry into those transcendent issues which stretch beyond private conscience and rational calculation" (FD, p. 13). The Bishops disparage "the narrow limits of all-too-typical religious arguments between the claims of individual conscience over killing and the rational calculation of justice by rulers" (FD, p. 24). For the moment, I pass by the latter question-begging description; it was reliably rumored that from its inception at least one member of the drafting committee was resolved not to fall into the trap of "rationalism," as the Catholic Bishops did. My point now is to say that I know no respectable Christian pacifist for whom *the point* is the purity of individual conscience over killing. Pacifism is, in their view, the politics Jesus introduced into our world, or at least it is the objective way the church's discipleship should go. Moreover, I would insist that the one thing Christian pacifists and just warriors have in common is that if anything is shown to be *per se* a moral atrocity, or to have no "just cause" *now*, it should be given Christian endorsement *no moment more*.

But I run ahead of myself. Let us see how just-war theory is played out.

"Three of those [just-war] principles are especially tested by nuclear war and have helped us form our own judgments" (FD, p. 13; cf. FD, p. 34). On first reading, that struck me as very odd language, and it still does. The Bishops do not say, "Three especially of the just-war tests have formed our judgments." That would have accorded those tests too much credit as enduring criteria for justice in war. Then do they mean to say the principles are especially tested and found wanting? That goes too far in the other direction. It would be like saying the Sixth Commandment and Jesus' teachings are especially tested by coeducational dormitories in Christian colleges and by Methodist divorce and remarriage practice, and found wanting. Evidently the Bishops do not mean this, since by analogy the principles and the commandment still "help." Do the just-war tests—as they fall exhausted from their final, supreme, breathless act of condemning nuclear war and deterrence, or fall far behind in their desperate attempt to keep up in endless relay race with military technology—pass the baton to the Bishops'"new theology of a just peace"? This, some have supposed to be the meaning, from newspaper accounts; but I think not.

The Bishops share with Enlightenment liberalism a reluctance to call any war or resort to violence "just." So they distance themselves from the three principles of reasonable hope of success, discrimination, and proportionality even while using them to form their own condemnation of nuclear war and deterrence. True, their account of these principles is only minimally accurate. The explanation of discrimination as "the moral immunity of civilians from *direct* attack" is correct. But the Bishops still seem surprisingly reluctant to *teach* their constituents that the technical word "direct" prohibits (only) the deliberate human act of intentionally aiming at civilians, not their foreseeable destruction collateral to aiming at legitimate and important military targets. The reader is still permitted to believe that the principle of discrimination can be violated "whatever the intention of political and military leaders" (FD, p. 34). That could be a violation of proportion—doing the greater evil—but again this would be immoral only if such destruction was the intention (or the only intention that can be imputed to military commanders or reasonably construed from their actions). Plainly, the Bishops are straining to produce from these tests verdicts that acts of modern warfare are *wrong* or *unjust* without suggesting to someone, or instructing someone, that by the same standards some military actions or policies today could be *just*, or that immoral military policies (deterrence) could be reshaped to fit just-war norms.

Sure enough, there it is in the *Guide for Study and Action* (p. 7, col. 1): "the principle of *discrimination* (which prohibits attacking noncombatants)." At my suggestion, and I presume that of other respondents as well, the Bishops corrected #17 of their "Guiding Principles" (FD, p. 37) to read "refrain from *directly* attacking noncombatants." In my response to the first draft, I had written that, if the telescoped expression "attacking noncombatants" were retained, the Bishops then should explain that by "attack" they mean intentional or deliberate attack upon civilian life. Without some such elaboration, I pointed out, they would be expecting ordinary readers to understand a too abbreviated expression of the just-war norm. Now there will be pastors and teachers throughout the UMC using the "explanation" (in the *Guide for Study and Action*) of the three just-war principles, which the Bishops conclude "cannot be met by any nuclear war." If so, church people likely will be told by their class leaders that *discrimination* "prohibits *attacking* civilians" (Session 2, p. 7, col. 1)! Of course, the Council of Bishops is not responsible for everything done in the name of its initiative. Still the door was opened to abuse of just-war norms by the fact that the Bishops needed only the "principle of *proportion* (which requires that the benefits of war-making outweigh the harm it causes)" (ibid.) to condemn *nuclear war*. Nuclear *deterrence* required more *nuanced* understanding, as did issues of non-nuclear war-making and deterrence.

The list (FD, pp. 33–34) of the seven criteria of just war has been rearranged (in response to my suggestion, and doubtless that of other respondents) to begin with "just cause" and "just intent," and not with "last resort" as in the first draft. "Last resort," I wrote,

is the criterion that states the just war presumption against violence and war. [I reminded them that] this means "last politically reasonable resort," and not, e.g., letting Hitler take the Rhineland, etc., requiring far greater violence and destruction to stop him later—as Bonhoeffer realized inside Germany at the time. [Therefore] the presumption against violence built into "last resort" is set within the larger context of a *presumption against injustice* in the just war tradition.

Just war and pacifism do not share an equivalent rejection of violence. Pacifism's presumption is in favor of *peace* (or else peace and justice are believed never to conflict). Just war's presumption favors the defense of an ordered *justice* (which sometimes may not consist with peace). *Just cause* is overarching in just-war theory; *within that*, last resort comes into play. If and only if there is found in justice a possible cause of war is there a presumption against resorting to violence to be taken into account. Thus a presumption against *injustice* is a lexically *prior* presumption to the "presumption against going to war" under "last resort." Confusion, not clarity, comes from saying that this is *like* pacifism's rejection of any use of violent means. So, I seriously suggested that the listing of these tests be rearranged to reflect the logical priority of just cause and just or *right* intention—unless the Bishops wanted deliberately and intentionally to retain a sequence that, by placing last resort first, begs the question about the shared equivalent presumption against violence.

The final draft adopted by the Bishops removed "last resort" from first place. But everywhere they continued to assert and build upon the supposed common presumption against violence. And the rearrangement did not persuade the Bishops to admit "just cause" into their own arguments except "to say *No*, a clear and unconditioned *No*, to nuclear war and to any use of nuclear weapons" (FD, p. 13). The most remarkable single-sentence avoidance of the very notion of "justice" in the cause of war today is this: "There are morally significant differences among the world's political, social and economic systems," the Bishops observe (FD, p. 35). "That," they go on to say, "is the lingering kernel of truth in *the crusade tradition*." I should have thought it to be a kernel of truth in the just-war tradition. It is elementary that a *just* cause need not be holy (indeed, should not be deemed holy). Then it is realistic to expect that "just cause" may sometimes be found among the *morally* significant differences among the world's political systems, as without cessation they clash and cooperate, cooperate and clash, by night and day, to the end of the world (or until there is a *just* world authority capable of preventing all war and of removing all threats of war).

There's something deeply troubling—something at once ingenious and disingenuous—in recent publications that (1) advocate pacifism, condemn all Christian participation in war or its preparation, and then (2) adopt the hypothetical assumption that the just-war tradition is correct in order to show that this leads to these same pacifistic conclusions in the nuclear age (or for that matter for the entire twentieth century, with its arsenals of "modern" weapons). The Bishops do not do this. Nevertheless, it will become clear that they distance themselves from the just-war criteria even while using some of them. This cannot be regarded as an intellectually serious probe into the imperatives of government incorporated in those norms. Just-war tradition only blunts the force of a deep undercurrent of pacifism that runs throughout the pastoral.

The simple fact is that these episcopal documents are ambivalent. Traditional just-war morality provides "too narrow a base from which to discern many of the most salient issues of the nuclear crisis" (FD, p. 32). Yet the Bishops won't let it go: In the next sentence they disagree with "those who claim that nuclear weapons have simply nullified just-war tradition altogether." Indeed, they do definitely need to keep these criteria alive, in full force, in support of the sweeping claim (our Bishops believe, vs. the Catholic and Episcopal Bishops) that "the *logic* of this tradition ultimately discredits nuclear deterrence as a morally tenable position" (FD, p. 33). (This categorical verdict requires some discriminating assessment that I will introduce later.) Those three "tested" principles from "the still-valuable just-war tradition require us to say *No*, a clear and unconditioned *No*, to nuclear war and to any use of nuclear weapons." Still, the Bishops note that their *No* to nuclear war and weapons is more than a matter of "ethical calculation" (FD, pp. 13, 34). I do not see why Wesley's Quadrilaterals (FD, p. 10: scripture, tradition, *reason*, and experience) were mentioned in the final draft (not in the first) if the Bishops were resolved to prefer prophecy and vision over "rationalism." What can be better than rational calculation discriminating between justice and injustice in answering the questions, Whether to war? and, If to war, how?

Of course, proportionality (or economy of force, or prudence) is more than a *formal* principle. We need not wait to apply the principle case by case, or "measure for measure," force against force, to ever-increasing heights. We can with good reason determine that the present arsenals of armament in the possession of the two superpowers and their allies are *materially inordinate*. This became the case when first one side MIRV-ed nuclear missiles and then the other side did likewise. Whether with *three* or with *ten* nuclear devices on the lethal end of a missile from *one* base, separately targeted upon three or ten objectives, this mathematically meant that both sides would soon *run out of targets*—whether pointed discriminately at military or indiscriminately at "significant" civilian targets. This sort of deterrence can only fuel an arms race. It built overkill on both sides into the rightly intended end of mutually preventing the use of these weapons. Nuclear deterrence became inherently disproportionate, even if both "we" and "they" share the deterrence and peace is kept.

I know of no serious analyst of international affairs who does not endorse mutual riddance of this redundant, disproportionate, dangerous deterrence; or who would not acknowledge in a quiet hour the shared responsibility of the U.S. and U.S.S.R. for the present disastrous overdevelopment of deterrence.

Urgent warnings from church leaders concerning this situation are not for this reason themselves redundant, nor are calls for planned withdrawal from such issued to the churches and to the nations. Still our chief pastors needed to *articulate* deterrence *if* they aspire to be teachers of citizen-responsibility to their members. Plainly, by "deterrence" our Methodist Bishops mean the disproportionate deterrence just described. At least, their withdrawal of the church's blessing can only be from such deterrence, unless they mean to speak up for some version of pacifism. For the only way to get rid of deterrence is to get rid of nations (or to dream of nations without arms)—or collectives by whatever different name—in an international system. Deterrence, in short, is *a fact of life*, if there is not one government capable of ruling the world justly.

Most often the word "deterrence" is used in the Foundation Document without predicating any qualification on it. More qualifiers than the word "nuclear" are needed if we are to engage in an adequate discussion of deterrence. The question is justice in the posturing of arms to deter war and to project power abroad. Whether or not there can be and need be or must be a nuclear ingredient in a *moral* deterrent system was the question for voices of the church to address directly. How to reshape arms and deterrence policy is not even opened by episcopal documents that speak always and only (or even mainly) of the immorality of the present deterrence policies of the U.S. and the U.S.S.R. It may also be the case that there are *conventional* deterrence systems that should be deemed morally unacceptable. In general, if and only if a weapons system has no other use than for targeting populations in war-fighting or in deterrence, or for *disproportionate* deterrence, are those *weapons* immoral. The line to be drawn between a moral and an immoral deterrent cuts across the distinction between nuclear and conventional weapons, or may do so. These were the questions to be addressed.

So far, I have expressed my general bewilderment as to how to understand the claim that, "in the roundedness of *shalom*, a just-war ethic is never
enough" (FD, p. 35). Now we will turn to my puzzlement in detail. Here,
we shall see, puzzlement turns into doubt.

The Bishops distinguish between "primal" issues and "consequent" issues
(FD, pp. 14, 39). We must come to terms with these terms. By "primal" is
meant "blast, fire, fallout—the hard reality of nuclear weapons themselves,
their more- or less-direct physical impact" (FD, p. 39; cf. p. 14). We might
call these *proximate* issues, or, as the Bishops say, "the *elemental* questions as
to whether any possession or use of nuclear weapons is morally permissible" (FD, p. 40; my italics). (Other weapons are not given "primal" consideration, since the renunciation of *war* is assumed.) The Bishops pay tribute
to "some theologians who have earnestly sought to address these primal
issues," but who have "typically . . . drawn on pacifist and just-war traditions in their efforts" (FD, p. 39). Evidently our chief pastors believe that to
go beyond or transcend those Christian options we must be convinced to
give *primacy* to the "consequent" issues in questioning the morality of
Christian participation in modern warfare. It is in any case the "*consequent*
issues [which] stretch farthest beyond the classical war-peace debate" (FD,
pp. 14, 39).

An alert reader will ask at this point, Are there no other "primal" or
immediate issues than *nuclear* destruction? Are there no other forms of war-
prevention than our present deterrence policy, if among the imperatives of
government are the constraint of sin, "defense against enemies," and "national security" (FD, p. 25)? That the Bishops do not *here* ask about any
other weapons, do not *here* ask any other justice-questions, signals the fact
that they implicitly believe there can be no *just* cause for any resort to any
armed force in a nuclear age. By considering only nuclear weapons at this
point, the Bishops avoid balancing the well-known destructiveness of war
against injustice to be resisted, or, better yet, against innocent, wretched
lives to be protected or relieved from the systemic harms they daily suffer.
War becomes a "social justice" question only when we come to the remote
consequent issues.

Limiting their consideration of the primal issues to "the elemental questions as to whether any possession or use of *nuclear* weapons is morally
permissible," the Bishops offer an "Ethical Spectrum" of seven possible
positions, ranging from pacifism to extreme bellicism. They state succinctly
the inherent ambiguity or paradox of nuclear deterrence. "As a war-prevention strategy, deterrence represents a just cause. ["Right intention," intending an ordering of peace, better describes the good of deterrence.] As a

potential holocaust, deterrence represents unimaginable evil. Christian thinkers differ greatly in their attitudes toward this awesome moral ambiguity" (FD, p. 40). Hence the seven spectrum positions, two of which deserve some comment.

No First Use/Deterrence. This was the view of, among others, the Roman Catholic Bishops, who took their theme from Pope John Paul II's 1982 statement: "In current conditions 'deterrence' based on balance . . . as a step on the way toward a progressive disarmament, may still be judged morally acceptable." Our Methodist Bishops have succinctly stated the "awesome moral ambiguity" of deterrence. They have unambiguously announced (in disagreement with the Catholic Bishops) that "the logic of this [just-war] tradition ultimately discredits nuclear deterrence as a morally tenable position" (FD, p. 33). They are at work setting primal issues, just-war tradition, and pacifism to one side or behind them in developing "a *new theology for a just peace.*" Let the reader determine which ethic—the old or the new—is eccentric to the other. At this point I only want to emphasize that a close analysis of the discernible differences between the two councils of bishops on deterrence is requisite to an understanding of the ecclesial or the moral state of the question today.

First Use/Deterrence. This is better explained as First-Use *Option* against Conventional Attack/Deterrence. Paul Ramsey is said to be the "most notable exponent" of such *counterforce* strategies from a Christian just-war perspective. The seventy-word summary of a position I had taken is adequate enough. Four comments only may be needed to furnish the context. (1) I used the expression "counterforce" in contrast to counter-*people* war-fighting or counter-*people* deterrence. "Counterforce" has since acquired other meanings and connotations. "Counter-combatant" is a better term today. (2) My fullest exposition of preserving the option of "first use" dealt with tactical battlefield weapons *within the limits of another "rule"* to be unilaterally imposed on such use: only over one's own territory or the territory of one's allies, accepting the collateral damage ourselves, after an adversary's massive conventional attack had crossed borders deemed just to defend. (3) As a Christian ethicist I endeavor to place restraints upon myself as an advocate. My "office" involves thinking through and elucidating *possible* applications of just-war principles, especially discrimination and proportion. So I once elucidated stages in a *just* "graduated deterrence" that, if needed by states in the international system, included the Bluff. When subsequently I removed the latter peak from my sketch of a possibly justifiable deterrence, this was primarily because of conviction that the Bluff would be *immoral*, not because it wouldn't work politically. (This also I am competent to say as a citizen. On the immorality of a Bluff ingredient in deterrence, see pp. 206–7.) (4) In 1966–67, less than two years after my 1965 pamphlet, which the Bishops summarize, I explored the conditions that might make possible the exclusion of battlefield nuclears and the reduction of the ingredients of a graduated deterrence to the conventional-force level. (There is a reference to this, p. 201 below.) In other words, I was exploring the "No first use" position. Unfortunately many prominent advocates of "No first use" today emphatically do not want any alteration to be made in our immoral counter-population deterrent! Here is a devil of a moral dilemma that won't come out except by much prayer, fasting, and *concentrated attention* to the *primal* issue of justice in war and deterrence. So my retention of the option of First Use against Conventional Attack never excluded the option of war-fighting conventional forces readily perceived to be sufficient to deter conventional attack. We shall find a gaping hole here in what the Bishops have to say *morally* about conventional forces.

Spectrum positions 2 through 5 appeal to just-war norms. "We must now call attention to a disturbing fact: these sharply contrasting moral views on nuclear weapons, from nuclear pacifism to moderate deterrence to limited nuclear war and infinite escalation [?], all appeal to just-war doctrine to support their case. There is no consensus on the application of the just-war tradition to nuclear weapons" (FD, p. 44). Disagreement may be regrettable, but if contrasting conclusions are "disturbing" in the sense that a common framework of moral reasoning is believed to be thereby called in question, the reply is fourfold. (1) Disagreement on practical matters does not invalidate; indeed significant disagreement is impossible without commonly assumed moral norms. (2) As I have publicly asked whether the Holy Spirit informed the political prudence of the Catholic Bishops in their specific recommendations (and if He did, how we could *know* He did), so I now suppose that the question that needs to be asked of our non-authoritative Methodist episcopal initiative is whether the Holy Spirit accounts for their specificity, their discovery of a narrower range of options on war and peace in the nuclear age (defense or "development"—you can't have both). (3) In any case, "consensus" never proved anything to be right, nor can lack of it prove any practical judgment wrong. I might add, with an impish twinkle in my eye, that (4) We shall have to wait to see whether the Bishops' crypto-pacifist evacuation of meaning from "just cause" gains agreement today, and then ask *why* contemporary American Methodists may very well constitute some sort of consensus around that opinion, around documents that, the more I study them, sound more and more like the left wing of the Democratic Party at prayer. But again I run ahead of the texts.

At page 44 of the Foundation Document (quoted above and correctly at my "[?]"): "The Bishops imply that the just-war tradition is too flexible to be really helpful in the current situation" (*Guide for Study and Action*, Session 7, p. 17, col. 1).

"Infinite escalation" begs the question; indeed, it is quite false. By just-war teachings, any nation's military policy leading to "infinite escalation" was wrong *ab initio*. Perhaps the Bishops were thinking of one of the two final spectrum positions, either *Counterforce Superiority* ("Winning" or Prevailing, which is never distinguished, by the way, from a deterrence policy of being *inferior* to none) or *First Strike Policies*. The diagram provided for the use of teachers of Session 7, *Guide for Study and Action* (p. 17, col. 2), shows clearly that such policies would be condemned by just-war norms. No comment is needed on them—except that I must say that it went below the belt to illustrate *First Strike* by remarking that Soviet leaders "remember the years when some American political and military leaders blatantly advocated a preemptive strike," with no mention of how in plan after plan the U.S. tried to persuade the Soviets to join in "internationalizing" the Bomb when we alone were possessors of it. Bertrand Russell was one of those "perfect peace" advocates who urged that, while the West had the monopoly of atomic power, we issue an ultimatum threatening a devastating "first strike" if the U.S.S.R. did not agree to internationalization.

There are two transitional sections that should be given the closest possible attention before coming to the *consequent* issues on which ultimately depends the Bishops' understanding of the justice that alone is decisively pertinent to verdicts concerning the morality of war in today's world. The first of these passages is "The Idolatry of Deterrence" (FD, pp. 46–49). Serious *moral* questions can be raised concerning the Bishops' "justification" in this section of continuing support for something categorically declared to be morally unjustifiable. The second passage transitional to the morally serious *consequent* issues of social justice is the section on "Nuclear Weapons and Conventional Weapons" (FD, pp. 53–54).

The latter section (FD, pp. 53–54) I lift out of order, since the *consequent* issues were introduced in the section preceding it ("Nuclear Weapons as a Justice Issue" [FD, pp. 52–53; cf. FD, p. 15])—in a rhetorical sequence that eloquently proclaims "Justice, of course, is the prime concern [in letting the three "tested" principles condemn nuclear war and deterrence] . . . Justice is also offended . . . Justice is abused . . . Justice is forsaken . . . Justice is defiled . . . Justice is denied . . ."

Surely, whether *conventional weapons* are just and necessary for defense and deterrence is also a "prime concern," an immediate or proximate concern, under the first of these sequential affirmations. The Bishops chose not to consider conventional forces here, in context with the "elemental" questions of the "direct impact" of nuclear weapons. This was a major failure in moral/political thinking. Instead, the topic of conventional forces is brought up later, after or while consequent social-justice issues are discussed. Governments, on the contrary, must engage in some rational calculation, like it or not, of a number of weapon systems *before* or *as* any of the *consequent* issues of social-justice costs of national defense come into view.

1. The first passage begins with a seemingly softer claim: "We have said that the just-war tradition *does more* to discredit deterrence than to support it. We have discerned a lack of coherence in deterrence" (FD, p. 45). Presumably, consequent social injustices will clinch the final disaccreditation of deterrence. For our Bishops grant the short-term benefits of deterrence in inhibiting resort to nuclear weapons, though this effect is difficult to prove. They are profoundly correct in discerning the "fundamental flaw" in deterrence with redundant massive counter-society weapons, the "contradiction between inordinate confidence in the rationality of decision-makers and the absolute terror of annihilation. Nothing in our understanding of fallible and fallen human nature," they rightly say, "warrants the expectation that this relentless strain between reason and terror can endure indefinitely." The usual response that we *must* assume minimally rational decision-makers, and that there's nothing like deterrence (or being shot at sunrise) to alert the mind, are no answers to the Bishops' dismal prognosis. But neither, I regret to say, is answer to be found in their eschatological hope in a new Earth-ethics.

The thing most worth remarking upon in this section on deterrence, however, is its astonishing *moral analysis*. The Bishops refer to "some Christian leaders" who "have sought to *justify* deterrence as an *interim ethic* while nuclear-weapons states pursue arms reduction" (my italics). Pope John Paul II's "interim ethic" in his 1982 address to the United Nations is again quoted: "deterrence may still be *judged morally acceptable*" as a step toward "progressive disarmament" (FD, p. 47). Our Methodist Bishops reject that interim *ethic*, that provisional moral *justification* of deterrence, that statement of a context in which deterrence can be *judged morally acceptable*. They reject this outright. They will have no terms of moral approbation used of deterrence.

At a Southeastern Jurisdictional Convocation on the pastoral (Lake Junaluska, N.C., August 3–7, 1986), Bishop Roy Clark, a member of the drafting committee (and a former student of mine at Millsaps College), asserted that the best interpretation of the section on deterrence was in terms of an interim *ethic*. This goes against the plain statements in the text and does not comport well with the Bishops' well-known resolve to "go beyond" the Catholic pastoral. Unfortunately there was not time for me to find out what was in Bishop Clark's mind. He was not asked to respond to the addresses Hauerwas and I gave.

The evacuation of all moral language from the Bishops' temporary acceptance of nuclear deterrence is far more important than their probably correct, factual judgment that "deterrence no longer serves, if it ever did, as a strategy that facilitates disarmament, that deterrence now fuels the arms race." (I would say, *redundant* nuclear deterrence now fuels the arms race.) The point of nuclear deterrence always was only nuclear war prevention and nuclear peacekeeping; the Catholic Bishops are also in trouble over *what to say next*, having added states' purpose of disarmament extrinsically to purposing weapons for deterrence. For, if the stated conditions are not fulfilled, or not rapidly enough, church councils will be drawn more and more into doing the business of states—determining not only the moral aspects of deterrence but other questions of diplomacy and international relations as well.

The U.S. Catholic Bishops resolved in November 1986 that they "publicly recognize the increasing evidence that the conditions for the moral acceptance of deterrence are not being met." Once again a committee of Bishops was formed to study the question. The *Times* news report quoted Fr. J. Bryan Hehir, secretary of the Catholic department of social development and world peace, as saying that the new committee's function was to "examine the conditions set on deterrence in 1983" by the Bishops' pastoral letter, and "to see how or whether they are being fulfilled." Fr. Hehir elaborated: "When you give conditional acceptance to deterrence, you have committed yourself to stay in the nuclear debate, because you obviously have to measure whether your conditions are being met" ("Catholic Frame Deterrence Study: Panel of Bishops to Review Missile Defense Plan and Other Nuclear Issues," *New York Times*, May 4, 1986).

What to say next is a trap if, *but only if*, what was said went too far beyond essential Christian moral norms into particular options. The Roman Catholic Bishops may have preserved more than Methodists have of the common Christian memory of the ancient practice of the church's speaking truth to temporal power about all sorts of questions, *and getting something done about them*. Neither church would today seek such a merger of the ecclesial and the temporal powers. Here then is another reason for caution when speaking for the church: One might have to continue to deliver political wisdom about particular policies! Fr. Hehir noted that the Catholic pastoral letter conditionally accepting deterrence "set conditions that were basically of two kinds: first of all, that deterrence was justifiable as a framework within which one would be moving toward a different kind of security arrangement between the U.S. and the Soviets." Disarmament and/or World Order could be two things by which "to measure whether your conditions are being met." Unfortunately, it takes two (or more than two) to tango up to those peaceable ends of the nuclear age and/or of the international system. The *morality* of deterrence, or of a particular design of deterrence, with what weapons and what intentional targeting, are all questions *intrinsic to purposing deterrence*. Linkage of a proper assessment of the morality of deterrence with the goal of disarmament or world order raises questions of a different order, purposes other than deterrence itself. A form of deterrence is morally acceptable or unacceptable from its inception, and not because of those outcomes or replacements.

When I say it takes two to tango up to those peaceable worlds, I do not imply that, for sure, it's the U.S.S.R. alone that refuses to negotiate disarmament or international peacekeeping institutions. I mean rather to say that linkage of the acceptability of deterrence with other purposes—placing conditions on deterrence other than moral assessment of its own features or design—is bound to confuse the mind on the question of what to say or do next. Decent people and good Christians alike whose "acceptance" of what on the face of it looks threatening and wicked, and whose sleep is disturbed by dreams of peace on earth, must soon be persuaded that our own government is the one that refuses to tango. For the liberal premise is that it's always possible to dance. Christians have special reason to cultivate in themselves not only national self-criticism but also an awareness that "anticipatory reconciliation" can bias the mind against one's own nation.

It helps to free the mind from bias one way or the other to entertain the notion that a "balance of forces," arms control (not disarmament) for deterrence (if morally acceptable) are policy goals that need not be means to other ends (however desirable). Fr. Hehir also spoke of another kind of assessment of deterrence, more nuanced than, I believe, our Methodist Bishops could appeal to in the future. "The second kind of condition was what you might call *the character of the deterrent.* That is to say, if the moral justification of deterrence rested with preventing the use, then one had to examine each of the major additions to the nuclear arsenal precisely to be sure it did not lead in the direction of use rather than deterrence." Was the Catholic pastoral's acceptance of deterrence provisional in this sense, or conditional on progress toward a world in which no deterrent is needed?

In any case, there are already voices calling upon the U.S. Catholic Bishops not to address again the "moral principles" but to focus attention upon the "moral judgments" in their pastoral letter. "One need not delegitimate deterrence as such," writes David Hollenbach, S.J., "in order to reach a conclusion that there are fundamental flaws in current policy" ("Whither Nuclear Deterrence?: The Moral Debate Continues," "Moral Notes," in *Theological Studies*, 47/1, March 1986, pp. 117–33). That advice is exceedingly apt to lead in the direction of more particular dictates to government coupled with an unintended collusion with the powerful forces that would keep in place the present deterrent that has kept the peace for three decades by exchanging hostage populations as targets.

If deterrence is emptied of every possible *moral* justification, even in an interim *ethic*, what then should Christians do? That would settle the matter for any traditional pacifist, nuclear pacifist, or just-war Christian, if so convinced. (Indeed, a nuclear pacifist is simply a just-war theorist so convinced!) The deterrence system would have to be dismantled immediately; or if not, Christians would have to disentangle themselves from complicity with it for as long as it continues to exist. The one thing Christian pacifists and just warriors have in common is that, if anything is shown to be *per se* a moral atrocity or to have no "just cause" *now*, it should be given Christian endorsement *no moment more*. Our Bishops do not concur in this. They avoid this conclusion by a line of "reasoning" I find impossible to understand. Have the Bishops not abandoned moral reason and spiritual guidance when they write:

The rejection of nuclear deterrence, however, does not necessarily mean immediate unilateral disarmament. Those who regard themselves as nuclear pacifists do not hold a fully responsible position if they only say No to nuclear weapons: they must share in the difficult political task of working out a strategy of phased arms reductions. . . . Deterrence must no longer receive the churches' blessing, even as a temporary warrant for the maintenance of nuclear weapons. The interim possession of such weapons for a strictly limited time requires a very different justification: *an ethics of reciprocity* as nuclear-weapon states act together, in agreed stages, to reduce and ultimately to eliminate their nuclear arms. (FD, p. 48)

How does "interim possession" differ from the "interim ethic" the Methodist Bishops reject? What is the "very different justification" of their "interim possession" if it is not (which nevertheless they claim) *an ethics* of reciprocity? At first I thought the Bishops' chief proposal would better be called "a *process* of reciprocity." But then they have a still better name for it. They call for unilateral initiatives that would be "an *invitation* to reciprocal national restraint," and even give this an acronym, RNR (FD, p. 77). This is a process that diplomacy should always seek: *invitations* to tango, which requires two partners. To call this *an ethics* is only a fig leaf covering the fact that the Bishops never adequately analyze the *primal justice* questions confronting statesmen and citizens alike concerning either the use, preparation, or maintenance of military forces. But suppose there is such a thing as *an ethics* of reciprocity (distinct from a *policy* seeking reciprocity). What is *that* if it does not include judging deterrence to be "morally acceptable" within and for the duration of staged steps in disarmament? What is the meaning of the word "responsible" in the Bishops' charge that nuclear pacifists do not hold a "fully responsible position" if they simply say No to nuclear weapons now? What could "responsible" mean besides *morally* responsible (or morally irresponsible) in some sense? Are the Bishops telling us to do what simply *must* be done because a totally immoral deterrent still works, or that something that must no longer "receive the church's blessing" (FD, p. 92) even by interim *moral* warrants should be upheld as a temporary *expedient*, lest worse befall? Are we to sin (or let others in silos sin for us) that the grace of disarmament may abound? Such a *consequentialist* ethics may fit the *consequent* issues on which the Bishops finally rest almost every statement about justice; but in this there is no *principled* ethic. For the Bishops there is no *just cause* for participation in political tasks that meanwhile *uphold* the "interim possession" of nuclear weapons.

2. Under their spectrum position *No First Use/Deterrence*, the Methodist Bishops noted that, to endorse "no first use," the Catholic Bishops "reluctantly" raised the prospect of "some strengthening of conventional forces" (FD, p. 42). Our Methodist Bishops will have none of that either. So when they take up "Nuclear Weapons and Conventional Weapons," they categorically reject any coupling of nuclear with conventional defense policies. (This proves that conventional weapons are one of those "primal" issues nuclear-weapon states must confront, and which should have been considered earlier.) "We cannot support the view that NATO would have to undertake a massive build-up of conventional forces before renouncing its option to respond to a conventional attack with nuclear weapons," the Bishops declare (FD, pp. 53–54). The word "massive" serves to make that sound plausible. Still we must ask the reasons offered for rejecting the need for a build-up of conventional forces coupled with the adoption of a "no first use" policy. The need to strengthen conventional forces is based on "two assumptions that appear very dubious to us." The first is the belief "that the USSR would seriously contemplate an invasion of NATO territory" (FD, p. 54). If that is dubious in Soviet contemplation, it must be because of the war-preventing effectiveness of deterrence maintained by "preserving the option." We have just considered the baffling moral reasoning by which the Bishops urge traditional pacifists and just-war nuclear pacifists, while still alive, to keep alive the wholly immoral interim possession of nuclear weapons. And we are about to learn that conventional weapons serve no just cause either, and are only to be possessed for a similar morally dubious interim.

The second reason offered for there being no need to strengthen conventional forces is a factual one: "the Warsaw Pact conventional forces would [not] overwhelm NATO conventional forces." I hope our Bishops know that to be true. I do not. But the following can surely be said. Among the factual reasons cited in support of the episcopal judgment that "a major conventional escalation by NATO is hardly necessary" is the "lingering Soviet suspicion that NATO *might* resort to nuclear weapons even after a 'no first use' declaration" (FD, p. 54). Now, how did that piece of hypocrisy get in there? In this fact warranting no build-up of conventional forces, nuclear deterrence returns in full array, and maybe bluff-deterrence at that! We are to count on that, among the *facts*—not, however, as something "morally acceptable." I venture to say "hypocrisy" because in other contexts it is not. The reality is that only the nuclear power that has and maintains believed-sufficient conventional forces can seriously adopt a "no first use" policy—and mean it.

The section ends, as it must, with a secularized eschatological expectation that the harmony of *shalom* will harmoniously come to pass. The call is to "create the climate" in which conventional-force reductions could also be negotiated even as deterrent nuclear forces are dismantled. We must "find ways to combine" both disarmaments. "The war system itself must be overcome."

We have now arrived at the *midpoint* of the foundation study document. This reader has moved from bewilderment in general through puzzlement over details to holes in the practical reasoning large enough for the Clydesdale horses to pull a moral argument through. A beautiful sight, but hardly edifying. The gaps in the argument are identified in the two numbered paragraphs above. Having stipulated that "in the roundedness of *shalom* a just-war ethic is never enough" (FD, p. 35), our Bishops were *necessarily* left with only two outcomes: inadequate or even shoddy just-war (or other) moral argument concerning the pressing *primal* issues of government; and utopian visions emblazoned over the *consequent* or long-run social-injustice issues.

With a full half of the Foundation Document yet to come, what more can the Bishops say? This must be the center of gravity of their *"new theology for a just peace,"* for which end they have transcended and gone beyond traditional options for Christian conscience. All praise to any effort to say something new addressed to new situations! But something so *entirely* new is a different matter. Despite all talk about keeping alive the traditional options of pacifism and just-war norms, in surpassing these positions the Bishops have in effect *evacuated* all terms of discriminating moral approval or disapproval that might be applied to the interim possession of systems of armaments they both blanket as totally evil and nevertheless urge be upheld a while longer. Specifically, there seems to be no "just cause" *prior to* or *contemporary with* any war-fighting or war-fighting *capability* (we Methodists long ago "renounced war"); and there is no deterrence *now* that can ever be deemed to be "just" war prevention. It is impossible to imagine a greater denuding of the moral language in which war and peace issues, and the task of governments, have been discussed. "Justice" and "injustice" talk is finally reserved for the *consequent* issues; and, of course, of these two terms it is "injustice" that does the work of the latter half of the Bishops' document.

The *consequent issues* are introduced and summarized in the "Justice is offended . . . outraged . . . abused . . . forsaken . . . defiled . . . denied" passages (FD, pp. 15, 52–53). Another summary passage describes consequent issues as "second- and third-generation issues," the "many long-term ramifications of nuclear technologies not only for the physical environment but also for all human institutions and behavior: political, economic, scientific, educational, cultural, and psychological" (FD, p. 39). There is "a web of influence" in which all basic institutions are implicated: a "military-industrial-political-scientific-educational-recreational-media-religious complex" (FD, p. 56).

The *Guide for Study and Action* speaks of the "Jerusalem web of influence" in connection with Bible study of Jeremiah 27–28 (which see!) and comments, "One cannot always trust the web of influence to speak the truth" (Session 8, p. 19, col. 1). The description of "this web of influence" (used twice, FD, p. 56) is quite enough to convince anyone that this, indeed, is a fallen world!

The human cost of arms build-up in the name of "defense" is memorably stated: "US 'rearmament' is being purchased with foodstamps" (although a Congressman is quoted as saying that our contempt for the poor is such that there is no assurance that, if the arms race were to stop tomorrow, the funds would be transferred to human needs) (FD, pp. 56, 58). Then there is "the strain of psychological contradictions" everyone is under: the "rational management of suicidal terror" (FD, p. 59) and the constant fear of "futurelessness" (FD, pp. 60–61). Also, there is the "new cold war," a "fractious force within many nations" and a "major source of injustice to the world's poorest people," which turns every North-South justice issue into an East-West confrontation (FD, p. 69). The arms race or development: The world cannot have both.

I cannot omit comment on the first of the series of statements about justice: "*Justice is offended* in the double standard under which some nations presume nuclear weapons for themselves while denying them to others" (FD, p. 15), "seeking by every moral, legal, and technical means to deny them to others" (FD, p. 52). This offense against justice is elaborated and listed among the bitter complaints of the "South" against the social injustice of the "North": "This simultaneous inequity of being economic have-nots and nuclear have-nots is storing up a reservoir of bitterness with unpredictable consequences" (FD, p. 69). I understand and agree with what the Bishops were indicating by that statement; but is it not strange to press the moral claim to *equality* to the point of demanding *equity in iniquity*? To the point of demanding equal access to the possession of weapons on which has been pronounced an unqualified No? To the point of demanding fairness in a sort of "having" that cannot receive the church's blessing? Does not this particular instance of consequent social-justice advocacy come close to taking advantage of the poverty of undeveloped nations to seduce them into wickedness, rather like the contention in the matter of abortion (let us suppose a sort and circumstance of abortion that *we agree* would be immoral) that, since rich parents can procure them, poor parents should be given access to them also? We ought not to add the inequity of being abortion have-nots to the inequity of already being economic have-nots!

My first thought upon reading *In Defense of Creation* on the *consequent* social-justice issues (which means social-*injustice* issues!) was the slogan repeated often in the "pacifism between the wars." I am certainly older than any of the voting Bishops; so I drank more deeply than they of the heady hopes of that pacifism even in face of the plain signs of the times in the gathering storm of World War II. "There are many, many evils worse than war," we used to say, "and war is the cause of them all." This is part of the context in which it is correct to say that "many of the most prominent United Methodist leaders of the twentieth century have been pacifists" (FD, p. 31). In the same breath it should be acknowledged that the pacifism between the wars (reacting against the failure of World War I, fought with "holy war" zeal, to achieve unearthly Wilsonian goals such as ending war) weakened the will and the readiness of the Allies in taking the "last *timely* resort" that reasonably could have stopped Hitler without the terrible destruction needed later.

As a student at Millsaps College from 1931 to 1935, I listened (with earphones, over my crystal radio set) to the silver-tongued oratory of Harry Emerson Fosdick. Kirby Page and Sherwood Eddy were principal speakers on college campuses and at YM and YWCA summer conferences. So I know all too well the lure, the siren song, of consequent social-justice issues summed up in the slogan that war is the cause of every evil worse than war. Even nations had ritually renounced war as an instrument of public policy in the Kellogg-Briand Pact.

Not much more need be said concerning the consequent social-*injustice* issues, on which depends almost the entirety of the Bishops' *moral* reasoning. If only they had first shown (among the *primal* issues) that there are and can be no more *necessary* wars that may or could be *just*. (No one wants anything other than to reduce drastically the weight of armaments upon the people of the world.) If only they had not exhausted the just-war doctrine in proving the obvious: Nuclear *war* should never be fought and cannot be won. If only they had not earlier evacuated any use of the discriminating moral language of justice and injustice in relation to war-fighting forces other than nuclear war. If only the nuanced principle of discrimination had not been melded into disproportion. If only the Bishops had really come to grips with more than a passing need for deterrence and had dealt with the *morality* of deterrence (in distinction from the justice or injustice of nuclear *or* conventional war-fighting). If only the movement had not been so rapid toward consequent social injustice. If only the Bishops had found an exit from all they rightly say about the immobilization of politics other than by visions of perfect harmony—after long and arduous peacemaking, no doubt. If only—now we come full circle—to proclaim *shalom* had not been *decoupled* from a proper Christian theology of Last Things/Ultimate Things and mislocated among the *direct* aims of the international diplomacy of earthly cities in which the church is a pilgrim.

This leveling-up of worldly peace and leveling-down of Christian hope in a new heaven and a new earth into a one-world, linear aim at peace by institutional good works formed the basis of my written response to the Foundation Document, chapter 6, pages 82–90, on "The Church as Peacemaker" in the first draft. I must report, I wrote the drafting committee (among other things), an increasing sense of oppression, suffocation, even of totalitarian claims for peacemaking. The church, the family, worker or professional guilds, seminaries, "every aspect of their [pastoral] ministry . . . can be an opening for peacemaking." Every aspect? Grant that understanding the Gospel's imperatives in political life is not optional, that this is "integral to our pastoral care of souls in a warring world" (FD, pp. 87–88). Still, have not transcendent dimensions in the care of souls in such a world been drastically omitted? All lesser communities and relations appear co-opted for one cause, and co-opted to the whole extent of their being and value. Perhaps I read not prayerfully enough. Still the Bishops might remind themselves that in their *next* episcopal initiative they may want some energy left over to serve other causes, or specialized "vocations" for different goals! And I'd say the family has as one of its purposes going fishing, without contemplating whether this activity fosters *shalom*. The family may be a "potential greenhouse of all peacemaking" (FD, p. 85); but the family is also to the glory of God, into which children are born to be reborn and baptized in Christ's name, incorporated into his church forever. I confess the same recoil from the expression "Christian nurture for *political ministry*" (FD, p. 88). Such reduction of the Gospel can only produce young Reinhold Niebuhrs who find in their ministry that they really have nothing to say to people caught in industrial and other *strife* and nothing to say to the simple old woman of great faith in her dying (*both*, it is usually forgotten, reported in *Leaves from the Notebook of a Tamed Cynic*).

One additional aspect of the Bishops' call to peacemaking should be singled out and lifted up to view. There is special place for "the ministry of the laity" (although it is said—questionably, indeed—that "those who serve in *church* vocations are primary gatekeepers who can either open or close the opportunities of corporate witness to the things that make for peace") (FD, p. 87). I should have thought "the universal ministry of the faithful" was our belief, and that, if distinction is to be made, in *politics* the laity would be the primary gatekeepers. Be that as it may, the Bishops call upon the laity to be "vital bearers of *shalom*, working through *vocational* guilds (occupational groups) in ways that are appropriate to each field of work" (FD, p. 87). One such occupational group urged to study the tasks of vocational peacemaking consists of Methodist men and women in the armed services. The sole word that may, by a stretch, be taken to be addressed to these, our fellow Christians, is:

> We know that scientists, engineers, and other workers involved in defense industries face difficult questions of conscience. We want our churches to help such persons confront these questions eth-ically; we urge the churches to provide a supporting fellowship for such persons in whatever vocational choices they make. (FD, p. 87)

Is that not a lame word to persons in military and defense-related vocations integral to the care of souls in a warring world?

In this the gap, the fault, in the Bishops' *moral* argument (discussed in the paragraph numbered 1 above) is clearly evident. I see some sentimental sense in asking the churches to provide a "supporting fellowship" for such persons. But what can it mean to "want our churches to help such persons confront these questions *ethically*," when their vocations *consist in* activities the Bishops have declared cannot "receive the church's blessing," can never be "judged morally acceptable," not even as an interim *ethic*? Unless these judgments are withdrawn or nuanced, all that joins us together with men and women in the military services, defense industries, etc., is "responsibly" working together with them (under the immoral umbrella of the possession of arms, not nuclear alone) to advocate a *policy* of reciprocal arms reduction, the issuance of "invitations to reciprocal national restraint (RNR)." Where are the "difficult questions of conscience" in that? Methodists can, of course, do *that* till Kingdom come—and seem likely to do so. The question of questions, however, is our *systemic* complicity meanwhile in activities for which our chief pastors have found no moral justification.

Here was the point at which the Bishops should have fished or cut bait. If they mean our church to renounce war as an instrument of national policy, if they mean to go for broke for a world without war as the only world that can be *morally* acceptable, then we should tool up to become a pacifist church now. Then let the call go forth for Methodist men and women to come out of the military and out of the defense industries. Let our theolo-gians and pastors in their care of souls in a warring world attend to the problem of conscience in discerning acceptable and unacceptable "degrees of *complicity*" ("cooperation," this has been called for centuries) *in grave evil*. Is there a difference between proximate and remote complicity, material and formal (rational) cooperation, in the web of evil that is the deterrent state, a warring world? Should an engineer who uses his highest human faculties in weapons design leave his post, while a Methodist working man, with five children, who sweeps up at night is morally permitted to continue to earn his living in a defense industry? The Bishops have raised again Luther's question "Can a soldier also be saved?", as well as questions of political conscience all along the line: *Voting* for Senator Sam Nunn of Georgia could be one of these. Some such morally and theologically serious pacifism as I have suggested would be a forthright expression of the spirit that pervades *In Defense of Creation*.

Return with me one moment more to the just-war teachings, to a point to be conveyed in the church-wide educational program that was launched. The teacher of Session 5 is advised to write on a newsprint sheet the *seven* main principles of just-war assessment and to "explain that *all* of them must be satisfied for the use of violence to be considered to be *just*" (*Guide for Study and Action*, p. 14, col. 2). The statement that all the just-war norms must be satisfied is in itself quite correct. The need for *teaching* Christian traditions is short-shrifted, however, when class members are asked to begin by indicating how close they stand to one or another of the three classical positions and whether they agree with the Bishops that any use of nuclear weapons would violate three of the criteria of just war. *No profound search* for the meaning of the three classical positions or the seven just-war norms or the three that bring in the verdict of "guilty" against nuclear war and deterrence is acknowledged to be needed. What is the reasonable meaning of "last resort"? Must "*every* possibility of peaceful settlement of a conflict . . . be tried before war is begun" (FD, p. 33; my italics), even if there is the possibility of greater destruction later if resort to arms is unreasonably delayed? Does "last resort" encompass "*timely* resort"? Who or what process in the world of today has "legitimate authority" to initiate use of violence? There needs to be a relentless search for the *meaning* of just-war tests in contemporary contexts in order to use them rightly in moral reasoning. If the Bishops treated them in passing, this will be the case even more so in church education.

But set these questions aside. More important, the explanation that *all* the tests must be met—no more said—can become a thoughtless, legalistic way of condemning all wars one at a time, and any war test-by-test. No wrestling is begun to discover political wisdom in this long-standing Christian tradition. No allowance is made that morally acceptable, necessary wars may be more or less just, or that violation of one test may be more or less serious than another.

The most deplorable failure, however, is the omission of any sense of

tragedy or sorrow Christians may have to endure, and should cultivate
under the tutelage of these norms, when resort to violence in a palpably just
cause cries to high heaven for us to rescue the perishing and *we cannot do so*
because in the attempt greater evil would be caused than prevented or
corrected. I find one mention of this mortal sorrow in *In Defense of Creation*.
Following a short list of blunders on both sides in the history of U.S.-
U.S.S.R. relations since 1917, the Bishops draw attention to the abounding
moral ambiguities in most international conflicts, and they rightly urge that
"we must cultivate a profound sense of tragedy about the suffering that
might have been prevented by sounder understanding" (FD, p. 65). Sad as
such lack of understanding may be as a cause of suffering, that is not tragic.
And "regret" is a better word for it than "sorrow." The Bishops' sense of
"tragedy" is over "might-have-been's" that, they intimate, might not have
been. That is mistake or misfortune, not tragedy. The sense of tragedy
inculcated by a proper use of just-war political wisdom is, by contrast,
moral anguish over inevitable clashes between *justice*-reasons for going to
war and *disproportion*-reasons prohibiting it. The sounder our understanding, the more the moral anguish over suffering we *ought* to let continue
unrelieved because to topple the oppressor would bring on as great or
greater suffering.

   This is the chief lesson to be drawn from learning that all the criteria must
be satisfied for a use of violence to be fully justified. Along with that, there is
another very important lesson, namely, that more is at stake for the Christian in political life than mere "justice." The Catholic Bishops' pastoral
stated this when it said that the "central premise" of the many forms of just-
war argument over the centuries is "the Augustinian insight that from love
we should restrain an enemy who would injure the innocent." All that I
myself ever attempted to explicate from that Augustinian insight has been
the *logic*, the heart and soul, of such protective love: If one is permitted to
war to protect the innocent from continually being killed by an oppressor,
then one is *prohibited* from injuring the innocent as a means of stopping that
oppressor. Hence the principle of discrimination: that noncombatants must
be held "morally immune from deliberate, direct attack." It *cannot* be a work
of love to *aim* at innocent life to relieve the suffering of other innocents.

   The fundamental move, out of Christian love, to *resistance* of evil was made in my
Basic Christian Ethics (1950; ch. 5 pp. 153–57, 166–90), before I had read the
landmark article by John C. Ford, S.J., on "The Morality of Obliteration Bombing,"
which decisively influenced my chapter on "The Genesis of Noncombatant Immunity" in *War and the Christian Conscience* (Durham, N.C.: Duke University Press,
1961).

Even to express the clash between the love-and-justice reasons for engaging in resistance (violent or nonviolent) and the reasons of disproportionate evil for not doing so exhibits rather well the moral anguish of placing oneself under obligation to all the rules of just warfare. Anyone who for the love of Christ is morally bonded to both the oppressor and the oppressed, and to the bystanders (e.g., the children) of both, is not likely to come through with hands unclean only from the suffering of others that might have been prevented by sounder understanding. I cannot be certain that our Methodist Bishops understand this. Reluctant as they are even to use the word "just" of a nation's use of violence, it seems too much to ask that they understand just-war teachings to be the "alien" work of *love*. They define "just cause" as the vindication of justice in response to some serious evil; and to illustrate "serious evil," they add "such as an aggressive attack" (FD, p. 33). Not too much should be made of this illustration, but it does suggest that *defense* of oneself, one's own, one's own nation is the chief motivation in *jus ad bellum*. That is the language of the modern period—the aggressor-defender doctrine. The language of just-war teachings is that of positive protection of the neighbor. Hence, again, the moral anguish in a world of conflicting neighbor-relations. Hence, also, the need for thoughtful reflection on the "just" and right thing to do amid these conflicts. Such reflection is required by the tension among just-war teachings, by the fact that we are obliged to observe all the norms. So to relieve the tension,

> As we ring down the curtain,
> We believe in intervention
> Provided it's uncertain.

A Christian pacifist, on the other hand, has reason to complain that the Bishops—in going beyond pacifism, or nuclear pacifism—never say what's wrong with that position ethically or biblically. A standard objection to the pacifism of nonviolent resistance is not open to them. *In Defense of Creation* assumes the primacy of a moral distinction between nonviolent resistance and violence. Language rejecting *violence* and assessment in terms of degrees of violence (a quantitative understanding of "proportion") are used throughout. So the Bishops cannot consistently adopt Reinhold Niebuhr's telling point, that Christlike love is *nonresisting* love (and does not mean nonviolent *resistance!*). In saying this, I do not mean that the *agape* of the New Testament is *passive*, or that Christian pacifism is *passivism*. It is rather the simple and sound New Testament conjunction of the imperative "do not *resist* evil" (Matt. 5:39) with the imperative "*overcome* evil with good"

(Rom. 12:21). Overcoming evil with good is surely positive, active, ever alert in the service of God and of our neighbors in God. This does not say, however, always "overcome evil with good" when you can; but when you cannot, go ahead and "*resist* evil nonviolently!"

So one line of Christian moral reasoning concludes (as, I think, it is not open to the Bishops to object against the pacifist position) that the distinction between resistance and nonresistance is primary; that the distinction between violent and nonviolent resistance is secondary; that just-war sorts of assessments *govern either type of resistance* and govern the choice between them; that, of course, one chooses nonviolence rather than violence in every conflict situation in which there is *proportionate* reason to do so, that is, when the benefits of nonviolent resistance outweigh the harm it allows to continue to be done. Measured by nonresisting love overcoming evil with good (not to mention sweet reasonableness), nonviolent resistance is also an *ultima ratio*, an appeal to the arbitrament of strength for the settlement of disputes. "What an amazing way of deciding controversies! What must mankind be, before such a thing as war [or nonviolent resistance] could ever be known or thought of upon earth?" (Wesley, FD, p. 83).

Whether or not the Bishops understand the pacifism they reject, I do not know. If they understand the "classical" pacifist position to be the same as nonviolence, then a part of the reason they never fully state their moral objection to it must be because *In Defense of Creation* is a quasi-pacifist document *in that sense* of pacifism. Thus, the Bishops "encourage special study of nonviolent defense and peacekeeping forces." Much is made of Gene Sharp's proposals, drawn from twentieth-century instances of non-violent *defiance*, and of the proposal of Ronald Sider and others that an International Christian Peace Guard be established in such conflict areas as South Africa, Northern Ireland, and the Polish-Soviet border. Nonviolence as a political or military strategy seems to me to be war (or *revolution*) by other means, under another name. Gandhi and Martin Luther King taught us something. Let us agree that there is need for cadres of people trained to lead a population in nonviolent resistance for justified revolution or just defense, no less than there is need for armed resistance. "Command" and "control" of these "forces" would require that the two kinds of *resistance* of evil be kept separate. If the same "troops" were trained in both forms of resistance, nonviolent resisters, sensing failure, might become trigger-happy and not wait for "command" to raise the level of resistance; and, if violent resistance of evil began to do more harm than any likely good to come from such resistance, prudent "control" must assuredly be able effectively to return to the level of nonviolent resistance. For much the same reasons, if there is any role for battlefield nuclears, these weapons should not be in the hands of the troops that man the conventional weapons. These simplified suppositions indicate vividly that prudence, or the principle of proportion, governs the movement up *or down* any scale of *resistance of evil.* These distinctions are morally very, very important; but the gradations are each and every one *not* nonresistance of evil or overcoming evil with good.

I myself cannot comprehend how the nonviolent resistance the Bishops commend consists with, for example, their fine little section on "A Peaceable Spirit" (FD, pp. 83–85). Violent *or* nonviolent resistance must be an alien work of such a spirit. Or so it seems to me.

The equivalent argument for nonviolence as a crypto-military strategy influential in the "pacifism between the wars," even under the shadow of Hitler, was Richard B. Gregg's *The Power of Nonviolence* (Nyack, N.Y.: Fellowship Publications, 1959; first published, 1934), with its justly famous chapter on nonviolence as "moral ju-jitsu." There is some sense that nonviolence is an alien work of love in William Robert Miller's *Nonviolence: A Christian Interpretation* (New York: Association Press, 1964); still I found that book so much a matter of *technique* that some journal is still waiting for a review of my well-marked copy of it. It needs also to be said that *either* means of resistance, *any* means of pursuing victory, needs moral governance. A morally serious use of nonviolence as power strategy must observe the same moral limits as the just-war tests impose on violent resistance, as I tried to show concerning blockades, sanctions, and incapacitating gases in *The Just War*, pp. 465–78, 352–53, in *Christian Ethics and the Sit In* (New York: Association Press, 1961), and as did Richard John Neuhaus in *Movement and Revolution* (with Peter L. Berger; Garden City, N.Y.: Doubleday, 1970).

In Session 3 of the *Guide for Study and Action*, the class leader is to write the words of Matthew 5:9 on newsprint and to "be sure to note that those who are blessed as God's children are those who actively *make* peace, not just those who are *peaceful.*" Then the study guide says: "Jesus offered a description of what it looks like for one to be a peacemaker later in the same chapter. Read, or have a participant read aloud, Matthew 5:38–48." Those are the words of Jesus that include, "But I say to you, Do not resist one who is evil. But if anyone strikes you on the right cheek, turn to him the other also . . . Love your enemies, and pray for those who persecute you. . . . You, therefore, must be perfect, as your heavenly Father is perfect." Then the class leader is told: "Hold a discussion of this text around such questions as [the following.]" I quote the first three questions: (1) "What would happen if you tried to live this way in your personal relations?" (2) "What would happen if you tried to live this way *as a society or nation?*" (my italics). (3) "What would happen if you did *not* live this way?" (italics in original). Would not readers of the present volume like to hear the answers to the second question? And the answer to the third question is that if we did not live that way, if nations did not, we would have a world very much like the world as it is.

In the passage (FD, pp. 80–81) in which the Bishops emphasize Gene Sharp's research into nonviolent resistance, they "recall once more that pacifists and just-war theorists share a moral presumption against violence." I have said enough about the *difference* between these presumptions against violence. I defer to Christian pacifists, such as Stanley Hauerwas, to say whether nonviolence as a power strategy approaches what they mean by Christian peacemaking.

At the end of this section on the flawed moral argument of *In Defense of Creation*, I searched in memory for a near analogy to it in the wrestling for the truth to be done during those years of pacifism before World War II, as the world moved into the necessary and just war against Hitler. Only the editorials written by Charles Clayton Morrison in *The Christian Century*—beginning with the outbreak of the war and published in 1942 as *The Christian and War* (Chicago and New York: Willett, Clark and Co.)—came to mind. The *Century*'s pacifism was replaced by no conception of the justice of participation in war. Likewise, the Bishops see no justice in ever participating in war. On the other hand, Morrison wrote, "War is not sin; it is Hell," that is, the inexorable *judgment* of God. "Hell is that realm or condition or situation . . . where good and evil have lost their distinction." "God does not command us to fight; he *condemns* us to fight." In less strong language, our Bishops "accept" the morally unacceptable; they urge responsibility within the war system the church never can bless. Not entirely unlike Morrison, the Bishops seem to say that the war system is "not the pure will of God" and cannot receive the church's blessing; but that it is "the frustrated will of God" that we should live "responsibly" within it until the time of war passes. The peace, freedom, and morality that, for Morrison, were real before the war are, for the Bishops, possible "after" war. No principles govern government in both peace and war. Peacetime is one time, wartime is another, a time of God's wrath (Morrison) or inexplicable necessities and lost opportunities (the Bishops). In a mood of memory and *déjà vu* stirred by writing these pages, I dug out a review of Morrison's book written for the *Garrett* (Seminary) *Tower* (November 1942). I wrote then some words that are not entirely inappropriate now:

> To re-read these editorials is to gain a new sense of the white heat of intellectual activity and Christian sensitivity in which the viewpoint of Christian "realism" toward the war was first struck off. Admittedly a position unformulated prior to the actual outbreak of war, there is nevertheless continuity and consistency in the *Century*'s editorial development, however reluctant pacifists and liberals, who on certain points have lost an ally, or [neo-orthodox], who to a degree have lost an opponent, may be to admit it. A chief weakness of the book, indeed, arises from the fact that Dr. Morrison retains too many of his pre-war conclusions. If he had been a little less "moralistic" with regard to his conception of God's will in peacetime, he need not have excluded all moral distinctions from the judging will which condemns us to war, and need not have gone to the extreme of finding in war itself no place at all for the conception of a redemptive counterpart for discriminating human action with regard to the war itself.
>
> Even in the chapter on "The Inexorables of Life," the thesis of which is the promising one that "the principle of necessity inhering in actual war is not unique in our experience," a too sharp distinction is still drawn between the "ethical" freedom, or arbitrary choice, of which the freedom to have pre-

vented this war is an illustration, and the "religious" freedom involved in our ability to make an affirmative or negative response to life's inexorables, of which our attitude toward the "meaning" of war as a judgment of God is a case. It is notable that these two types of freedom are brought together by the assertion that "unexpected ethical alternatives" spring forth from the surrendered will, and that "the exercise of our religious freedom, the freedom to say Yes to the inexorables with which the Lord of history evermore confronts us, is the ground of our true moral freedom," and, finally, that "We are not even morally free until we have surrendered our human will to the will of God as he reveals it in the events and situations of life that are not open." This, the deepest insight of the book, is insufficiently developed. One may venture to predict that Dr. Morrison will need to stress this aspect of his thought before this war is over and those conditions for "ethical" action are restored which he presumes to have been the case prior to war and to be necessary for any action that is "free" and not under the condemnation of the inexorable judgment of God.

Turn that around, recapitulate it as the relation of the necessities of our present time to a time of peace and justice to come, throw in a measure, heaped up and running over, of the optimism required by the great reversal of the sequence "peace-war" (Morrison) to the sequence "war system/peace" (the Bishops), and you have fair comment on *In Defense of Creation*. At least, I'll say so, as long as I am capable of being self-referential.

4

An Ecumenical Consultation

"WE would welcome a continuing ecumenical discussion of this issue." The issue these words refer to is the most difficult question of all: the morality or immorality of nuclear deterrence. Our Methodist Bishops "are persuaded that the logic of this [just-war] tradition ultimately discredits nuclear deterrence as a morally tenable position." They understand the 1983 Roman Catholic pastoral letter and a report adopted by the 1982 General Convention of the Episcopal Church to "finally appeal to just-war arguments to support nuclear deterrence" (FD, p. 33).

Here, then, is a contradiction between the *conclusions* of recent church statements on deterrence, each avowedly using just-war reasoning. God cannot be a God of contradictions. Hence the Methodist Bishops invite continuing ecumenical discussion of whether the Deterrent State should receive the church's blessing. If ever such a searching interchurch debate were to take place, this would have to be more than an interchange of categorical No's and conditional Yes's among the *results* of recent ecclesial deliberations. We would be driven back upon our premises to a reexamination of the just-war criteria themselves, and the use made of them.

We can begin that ecumenical discussion here. The Methodist rejection rests upon the document's *primal* consideration of deterrence as a moral issue distinguishable from nuclear war itself. The one passage that does this is the *sole operative use* by our Bishops of the Christian theological doctrine of fallen human nature.

The dilemma of deterrence was well stated: "As a war prevention strategy, deterrence represents a just cause ["right intention"]. As a potential holocaust, deterrence represents unimaginable evil" (FD, p. 40). The moral dilemma is how to resolve—can we resolve?—the conflict between the *human intentions*, the purposes or objectives, expressed in these two statements. Unless these are intentions of policy, there is no *moral* dilemma. But as such, they conflict. Our Bishops probe this paradox, the "awesome moral ambiguity" (FD, p. 40), of deterrence no further. At the level of moral argument they "find no coherence in deterrence" (FD, p. 44); but I take that to mean, in context, no agreement or consensus in general from appeals to overly flexible just-war tests. Still at the level of moral argument, they reject deterrence because it "no longer serves, if it ever did, as a strategy that facilitates disarmament" (FD, p. 47). But that links deterrence with *another* matter. *If* the *logic* of just-war tradition discredits deterrence itself—even as a war-prevention strategy—that must be proved by an examination of the *immediate* bearing of just-war criteria upon deterrence postures, not by its connection with something else. Theologically, the Methodist Bishops deplore "nuclear idolatry that presumes the power of ultimate judgment and destruction of other nations" (FD, p. 46). But that assumes what has to be proved, namely, that the "awesome moral ambiguity" has been resolved simply and only into "unimaginable evil" and that, as a war-prevention strategy, deterrence does *not* represent a right or just cause (cf. FD, p. 40).

So we come to the single paragraph in which effective use is made of human sinfulness in an immediate moral appraisal of deterrence.

> We believe there is a still more fundamental flaw at the very core of deterrence doctrine: a contradiction between inordinate confidence in the rationality of decision makers and the absolute terror of annihilation. *Nothing in our understanding of fallible and fallen human nature* warrants the expectation that this relentless strain between reason and terror can endure indefinitely. (FD, p. 48; my italics)

That is true. But anyone who actually uses "fallen human nature" in theological-political argument knows that the *meaning* of that warrant requires its *universalization to all expectations*. Then the foregoing quotation cannot reasonably conclude with its astonishing alternative to deterrence: "The foundations of an enduring peace must be constructive and cooperative." Moreover, deterrence doctrine is not the only "doctrine" that places inordinate confidence in the rationality of decision-makers; nor is deterrence the only system for insuring peace that, you better believe it, can be seized with idolatry and its consequent injustice.

That completes a brief but sufficient review of what the Methodist Bishops had to say about nuclear deterrence (disassociated from their condemnation of *war*) in arriving at their categorical No. Notably, there is little or no invocation of just-war criteria when deterrence is taken up as a separate issue and not lumped together with all-out nuclear exchanges. Yet their conclusion stands there in the text: that it is the *logic* of this tradition (and not idolatry or fallen human nature) that ultimately discredits nuclear deterrence as a morally tenable position. The Catholic and Episcopal churches are invited to continue ecumenical discussion of this issue on the assumption that their accreditation of it, however qualified, finally appealed to just-war arguments. So if the Methodist Bishops are serious about this, they will have to go again to the sources of political wisdom in the just-war tradition, which they use and treat in *In Defense of Creation* only in passing beyond to the consequent social injustices flowing from the costs of armaments in general and their warping effect on every social institution.

I propose to continue the "ecumenical consultation" on the premises set forth by the Methodist Bishops by a consideration of the just-war criteria as these were elucidated by the Catholic Bishops' pastoral. This will be another exercise in comparative pastorals, which I suppose would be welcomed by our Methodist Bishops. Indeed, one can imagine a program of church-wide education launched with the aid of another sort of Guide for Study, which combines lessons on both *In Defense of Creation* and *The Challenge of Peace*. The *difference* in the treatment given the just-war criteria is most illuminating.

The Methodist Bishops accord pacifism and just war generally equal worth. This led them, I suggest, to stress the alleged shared presumption against violence even after this mistake was brought to their attention, and after "just cause" (with its presumption against injustice) was listed first and "last resort" (with its presumption against war) was listed later among the tests. The Catholic Bishops do not accord equivalence to these two classical Christian positions, although they did not *explicitly* state, following the Vatican Consultation, that there is only one Christian teaching addressed to states and to citizens. But the just-war criteria were accorded pride of place.

Naturally, these tests were elucidated with more care, since the Catholic Bishops were not in the business of shifting their foundational moral arguments away from them. A major fruit of this fact is that just war is introduced with no admixture with pacifism; so the *presumption* of just war is very clearly stated to begin with. This is certainly not a presumption against violence (that comes later, under "last resort"). It is not even a presumption against injustice as ordinarily understood—unless justice is taken to mean a distinctly Christian sense of *protective* justice and not as merely a matter of self-defense against aggression.

> The moral theory of the "just-war" or "limited-war" doctrine begins with the presumption which binds all Christians: we should do no harm to our neighbors; how we treat our enemy is the key test of whether we love our neighbor; and the possibility of taking even one human life is a prospect we should consider in fear and trembling. How is it possible to move from these presumptions to the idea of a justifiable use of lethal force? (par. 80)

That is the opening question; there is a presumption against harming *any* neighbor. And the concept of the enemy-neighbor clarifies that our attitude toward *any* neighbor is flawed if *defense* of one's own—one's own life or nation—against *aggression* against even *unjust* aggression, is the exemplary "just cause." How then, in a world of conflicting neighbor relations, is it possible to move from the presumption of universal love for all to preference for some neighbors, and to the idea of a justifiable use of lethal force?

"Historically and theologically," the Catholic Bishops say, "the clearest answer to the [opening] question is found in St. Augustine" (par. 81). For he was impressed by the fact that universal sinfulness has refracted the possibility of manifesting universal, equal love-in-action by never doing harm to anyone. Whether we say that the residence of just-war teaching is in a world *fallen* from the Adamic peace of the Garden of Paradise or in a world "not yet" the Kingdom, the consequence is the same.

Thus, the Bishops continue (and notice that we have yet to locate the fundamental *presumption* of just war as a Christian theory of states' actions):

> In his [Augustine's] view war was both the result of sin and a tragic remedy for sin in the life of political societies. War arose from disordered ambitions, but it could also be used, in some cases at least, to restrain evil and protect the innocent. The classic case which illustrated his view was the use of lethal force to prevent aggression against innocent victims. Faced with the fact of attack on the innocent, the presumption that we do no harm, even to our enemy, yielded to *the command of love understood as the need to restrain an enemy who would injure the innocent.* (par. 81; my italics)

So here we have it: "this Augustinian insight is [the] central premise" of just-war argument in its several forms in the history of Christian theological-political ethics (par. 82). The Catholic Bishops emphasize this point by a footnote to the effect that "Augustine called it a Manichaean heresy to assert that war is intrinsically evil and contrary to Christian charity." Indeed it is a *dualistic* or *spiritualistic* heresy to say that there is for Christians a *principled* (in contrast to properly prudential) presumption against killing and in favor of nonviolence *in a fallen world*. Instead, *the presumption is to restrain evil and protect the innocent.*

In my words (by way of Luther), protective violent or nonviolent *resistance* is an "alien" work of love that for one's own life alone would not resist evil. Or *jus ad bellum* and *in bello* can be spoken of in Brunner's language as the "relative natural law" tailored to a fallen world. Strange that the Bishops of a post-Reformation church should allow the theological doctrines of the Fall and the eschatological "not yet" *less operative influence* in a pastoral letter on war and peace in the nuclear (or any) age than do the Catholic Bishops. The Catholic pastoral letter is apt to persuade the reader that the restraint of evil to protect the innocent is a not-so-alien work of Christian charity. Only the circumstances have changed; service of the neighbor remains the same—provided the crucially different circumstance is understood to be that "the enemy" is *another neighbor's* oppressor.

How, then, does the notion arise in the Catholic pastoral that something else is the bottom-line presumption of just war? Disproportion does it. Prudent political-military decision must balance evil prevented against the greater or lesser evil of resort to armed force. The destructiveness of modern warfare in particular severely limits protecting the innocent among the *jus ad bellum* criteria.

John Courtney Murray's article "Remarks on the Moral Problem of War," in *Theological Studies*, vol. 20 (1959), pp. 40–61, is the definitive study of the limits the destructiveness of modern warfare places upon *jus ad bellum* permissions. See also my discussion in *The Just War* (New York: Scribner's, 1968; Lanham, Maryland: University Press of America, 1983), pp. 204–10.

Disproportion may not be the sole explanation of the pastoral's admixture of a presumption against killing seemingly coeval with just war's presumption against injustice. Just before listing the just-war principles, footnote 35 to paragraph 84 refers to a 1970 article by Ralph Potter on "The Moral Logic of War" (*McCormick Quarterly*, vol. 23, no. 4, pp. 203–33) and James Childress's account in his "Just War Criteria" (published in T. Shannon, ed., *War and Peace: The Search for New Answers*, 1980). These citations, the footnote tells us, aim simply to provide the reader with two additional analyses of "the content and relationship" of the just-war criteria. As a matter of fact, the logic of just war for Potter does seem to begin with a foundational presumption against killing, and this is also the case in Childress's translation of the criteria into *prima facie* and *actual* duties. So I make the friendly suggestion that Bryan Hehir's early education had something to do with the pastoral's degree of ambiguity concerning the "central premise."

These sources deserve closer attention. Potter's article was first published by the Department of Church and Society of the United Presbyterian Church U.S.A. as Occasional Paper on the Church and Conflict, No. 5, following its delivery at Occidental College, November 1969. The author asserts over and over again the primacy of the principle that we must do no harm or injury to our neighbor. When first translating this into our "prima-facie duty not to injure and kill others," Childress acknowledged Potter's "moral logic" to be "one of the best systematic examinations of the just-war criteria" ("Just-War Theories: The Bases, Interrelations, Priorities, and Functions of Their Criteria," *Theological Studies*, 39 [1978], pp. 427–45, at 428, n. 4). It is significant, however, that Childress *rejects* one of Potter's formulations of this principle:

> First, he states that our "common life is sustained by a strong moral and legal presumption against the use of force." . . . Second, he holds that the use of force "always involves an exception to the rule which forbids us to do harm to our neighbor *without due cause.*" . . . This second statement is faulty; for if the rule forbids us to do harm without due cause, the just-war criteria are designed to establish when there is "due cause." Thus a just war is not an exception to the rule stated; it is rather built into the rule. (Ibid., p. 431, n. 9)

Just so! Childress had greater or equal reason to object to Potter's assertion, "The justifications for the institution of war rest upon its presumed utility as a necessary means of serving the common good by protecting the innocent from *unjust* attack, restoring rights *wrongfully* denied, or reestablishing a social order necessary for decent human existence" (Occasional Paper, p. 15).

"Just cause"—and the intention of a "better" peace—does, indeed, establish when there is *causa belli*, when there is *jus ad bellum*. Just war is built into the defense of an ordered justice in a less than ideal world. Potter *begins* with *justice* in tracing the interconnection and reasons for the other criteria, no matter how frequently he repeats the supposed primacy of the presumption against injury. It is the latter, secondary principle from which "last resort," etc., derive; and Potter is right on target in deriving the moral immunity of noncombatants from direct attack from precisely the *jus ad bellum* principle of protecting the *innocent* from *unjust* attack. Childress anatomizes the connections among the criteria quite differently. He begins with "last resort"—which is correct if but only if the primary presumption is against the use of force and not against injustice.

Because they know their just-war tradition, the Catholic Bishops hold the view that there is one and only one teaching addressed to states in their pursuit of an ordered justice in a less than ideal world. However, disproportion is so forceful a reason limiting a determination that war is morally permissible that the Catholic Bishops state the derivative presumption as if it had joint ultimacy with the restraint of evil to protect the innocent. "Such a decision, especially today," they write, "requires extraordinarily strong reasons for overriding the presumption *in favor of peace* and *against war*" (par. 83; italics in original). But this statement is surrounded by implicit references to the Augustinian insight. For example, "if war cannot be rationally avoided" entails that war *could* be avoided negligently or irrationally, whether this is judged in terms of a primary presumption against injustice or against abandoning the innocent. (The clause just quoted entails also that, as I have suggested, "last resort" must mean "last *reasonable* resort" or "timely resort.") And the next paragraph (84) states, "The determination of *when* conditions exist which allow the resort to force in spite of the strong presumption against it is made in light of *jus ad bellum* criteria." If this is so, then the *jus ad bellum* criteria of justice and the restraint of evil to protect the innocent are the primary presumptions of just war, not the subordinate and derivative presumption against resort to force.

We may ask, parenthetically, why the Catholic Bishops inserted the infravalent presumption *in favor of peace* and *against war* in paragraph 18, when obviously the supravalent presumption of just war is in favor of justice and against assaults upon or tyrannizing over the innocent. My speculation is that the Bishops wanted to *elevate* the right of conscientious objection, of which they speak in the next sentence. "This," they write, "is one significant reason why valid just-war teaching makes provision for conscientious dissent." Such general language covers both *selective* and *universal* conscientious objection. It could refer to (erring) consciences that object to war in any form, to consciences that have not searchingly borne the burden of proof against the judgment of legitimate authority that a particular war is just, or to those who, after due respect to the duties of states and the duties which they have as citizens, must still refuse to fight in a war they deem to be unjust. Fr. John Courtney Murray was a notable champion of the consistency of just-war theory with objection to particular wars (just-war pacifism). The Second Vatican Council had called upon states to grant legal exemption to conscientious objectors to military service in order not to burden consciences excessively (cf. *The Challenge of Peace*, par. 118). But that did not elevate universal pacifism to parity with just war as a second Catholic teaching on war and peace. As we have noted, the U.S. Catholic Bishops were admonished that the first draft seemed to propose "a double Catholic tradition: a tradition of non-violence and a tradition along the lines of the just-war theory." There is "only one Catholic theory: the just-war theory," addressed to states and to Catholics in their capacity as citizens.

So my speculation is that the American Bishops did not want to go *that* far, or so expressly; yet they wanted to advance beyond the Second Vatican Council. Hence the insertion of the infravalent presumption *in favor of peace* and *against war* as "one significant reason" for "provision for conscientious dissent." The *next* sentence states the real ground for that presumption; namely, that "all sane people prefer peace, never *want* to initiate war." This appeal to *natural wants* may or may not be a universal description of all sane people. In any case, such an appeal in no way establishes that pacifism and just war are "double Catholic traditions," or that these two views spring from the same natural wants, or that just-war tradition *formulates* the natural preference for peace into the premise we are discussing. Paragraph 83 concludes by affirming of "conscientious objection" (still not specified) that "only the most powerful reasons may be permitted to override such objection." It is impossible to comment on such overriding reasons without knowing what *specific* objection to war the Bishops had in mind. In any case, the words quoted from Pope Pius XII do nothing to support locating the presumption *in favor of peace* and *against war* as the bottom line of just-war reasoning. For Pius's words say only that we must *be careful* in resorting to "the force of arms in defense of rights" lest those rights, however legitimate, "do not offset *the risk of kindling a blaze* with all its spiritual and material consequences" (par. 83; my italics). That would be "just-war" conscientious objection which, in this instance, offers "disproportion" as its final appeal. This in no way opens the door to pacifism in general as one teaching addressed to citizens or to "nonviolence" as one teaching addressed to states.

I spent a long time within that parenthesis because at other places the Catholic pastoral mentions "the presumption against war which stands at the beginning of just-war teaching" (par. 93, 120). There, as here, a reader must be careful to avoid recourse to the wrong presumption.

Next in our exercise in comparative pastorals, let us examine some details in the list and presentation of the just-war tests in each document. Most important is what the Methodist and the Catholic Bishops say about "just cause." Placing side by side these passages elucidating the *first* just-war norm conclusively demonstrates, I judge, that the two councils of Bishops disagree about the primary presumption or premise of the just-war tradition. Also there is remarkable difference in their understanding of the meaning of "just cause" itself.

METHODIST: A decision for war must vindicate justice itself in response to some serious evil, such as an aggressive attack.

CATHOLIC: War is permissible only to confront "a real and certain danger," i.e. to protect innocent life, to preserve conditions necessary for decent human existence, and to secure basic human rights. As both Pope Pius XII and Pope John XXIII made clear, if war of retribution was ever justified, then risks of modern war negate such a claim today.

The single word "justice" in the Methodist statement says too little, and likely also only the minimalist thing, if the Catholic Bishops understand our common Christian justification of participation in war. The "vindication of justice in response to some serious evil" settles comfortably into "aggressive attack" as the most obvious example. By contrast, the Catholic account of the "justice" of Christian participation in war ranges from justice ("to secure basic human rights") to the protection of innocent life and the preservation of decent human existence. These are more *positive* causes, certainly for Christian conscience. Love of neighbor is a forthcoming and, I'd say, a *generous* and *generative* principle. This is its nature even in the midst of conflict among neighbors. So generous and generative, indeed, that the Catholic Bishops were impelled to state, here at the outset, that "wars of retribution" to punish long-established wrongs or to restore basic human rights (in contrast to "a real and certain danger" or present danger to their security) cannot be justly waged today. Why? Not because a claim to retributive justice is invalid, or because past wrongs do not call for correction, but because "the risks of modern war negate such a claim today."

I don't suppose that the average Methodist has thought much about retributive justice (although any system of criminal justice depends on it). I suppose that if the thought of retribution occurs to us, especially in the lawless world of international relations, the issue is simply settled by leaving *vengeance* to the Lord, as the Scripture saith. And of course politically purposeless nuclear or other retaliation is quite senseless, and deserves condemnation in advance.

So I propose to pause here to explore what other sorts of *just* claims may be "negated" from being exercised through recourse to arms. The Catholic Bishops affirm, in effect, that the destructiveness of modern warfare (proportion) utters a conditional No to the use of armed violence in the service of retributive justice. What else would be negated because, in reason, it is likely to cause greater harm? Suppose, as a first suggestion, that we add deterrence of future crimes against humanity to retribution, and correctly describe this as "*protective* retribution." States very often do this. Are we to say there can be "justice" in military action that claims both retributive justice and protection from future similar harms as its joint justifying cause? The point I wish to make is that, even if the answer to that question is Yes, the risks and destructiveness of modern war, under many real-world circumstances, may negate the claim and forbid its exercise. So, I believe, the Bishops reason. They have written into their brief statement of "just cause" a warning drawn from *another* criterion to be taken into account in any *jus ad* (or *jus contra*) *bellum* judgment. That additional norm is proportionality.

So here is the place to ask, Are there other instances in which the generous and prudent judgments of statesmen and citizens are torn between these two norms? What of a war of liberation (e.g., of Latvia or Poland)? It may not be possible to justly wage such wars in today's world. Disproportion may utter a conditional No to recourse to armed violence even in the service of deliverance. Is this a hard doctrine to you, the reader? If so, is it a hard doctrine because of the *violence*, or because *serving* our neighbors under tyranny and delivering them from oppression are frustrated? We are close to the heart of the matter. Given that the basic presumption of just-war traditions is against injustice and in favor of the protection of the innocent, in principle there could be just intervention in domestic injustice of another nation, an *aggressive* just war, a war of liberation. That claim upon us does not cease to be morally valid; its exercise, however, is most often frustrated and vetoed by the destructiveness of any war today and by the risk of major escalation.

And what of revolutionary justice? Today we ache to do the right thing in South Africa. Our overwhelming impulse is to help cleanse that troubled land of apartheid. We are at war with ourselves. Some call for punitive sanctions sufficient to compel revolutionary institutional change: Thus justice calls for *intervention* abroad by some means. Others are more aware of the risk of greater harm to come from *effective* intervention (nonviolent or violent) on behalf of justice to the oppressed.

Responsible politics walks this narrow ridge. It is too easy a solution to deliver oneself of this moral anguish by absolutizing the distinction between nonviolence and violence. After all, a total blockade of a nation to bring about some change in its government's policy is counter-*people* warfare (a violation of the discrimination requirement), and it may well be more devastating to noncombatants and a greater violation of the lesser-evil test than a timely use of armed force (if the times and circumstances allowed such action). There is always need for prudence in determining the measure and means of violent or nonviolent resistance to be used. Economy in the use of force applies to any politically sponsored resistance. The alternative for Christians is pacifism, that is, refusal to participate in that function of government. We who are not pacifists are put at war with ourselves, as I pointed out, by the requirement that *all* the just-war norms be fulfilled in any use of any force. The Catholic Bishops at least opened these troubling vistas in their brief statement of the first criterion. Any *generous* understanding of "just cause" will generate these claims; a realistic political understanding will limit them. In the previous chapter I called this *moral anguish*—the anguish of being bonded to rescue the perishing in a fallen world, where justice and peace do not (yet) lie down together and the wretched of the earth are trodden upon daily. To do justly and love mercy cannot *in principle* be limited to responding to aggressive attack upon our own nation or our allies. Prudence or proportionality sets that limit; and if so, such proscriptions are not to be breached even for just cause. Prudence also determines whether nonviolence or violence is opportune or not. Both pastorals call for greater consideration of nonviolence by the church—one, as a pacifist substitute strategy; the other (I believe) as gauged by proportionate reason.

Under *Jus ad Bellum* (par. 85–100), *The Challenge of Peace* lists the following specific tests: (a) Just Cause, (b) Competent Authority, (c) Comparative Justice, (d) Right Intention, (e) Last Resort, (f) Probability of Success, and (g) Proportionality. Such listings vary, of course; but the surprise is the U.S. Catholic Bishops' *Comparative Justice* (par. 92–93). Ordinarily it is Proportionality that serves to "relativize" Just Cause—in the way we have been discussing. Before looking at the elucidation of comparative justice, a student of the Catholic pastoral should note that proportion is by no means a merely quantitative assessment. The "lesser evil" outcome of such a judgment involves more than body counts or the extent of war's destruction. Instead, "a spiritual dimension" is included in balancing "damage," "cost," and "the good expected" (par. 99). This means that the values and heritage of a people to be preserved must be "weighed" against the material or quantifiable cost of war. This I call an "indeterminate" decision, one that can nevertheless be made. So there are relative values incorporated in this criterion; nevertheless, proportion sometimes "negates" "just cause."

"Comparative Justice" must mean something else. A comparison of "justices" is at issue, where ordinarily it is supposed that "just cause" has settled *that*. Such questions as the following are asked here: "Which side is *sufficiently* 'right' in a dispute?" "Are the values at stake *critical enough*?" (my italics). This test, stated positively, is: "In a world of sovereign states recognizing neither common moral authority nor a central political authority, comparative justice stresses that no state should act on the basis that it has 'absolute justice' on its side." This, I say, relativizes "just cause" itself. The Bishops stress this in order to add weight to the need to limit war. They say, in effect, we need all the more to *limit* "limited war," dampen down its destructiveness, because in a comparison of justices none escapes moral criticism. Thus: "Every party to a conflict should acknowledge the limits of its 'just cause' and the consequent requirement to use *only* limited means in pursuit of its objectives" (italics in original). Otherwise "just war" would legitimate a crusade mentality, paragraph 93 concludes; "comparative justice" is designed to relativize absolute claims and to restrain the use of force in a 'justified' conflict."

In the middle of this passage stand two statements of the "presumption against war" that, I claim, the Catholic Bishops do not and cannot mean to be the bottom-line presumption. Where above I copied, "Are the values at stake *critical enough*" (italics mine), the Bishops continue, "enough to override the presumption against war?" And paragraph 93 begins: "The category of comparative justice is designed to emphasize the presumption against war *which stands at the beginning of just-war teaching*" (my italics). That cannot be right, for this passage itself says that comparative *justice* stands at the beginning of just-war theory! The sentences just quoted easily mislead, since the clear intent is to de-absolutize any nation's "just cause" in order to limit (*limit!*) "limited war" all the more. Hitherto I thought proportion did that; indeed, it often negates just war. This test of *jus ad* (or *contra*) *bellum* is thought-provoking to contemplate. Here, too, the Catholic Bishops speak of a "justified" conflict, not of "just" war.

It was not only the absence today of any "central political authority" to give legal definition to justice, and to settle disputes over justice itself, that led to these reflections. It was also the lack of a "common moral authority" in the world of today. This authorizes me, I think, to draw another implication from the fact that adversaries may be more or less "right," only comparatively just—an implication which the Bishops do not state. Left behind is the juridical model of just-war thinking, whereby for there to be just cause the other side must be declared "unjust" by "competent authority," soldiers then presumably "executing" the sentence of that authority. Grant, if we must, that *objectively* greater justice must be with one side, while the other *objectively* fights with less-sufficient justice, or unjustly. The Bishops say more than that, however, it seems to me. Who knows the objectively just cause in a world of sovereign states that recognize not only no central legal authority but also no "common moral authority"? So I suggest that comparative justice, relative justice, means that—at least *subjectively*—there can be a two-sided just war. Christians and other just men have fought and do fight honorably on opposite sides. This, indeed, is the meaning of an "arbitrament of arms." Christians who do not withdraw from government's imperative to resist injustice to protect the innocent will be impelled sometimes to resist evil (violently or nonviolently) in mankind's unending struggle to maintain a relatively just ordering of the human dwelling place. This struggle often takes the form of conflict over what justice means or requires. Only justice-seeking animals engage in intra-specific conflict. Generous, caring human creatures find also that in a fallen world there is no "universal view" of justice, only "views of universal justice" which they are bound to pursue in their political vocations. They also know in their hearts why some of their fellow Christians are pacifists.

Bryan Hehir tells me that a source for "Comparative Justice" in the Catholic pastoral was LeRoy Walter's account of "Objective Offense vs. Subjective Guilt," "Probable or Certain Cause," and "Just Cause on One Side or Two Sides" ("Five Classic Just-War Theories: A Study in the Thought of Thomas Aquinas, Victoria, Suarez, Gentili, and Grotius," Ph.D. dissertation, Yale University, 1971, pp. 321–23, 326–29). The notion of comparative justice comes from the "simultaneous ostensible justice" of those Spanish scholastics who sought to preserve the just-war restraints in a world of sovereign states. This is precisely the sort of world to which the restraints have now to be addressed, not to hierarchical political authorities in a supposed Christian Empire (if such ever existed).

There is a final, possibly misleading statement of the "presumption against the use of force as a means of settling disputes" (par. 120, in a section entitled "The Value of Non-violence," par. 111–21). The context is clear. Nonviolence is a *political option* to be assessed along the same scale as violence. "Economy of force" (proportion) dictates (to oversimplify) a staged movement from diplomacy to nonviolence to resort to armed force. So it is here in the Catholic pastoral. "The 'new moment' in which we find ourselves sees the just-war teaching and non-violence as distinct but inter-dependent methods of evaluating warfare. They diverge on some specific conclusions, but they share a common presumption against the use of force as a means of settling disputes" (par. 120). "We believe the two perspectives support and complement one another, each preserving the other from distortion" (par. 121). In short, nonviolence and violence are distinct but interdependent methods of going beyond diplomacy in settling disputes among peoples. The shared presumption is against the use of force (here I and the Catholic Bishops use a neutral word) as a means of settling disputes.

So there are staged last resorts. Nonviolent strategies might be developed that are needed, timely, and effective; if this is not the case, just-war teaching would surely not counsel unreasonable delay in moving to armed force. Just so, the test of Probability of Success was "to prevent irrational resort to force or hopeless resistance" that is "clearly disproportionate or futile." Nevertheless, the Bishops were sufficiently instructed in the difficulty of determining that resistance to evil is futile. Therefore they recognize "that at times defense of key values, even against great odds, may be a 'proportionate' witness" (par. 98).

By contrast, the Methodist pastoral not only begins with a parity of pacifism and just war in Christian conscience and tradition but also tends to meld pacifism and nonviolent resistance. Hence, too, the shared presumption against war is equivalent in these two equivalent alternatives. We have seen that the latter presumption, stated also in the Catholic pastoral, is an *infravalent* presumption, not one on which the just-war tradition *bottoms*.

Consider a final significant passage from the Catholic pastoral. In a series of letters to Cardinal Bernardin, the Reagan administration stated that "[f]or moral, political and military reasons, the United States does not target the Soviet civilian population as such" (par. 179, n. 81). The Bishops address the question whether that targeting (unprecedentedly reported to them) rendered U.S. military posture "moral" even if arguably discriminate. Granting that our targeting policy involves (only) "'indirect' (i.e., unintended) but massive civilian casualties," the Bishops nevertheless assert, quite correctly: "These possibilities pose a different moral question [i.e., different from the moral question that would be posed by indiscriminate targeting] and are to be judged by a different moral criterion: the principle of proportionality" (par. 180). Then come the two sentences I ask the reader to pay special attention to:

> A narrow adherence exclusively to the principle of noncombatant immunity as a criterion for policy is an inadequate moral posture for it ignores some evil and unacceptable consequences. Hence, we cannot be satisfied that the assertion of an intention not to strike civilians directly, or even the most honest effort to implement that intention, by itself constitutes a "moral policy" for the use of nuclear weapons. (par. 181)

The point is that the term "moral" (or "immoral") is used in two different senses in this section applying "moral principles" to "policy choices."

This is indicated by the quotation marks around "moral policy" in the foregoing passage. I am reliably informed that Cardinal O'Connor contributed the wording of the passage. Still, the reasoning of the entire section is of one piece, an entirely coherent argument *for* the Bishops' *specific* judgments in assessment of both war-fighting and deterrence even if U.S. targeting policy is in accord with the principle of discrimination.

In this connection I raise once again the questions of (1) the *relation* of proportion and discrimination, and (2) the meaning of the Catholic Bishops' "strictly conditional moral acceptance of nuclear deterrence" (par. 186).

Do discrimination and deterrence *converge* on the same war-fighting policy choices in the nuclear age? I may have too quickly assumed that these principles limiting justified war do converge in condemning all-out acts of nuclear war. The Catholic Bishops grant that U.S. targeting policy may not be in violation of the principle of discrimination. Their moral-offense term "immoral" applies the other principle (proportion) in this section and is equally condemnatory of certain policy choices. Paragraph 181, if quoted in full, would introduce the indented passage above with: "While any judgment of proportionality is always open to differing evaluations, there are actions which can be decisively judged to be disproportionate." Parenthetically, in thus stating their own policy judgment, the Bishops grant that others may reasonably draw "differing evaluations." It is the *distinction* between these norms, however, that admits the *logical priority* of the unexceptionable criterion of discrimination over varying, balancing proportionate judgments, while the extraordinary destructiveness of modern weapons permits the *lexical ordering* of our moral judgments concerning resorts to war: In the nuclear age war could become disproportionate before (or even if not) indiscriminate. Moreover, this lexical order allows us to conceive of sufficient *graduated* mutual deterrence that need not be intended to strike civilians directly.

Thus we come once again to the Catholic Bishops' "strictly conditional moral acceptance of nuclear deterrence." In order to accept morally any possession of nuclear weapons for deterrence, there must be (in the expression coined by J. Bryan Hehir) "*a centimeter of ambiguity* regarding the general question of the *use* of nuclear weapons" (my italics).

See Hehir's paper "The Nuclear Debate: Ethical and Political Implications," World Order Studies Program, Occasional Paper No. 12, ed. Robert C. Johansen (Center of International Studies, Princeton University, 1984). The words "general question" have the effect of averting our eyes from war-fighting use and decoupling that from another sort of use, namely, for prevention.

This "centimeter of ambiguity" as to use ought not to be understood to rest upon justifying an actual use in trivial war-fighting instances, say, to destroy a ship at sea (or—a "use" I once proposed—to fry an egg on Uranus!). What then is the ambiguity regarding the "general question" of use? The use in question is deterrence. The ambiguity is resolved in favor of deterrent possession (to preserve a peace of sorts) on two conditions: (1) a requirement placed extrinsically upon deterrent use, and (2) a severe caution concerning "the character" of that deterrent use.

The requirement placed extraneously upon deterrent use is that the nations take significant steps toward nuclear disarmament. Pope John Paul II's Message to the Second Special Session of the United Nations on Disarmament in 1982 is cited as authority:

> In current conditions "deterrence" based on balance, certainly not as an end in itself but as a step on the way toward a progressive disarmament, may still be judged morally acceptable. (cited par. 173)

I have said enough about the *unjustifying* linkage of the morality or immorality of nuclear deterrence with the goal of progressive disarmament. The Pontiff's words must be true when the clause enclosed in commas is deleted, that is, if his statement read: "In current conditions 'deterrence' based on balance may still be judged morally acceptable"! There must be a centimeter of moral acceptability in deterrent use as a means of maintaining some sort of peace in our trembling world, if the Deterrent State is not now a moral atrocity.

To probe "the character" of the deterrent use is far more interesting, for here we find novel and scarcely noted issues. By "the character," the Bishops mean to rest their strictly conditioned moral acceptance of deterrence upon keeping the deterrent limited to "preventing the use of nuclear weapons or other actions which could lead directly to a nuclear exchange" (par. 185). In other words, deterrent use is justified if and only if limited to this one specific function in world affairs: the prevention of the use of these weapons.

There can be no quarrel with the Bishops' condemnation of other "uses" to which nuclear weapons could be put, for example, as a deceptive shield for planning war-fighting strategies, for nuclear blackmail to obtain *other* goals than preventing nuclear war, or for prevailing in nuclear war. If I understand this correctly, however, *pure* deterrent use is *per se* justified. It is only when deterrent possession fuels the arms race or is not an interim in which disarmament progresses, and if deterrent possession is devoted to other roles in international power politics, that the Catholic Bishops find deterrence morally unacceptable. So it seems to me that, if uncontaminated, the mutual possession of nuclear weapons to deter their use is quite justifiable.

To preserve the good "character" of deterrent use, the Bishops had to ignore or suppress the fact that nuclear-war prevention itself requires either (1) the feasibility and morality of a meant threat of nuclear retaliation, or (2) the feasibility and the morality of the Bluff. Since neither can be ignored or deemed morally acceptable, any review of *The Challenge of Peace* must include not only an examination of its "policy choices" but also a return to the sources to re-vision the meaning of its "moral principles."

In another respect the norms governing the morality of war and deterrence, and their practical import in a nuclear age, cannot be excluded from reexamination. We saw that the Bishops grant that U.S. targeting policy may pass muster before the criterion of discrimination but still, they say, "be decisively judged to be disproportionate." We noted the latitude allowed for "differing evaluations" than their own under the test of proportion. There is, however, a further subtle question to be raised about proportion. Are there not *correct* judgments of proportion that threaten to contaminate "the character" of deterrence? Under the head of nuclear-war prevention, we saw, the morally acceptable character of deterrence requires that this be devoted to *no other role* in the international system.

Take "nuclear blackmail" as the example of a prohibited use of these weapons. Certainly *mutual* nuclear blackmail would be but another name for an unlimited nuclear-arms race, which deserves unqualified condemnation. Nevertheless, closer examination of "the character" of our nuclear deterrent will require the Bishops to ask a more probing and difficult question: How can one nuclear power *respond* to actual or perceived nuclear blackmail by its adversary while still keeping its own possession of nuclear weapons *severely limited* to the prevention of its own and that adversary's *use* of nuclear weapons? Suppose the U.S.S.R. piles up vastly redundant nuclear firepower (overkill) whose sole and actual use is to "overwhelm" European public opinion, weaken the governments of Western Europe, and neutralize NATO. Is there a morally acceptable *response* to such nuclear blackmail? Do we not have to defend the proposition (under the norm of proportion, where the Catholic Bishops rightly place the question) that in the matter of deterrence "a threat of something disproportionate is not necessarily a disproportionate threat"? This is the nature of deterrence in any age with any weapons and posture of military forces.

In *War and the Christian Conscience* I saw no way to avoid *discriminate* threats proportioned to keeping an ordered peace in the world which if ever used in warfighting would prove to have been disproportionate. I see no way to avoid this now, if there is any morally acceptable response to nuclear blackmail. If such questions are not on the Roman Catholic agenda, they are on the agenda of any serious deliberation concerning principles in a moral-assessment deterrence. It takes two to abide my mutual proportionate deterrence and war prevention. What if one side adds to that a measure of *bonus* civilian blackmail? Assuming discriminating targeting, that could slowly but surely tilt the world or regional power balance, thus rendering satellites of allies, turning nations now neutral into buffer states, and possibly leading to armed encounters years later. Nuclear blackmail (or, for that matter, blackmail by a build-up of conventional forces) is not a one-time thing. If the international system is governed and peace preserved by power limited by countervailing power, there must be some response to only threatening civilian blackmail. Keeping deterrence *pure* seems impossible. This fact is perilous, indeed, in a nuclear age, but it is not novel. Today, an erosion of the balance of power *could* lead "*remotely* and *indirectly* to a nuclear exchange." Perhaps this was not excluded by the sentence quoted above from paragraph 185.

Next, I propose to bring into this "ecumenical consultation" the voice and recent writing of John Howard Yoder. This is needed in order to be truly ecumenical, since Yoder is widely recognized as the leading contemporary American exponent of Christian pacifism. The "fit" with the foregoing is that under "comparative justice" the Catholic Bishops so far relativize the absolute claims of "just cause" that they—this time only—speak of "a 'justified' conflict" (par. 93) instead of *just* war. The quotation marks around the work "justified" (in contrast to clearly or purely "*just*") indicate that political decisions are made with more or less sufficient warrant among comparative conflicting justices.

I myself have so far followed the pastorals in using the term "just war," although the modification "justified" (only) was an entailment of taking seriously Augustine's critique of the "pagan" virtues, including the social justice for which the kingdoms of this world fight, in my *War and the Christian Conscience*. The Catholic pastoral reached the same usage by, in effect, insisting that, given the destructiveness of modern warfare, *jus ad bellum* should always be written *jus ad/contra bellum*. This was to *write* the negations of disproportionate evil into the justice reasons for going to war. Such was always the meaning of *jus ad bellum*; but the *contra* needs emphasis when addressing the responsibility of states and of citizens in today's wars, or in those of any age to come. There are, then, two reasons—the bias in any adversarial view of justice, and the prohibitions of the greater- or lesser-evil test—supporting our speaking of a "justifiable-war ethic."

The first thing to notice about John Howard Yoder is that he regularly uses "*justified/unjustified* war" in writing. Attention to his *When War Is Unjust: Being Honest in Just-War Thinking* (Minneapolis: Augsburg Publish-

ing House, 1984) will add a significant partner to our dialogue. Two
chapters especially deserve careful study, for just as Yoder rightly undertakes to keep justifiable-war theory "honest," so he may need correction by
that theory's understanding of itself. These chapters are "The Tradition and
the Real World," in which Yoder traces a sliding scale in which the reality of
warfare "tests" the normative criteria and (to mix metaphors) puts them to
rout; and "Making the Tradition Credible," in which he recommends ways
in which mainline churches and nonpacifist Christians might manifest that
they know the difference between justifiable war and mere defense of
national interest. Any theological ethicist, priest, or pastor today should be
excited to engage in Yoder's invitation to dialogue (that's a noun, not the
execrable verb in current usage). I know no responsible way to do this
except by taking up each point in sequence in each of these chapters and
enacting a *conversation* with them. I hope that Yoder remembers that once at
a meeting of the Society of Christian Ethics he paid me what I thought was a
very high compliment, namely, that I *use* the just-war theory and do not do
rote-thinking with it.

The theme of the first of these chapters is introduced in a brief paragraph,
"The scale keeps sliding." Here is evidence that the author knows that just-
war thinking entails an elementary distinction between "murder" and "killing" in war. Whoever cannot imagine such a distinction, or willingly
suspend disbelief in it, cannot enter into conversation with this Christian
tradition. Yoder begins by saying that the search is for ways to limit war not
only quantitatively but so that participants in war "can be assured that what
they are doing is not murder." Let's not quarrel here with the fact that he
wants those limits to be politically *effective*, not only morally *valid*. Then
Yoder states the slippage he is going to trace, stressing (I regret to say) the
wrongfulness of *killing*! This rather quickly withdraws the credence first
granted to distinguishing between murder and killing in war. "Beneath the
basic concession that there will have to be some exceptions to the wrongfulness of killing," he writes, "we [will] find a set of exceptions to the need for
justification for exceptional killing" (p. 56). Am I incorrect to see peeking
through here an alleged presumption against violence (killing) such as we
have been discussing? Certainly there is that presumption for any Christian
conscience, but the presumption against injustice and abandonment of the
oppressed is greater in justified war.

The first three steps in declination we could freely grant. The steps are
"lowering the hurdles" in submarine and guerrilla warfare simply in order
to encompass more killing of civilians, the doctrine of military necessity,
and "They did it first." Perhaps we should simply pass by these points as not

worthy of serious debate. But Yoder makes his point in the first instance by concentrating only on the additional *number* or *class* of civilians *excepted* from immunity. The slippage is in sequential resolves to keep the rules that can be kept, while letting go restraints that are no longer being kept. So if "the principle of noncombatant immunity can no longer be effectively respected," it seems better to "declare it a dead letter" and build up restraints that are still realistic. Yoder's failure here to inquire into the *intention* or *aim* of those novel acts of war, and to assess whether noncombatant immunity was violated, manifests itself later (we shall see) in serious failure to understand just-war teachings.

Appeals to military "necessity" do reduce to "utility," to breaking just-war constraints "but only if you *really have to*" (p. 59; italics in original). We ought also to agree that "They did it first" is no excuse, not even when the "reprisal" can correctly be described as "protective retribution" or, as Yoder writes, if the infringement of the rules goes "no further than the enemy did," and if "the intent of the exceptional sanction [is] to restore the rules." He can grant there is some gain in the development of international conventions ("contract thinking") while still keeping us honest about the intrinsic immorality of some sorts of reprisals no matter who did it first. Everything is going to depend upon whether Yoder has in mind a correct understanding of the intrinsic morality or immorality of acts and policies of warfare in the tradition he (rightly!) wants to help keep honest. Protective retribution is certainly not wrong because it is retributive, provided the reprisal is not itself a violation of justifiable-war restraints. There can even be reprisals that are not reprisals in (the wrong) kind; then protective deterrence is all that is at issue, and this is entirely justified—if one has not focused exclusively on the "primal" act of killing.

The next step down the slippery slope—"They are unworthy"—is convincing in the several examples Yoder gives of it—except for one, and this because of his account of why it was an unwarranted relaxation of just-war teaching. His main point is generally correct, and always needs emphasizing. This is that the savagery of warfare is always increased by gross distinctions between Greek and barbarian, Christian and Turk, Whites and "Japs," Afrikaners and Zulus, the West and godless Communism. It is always wrong to depict the enemy in justified/unjustified war as "savages"; but this does not render unimportant the Catholic Bishops' criterion of "comparative justice." Yoder's conclusion or objection should have been: "The worse the enemy (or the worse the enemy is painted), the more room we think we may have to break the rules too." Instead, he writes, "The worse the enemy's *cause*, the more room we may have to break the rules too" (my italics). There is danger of yielding to that temptation also, but the need for greater nuancing of this *possible* consequence of warfare in a "just cause" is clear from the fact that Yoder classed the war of the Allies against Nazism along with those other examples of "They are unworthy."

Lumping that justified war of living memory unqualifiedly with those other extremes of emotions angered in the fog and fury of warfare is, I judge, questionable in itself. But it is Yoder's *account* of the justification of the war against Nazism that demonstrates that (with every intellectual effort at understanding a position he does not himself share) he falls far short of grasping and comprehending just war in its generating principles. Yoder refers to an actual justification of the massive bombing of German cities in that war. But *what he says* of that argument (Walzer's) can, I judge, be abstracted for examination as to its claims about *jus ad bellum*. The justification in an exceptional case of the obliteration bombing of German cities, Yoder writes, "must have made some previous global judgments about Nazism and civilization." But *of course!* Yoder continues by saying, "Once more we can discern here a shift from intrinsic to contractual morality," mentioned before in elucidating the move to international conventions permitting *reprisals in wrong kinds* under "They did it first." In sum, what Yoder fears will become of just cause by inevitable departures from this norm in "the real world" is as follows:

> We are not obligated to respect the humanity of the enemy population because they are human, but only because they have committed themselves to carry on the combat according to our rules. If their rulers deny our basic value system, the enemies forfeit the privilege of our respect. It was a privilege which we, being morally superior, had bestowed upon them, or a conditional right which they earned by meeting us on our terrain—not an intrinsic right by virtue of their humanity. (pp. 61–62)

I find it hard to believe that, even when drawing our attention to the escalation of evil in justified warfare, Yoder leaves standing the possibility that he himself believes that conflict entailing global judgment about civilization and Nazism can be reduced simply to a clash of "value systems" having ideological overtones. Christian pacifism itself has no need to suppose this about that war or about nonpacifist Christians. To believe this would be to refuse any moral acceptability to Christian participation in any war, to evacuate *moral* appraisal of just cause *now* (as the Methodist Bishops tend to do), and to replace just cause with clash of ideologies only.

Perhaps mine is only a surface reading. Perhaps the author meant to ascribe the reductionist maneuver to the escalator of violence. Perhaps he fears or only predicts that *jus ad bellum* can too easily become the obliteration of the humanity of the enemy. Even so, and even though it is all but buried, we surely have at this place Yoder's own understanding of the fundamental justification he believes is offered by the justified warrior. This understanding is only minimally accurate, and at most a minimalist account of nonpacifist churches and Christians. Unless his understanding is corrected or supplemented elsewhere, Yoder believes that just-war appeals are only and simply to *natural justice*, and that the limitation of war by noncombatant immunity is "an intrinsic right by virtue of their humanity." If that were sufficient, then the state's function in the use of armed force and citizen participation are based entirely on *another morality* than that of the Gospel; there is then a "double morality" needed to warrant Christian participation in the resistance of evil, however these two are joined together. Nothing said here acknowledges a more generous justice, the work of love in restraint of evil to relieve and protect oppressed neighbors. This minimalist justice could exhaust itself in defense of one's own life, one's own family, one's own nation against aggression; and it would require a doubling of loyalties to couple *that* or natural justice or universal human rights with Christian charity. That could be a defensible position, but it is not the heart and soul of justified-war ethics.

The next and fifth slide along the scale downward is "Situationism"— that is, the position of those "realists" about wartime situations who reject any sort of intellectual calculation or structural reasoning. "Philosophy" is not very convincing "when the lives of my men are at stake." The closest we have come in this ecumenical consultation to this rejection of any rule-like thinking about justice in and about war is the Methodist Bishops' resolve— to teach an opposite conclusion from that of situational realists—to eschew "rationalism" and instead to rely on vision and prophecy, supported by long-run consequent injustices that are nonpolitical in nature. I'd pass by this step along Yoder's slope except for the fact that here he gives an excellent reply:

> The normal penchant of the human heart for such excuses is precisely why we need rules. Precisely because there is not much time, decision makers need reminders of the fundamental rights of other parties in the conflict, which remain even in the midst of unavoidable conflict. Precisely because abstract analysis is not appropriate or easy under fire, the limits of our entitlement to destroy our fellows' lives and property need to be formulated firmly ahead of

time so as to be protected against our (partially, but not infinitely) justified self-interest.

This passage repeats, it is true, Yoder's view that universal and minimalist natural justice—"the fundamental rights of other parties in the conflict"—is the morality on which just war *bottoms*, with its readiest expression or exemplification in aggression as what gives us (in defense) "our entitlement to destroy our fellows' lives and property." Nevertheless, we may need to recall Yoder's reply—which surely does not require perfect effectiveness of the restraints—when we take up his recommendations for keeping the tradition honest and credible.

Leaving behind the foregoing "least worthy adjustments" that "use ordinary debating language," Yoder turns next to a celebrated systematization (pp. 62–67), to "one line of argument which claims deep roots in the tradition of the most intellectually careful moral theologians." This is the "doctrine of double effect," which claims the capacity to throw light on especially difficult choices, when in the case of "competing and coinciding values . . . in order to ward off one evil . . . one must accept another." That's a rather fine statement of the so-called rule of double effect, as is Yoder's list of four requisite elements, including "The evil which occurs should not be willed or intended."

It comes, then, as quite a surprise that Yoder's immediate verdict is that double-effect reasoning "constitutes a powerful intellectual argument *contributing to the downward drift*" (my italics). This is all the more amazing since Roman Catholic moralists are currently at work dissolving or jettisoning "double effect" because they deem this rule to be too restrictive. The state of this question should lead to some interesting and profitable ecumenical encounters if moral theologians consent to come out of their separate ghettos with a view to genuine dialogue.

Unfortunately Yoder's brief text in demonstration that double effect powerfully contributes to the drift downward does not prove that point and fails utterly to give "intention" the role he had (all too briefly, of course) prepared the reader to expect. The passage simply gives two interpretations of double effect ("Some argue . . ." "Others, however . . ."). Those two sentences state disagreement among interpreters over *what* the "rule" prohibits. Both of the two views may be true, and in any case prohibitions—not "downward drift"—are the upshot of either. Yoder's words seem not only harsh but without foundation when he concludes, "It is very difficult for the critic who wants to be fair at this point to know where the line runs between careful casuistry and plain cynical abuse."

As I read them, the two sorts of prohibitions of intended wrong acts in no way support the judgment (at the beginning and end of the passage) that double effect is an engine propelling a drift downward from credible restraints. "Some argue . . . that the just-war theory as a whole represents a case of double effect, where the *killing of enemies* is the regrettable and unintended result of the intrinsically good defense of national values" (my italics). If I understand that, the reply is that the dominant tradition never invoked double effect in order to justify the killing of enemy soldiers (combatants). Enemy soldiers were believed to be in solidarity with an adversary power's "guilt," and so they could lawfully be directly and intentionally killed. Double effect was not needed, except perhaps by moralists holding a minority opinion that enemies are at least *material* aggressors. *Stopping* the aggression can be the *aim* in killing them, not putting an end to their lives, just as killing an individual gone berserk may be the regrettable and unintended (though foreseen and unavoidable) result of intending to stop his aggression in the intrinsically good defense of oneself or others. I myself have used that argument in explaining the justified stopping of the "combatancy" of combatants or the innocent, material aggression of an unborn child upon its mother's life. These are only different *explanations*; neither weakens the point and chief relevance of double effect, which distinguishes between the intentional targeting of military objectives while permitting civilian death and destruction (if proportionate) *beside* that primary aim.

Yoder's "use of double-effect reasoning at the next lower level" is more difficult to understand. To put the best face on it, I excerpt these words: "Thus one can speak . . . of the acceptance of noncombatant deaths . . . as a lesser evil, not intended but regretfully accepted as a part of the price to pay for a higher good." Yoder seems to believe that one of the just-war criteria *prohibits the killing of noncombatants* and that the infraction of this rule is at issue. If an infraction of this rule is the lesser evil, Yoder needs to know that this can be accepted as the price to pay for a higher good *if but only if* those noncombatant deaths are not intended! On the scale of lesser evil and higher good, of course, nothing else stipulated, one can and should intend the lesser as a means to the higher good. One should do that. But justified-war ethics does not understand either killing *per se* or the infraction of somebody's rule against killing noncombatants to be *the* evil, or an evil to be scaled. There *is* no rule against *causing* the death of noncombatants, but only against intending to target them directly, or aiming at "bonus civil damage." Yoder's words (excerpted above) should have reversed the order of lesser evil and intentional action to read: "One can speak . . . of the acceptance of noncombatant deaths . . . if not intended but regretfully accepted . . . *and if this is a lesser-evil* price to pay for a higher good." That is the correct lexical ordering of the two principles, discrimination and proportion.

The foregoing is the best reading I can propose of this difficult paragraph. It is the footnote (to p. 63, n. 3, on pp. 84–85) that makes it crystal clear that Yoder is not reading us properly. The note is attached to his entire list of four elements or to the fourth proviso of the rule of double effect, which states: "The actual deed which triggers the evil by-product and is indispensable to *the good primary intention is not intrinsically wrong*" (my italics). Yoder's footnote comments on the "scholarly debate" recently "reviewed" by the book I coedited with Richard A. McCormick, S.J., *Doing Evil to Achieve Good* (Chicago: Loyola University Press, 1978). One sentence describes the position McCormick defended: "Some would tend to argue that all the four criteria for permissible 'double-effect' decisions can be reduced to sophisticated calculations of consequential utility." While I am glad to have Yoder as an ally in that debate, there is, of course, a teleological morality that is *not* consequentialist. McCormick never quite arrived at "consequential unity" in this exchange, although he did change his mind and withdrew some major opinions. The second sentence, I suppose, refers to my own defense of the irreducibility of double effect to proportionalism. Yoder's summary is (I must say) a muddle of "safeguarding some notion of multiple intrinsic moral duties and limits, even in situations of complex and tragic compromises."

I have publicly stated that ours was a failed book; my chapter in particular was insufficiently revised to make clear the meaning (to Yoder, for example) of an "indeterminate" decision. So let me say here that I, too, would short-shrift double effect if I took the meaning to be the texture of complex compromises Yoder comprehends it to be.

With "consequential utility" and "compromise" the alternatives, no wonder Yoder exclaims in frustration: "The skeptics who are unconvinced by the entire system point out especially that to say that one does not 'intend' the evil results of one's deeds, even though one chooses so to act with full knowledge that those results will follow, . . . is a sophistry."

Nothing, however, could be more revealing of Yoder's failure to comprehend justified-war teaching than that sentence; indeed, it would appear to reveal his lack of acquaintance with an entire literature dealing with the centrality of intentionality in ethical analysis (not by double-effect advocates alone). One can drop the whole modern elaboration of double effect, double intentionality. One need no longer speak of *indirect* effect, *indirect* intention, or the *indirectly* voluntary. But without the core notion of *intention* itself (which, then, encompasses directionality), no ethical analysis at all is possible. A *human* act, a moral (or immoral) act, a human, responsible "doing" *means* an intentional action. What falls within the scope or ambit of the intention of human agents—the *object* of their acts—and not what falls within the larger scope of awareness of events and causal connections in the world, determines the moral species of those deeds (and the good or bad characters who do them). "Conscious of" something is not identical with "doing" something.

Absent this understanding, Yoder cannot comprehend that there could be actual deeds whose "good primary intention is not itself intrinsically wrong" that trigger an evil by-product. (If this surpasses understanding, then the excision of a cancerous uterus to save the life of a woman who is pregnant cannot be meet and right to do in surgery because the by-product is the death of a helpless, innocent human being.) This fourth proviso Yoder dismisses as petitionary prayer, raised to heaven by people whose "entire argument is set up to explain why some things that are wrong in themselves must nevertheless be done because of complicated conflict situations." With that rush to judgment, Yoder's conclusion is the opposite of the truth: "The advocates of the adequacy of the double-effect theory have not made clear how to distinguish between intrinsically wrong things which one may *never* do and other intrinsically wrong things which one may do under the above restrictions" (italics in original). The author of that statement must surely believe that *killing* is the intrinsically wrong thing to do. That is debatable, and doubtless will continue to be debated; but justified-war Christians *do not believe that killing is intrinsically wrong.* They draw the line on intrinsic wrong at "evil-meaning minds," not at deaths wrought collaterally to just-war *means* or *ends.* Our "book-long debate does not even notice this challenge," that is, Yoder's challenge; but then, it's a challenge that is rather forgettable—except by someone who has not, at the time of writing this volume, succeeded in willful disbelief in his own pacifist premise. Elsewhere Yoder is more on target concerning what just-war tradition needs to be honest about to be credible.

A human action takes its *moral species* from its *object.* "Killing," then, is, as yet, not a human action, because its object has not yet been stated. A mere description of "killing" would be "physicalist" only. Such a "primitive description" would not be an "action" that is subject to moral appraisal. But certain describable circumstances do tell us the agent's objective in that act of killing, that is, "murder." Still other circumstances tell us that the person murdered was the agent's father; and the *moral species* of such a describable action is "parricide." Finally, there are circumstances (situation or long-run consequences) that do not enter into the *moral species* or the object of the human action. These may be justifying or excusing or extenuating "reasons," but they do not determine the *moral species* of the human action. *Of course*, parricide is not a part of the "world out there," though a case might be made for using the word "killing" with such a physicalist meaning only. *Of course*, murder and parricide do not exist apart from our human moral world. "Killing" *circumstanced* as "murder," or further as "parricide" (but not as loving kindness or the lesser evil or the proportionate good on the whole), states the *moral species* of a human action. A moral notion draws a circle around a certain sequence of events *and concomitant human intentions* and brands them morally significant. This is true whether the moral terms praise or censure. I believe this analysis of human action is consistent with that of Thomas Aquinas.

It is not clear to me why the next two steps in Yoder's account of slippage in just-war reasoning belong in the chapter under discussion. They would be more suitable in his final chapter, on "Making the Tradition Credible," where they would stand as just-war voices joining with his to call for the same credible clarity. The first step—titled "This far and no farther?" (pp. 63–64)—is Yoder's report of "the earliest firm landmark in the development of what we have since come to call 'nuclear pacifism'." This was the issuance of a World Council of Churches (WCC) study document on "Christians and the Prevention of War in an Atomic Age" (1957). This report stated:

> . . . [W]e are agreed on one point. This is that Christians should openly agree that the all-out use of these weapons should never be resorted to. Moreover, that Christians must oppose all policies which give evidence of leading to all-out war. Finally, if all-out war should occur, Christians should urge a cease fire, if necessary on the enemy's terms, and resort to non-violent resistance.

Yoder notes in passing that this "logically irreproachable" statement of the ordinary meaning of just-war tradition was "so threatening" that it provoked "a striking series of defensive measures on the part of the World Council of Churches." That, he says, "is not our present concern"; that is, he does not here point the finger at those incredible defensive measures. Instead, Yoder simply concludes: "If one cannot with moral legitimacy prosecute a war, then the only morally worthy alternative is not to prosecute it. The only remaining path is to pursue by other means the purposes which can no longer be legitimately achieved militarily."

I have suggested that a generous care for others and for a decent political dwelling place for all human beings, following the move from nonresistance to resistance of evil, may then move in sequence from nonviolent resistance to timely resort to violent means of resistance (under the constraints of discrimination and proportion). A main reason for quoting Yoder on the entailments of just-war nuclear pacifism is his testimony that a credible justified-war ethic can and ought to move in the reverse sequence, from violent to nonviolent resistance, if war cannot be morally pursued. This seems to me to be correct; these forms of resistance, unless *either* one or the other is indiscriminate in its resistance of evil, are simple alternatives to be prudently assessed in terms of effectiveness in meeting the lesser-evil test. But Yoder's urging that just-war Christians ought sometimes to choose nonviolence when violence becomes the greater evil does not entirely consist with his presumption that Christian nonpacifism can be counted credible if and only if we share Christian pacifism's absolute preference for nonviolence, or its presumption against killing.

Just-war nuclear pacifism's unqualified and unalterable rejection of all-out use of nuclear weapons (as stated above) is not the same as the unqualified No's uttered by the Methodist Bishops, or their No to nuclear deterrence, or the Catholic conditional No to deterrence, or both pastorals' call for no first use, etc., etc. Our study of the pastorals showed that there are many prudential judgments subject to variable opinions and legitimate disagreement among Christians. Yoder allows us now to suggest from another point of view that within a credible commitment to just-war principles (with its obvious No to all-out nuclear war) there is room for continuing honest and credible disagreement over, for example, particular "policies which [some say] give evidence of leading to all-out war" or some say lead away from it. No calls for clarity, forthrightness, and faithfulness to a structured or determinate set of principles for ethico-political decision-making can remove uncertainty and contingency from specific or particular policies.

"This far and no farther?" merges with—indeed, it is the same thing as—the next point: "Surrender rather than fight?" (pp. 64–67). Again, Yoder joins his voice to those of just-war thinkers. That of Paul Ramsey (1961) is mentioned and quoted, along with (earlier) John Courtney Murray's *Morality and Modern War* (1959). The obvious point is, in Yoder's solidly correct just-war statement, "If the only way not to lose a war is to commit a war crime, it is morally right to lose that war." Anyone who believes that no war should ever be fought that (among other tests) is *not* an instrument of purposeful national policy should understand that (as von Clausewitz said, quoted by Murray) "we must therefore familiarize ourselves with the thought of honorable defeat." There were just warriors who condemned obliteration bombing of cities *at the time*, the policy of unconditional surrender *at the time*, Hiroshima *at the time*. The expression "preemptive surrender" (which I used) was perhaps overly rhetorical. Yoder speaks for and from within the just-war tradition when he says that "there is a cease-fire line dictated by the doctrine" and that "Murray was no defeatist. He insisted that surrender is not the first but the last possibility." In other words, for just-war theory, both going to justified war and stopping a (so far) justified war can and ought to be the last timely resort. Perhaps I should cite the words of Courtney Murray, which Yoder quoted here without objection: "I think it is true to say that the traditional doctrine was irrelevant during World War II. This is no argument against the traditional doctrine. The Ten Commandments do not lose their imperative relevance by reason of the fact that they are violated. But there is place for an indictment of all of us who failed to make the tradition relevant." That discriminating self-indictment by an exponent of just-war norms needs to be remembered also for what it does not say. Failure to make just war *effective* in national policy formation, as well as failure to make a pacifism of nonviolence effective in national policy, is no argument against either. The imperativeness of neither is diminished by reason of the fact that it is violated. To be mealymouthed or lacking in seriousness about nonviolent resistance or about justifiable/ unjustifiable war is the indictable offense against the first principles of the proponents of either Christian position. But neither the charge that such pacifism *has not* become politically effective, nor the charge that just-war criteria are not shaping national military policy, counts against the credibility of adherence to those outlooks.

There are two steps to go before Yoder's slide becomes, in his view, a rout. "Category slide" he defines as "undercutting . . . the doctrine" by "centering [exclusively] on one or the other of the criteria." This might open a discussion of the moral anguish or tug-of-war in Christian conscience that results from finding oneself obligated to observe all the criteria. Instead, the passage consists of one or two examples of *selectivity*. Yoder's use of Robert Tucker's *The Just War: A Study of Contemporary American Doctrine* (1960) as an example of concentration only on "just cause" demonstrates again Yoder's own limited understanding of that criterion. For the contemporary American doctrine that is the subject of Tucker's critical book is the "aggressor-defender" doctrine. An adversary that is so wicked as to aggress upon us, our nation, deserves the holy-war zeal of our fighting no-holds-barred by *jus in bello* constraints. Other examples are the lack of seriousness among just-war thinkers who *omit* "competent authority" or "just cause" and concentrate only on what Yoder here calls "questions of discrimination: proportionality and immunity." Only such formal questions are asked, he implies, "because for the others no one can give an answer." Then Yoder wryly observes that "in a backhanded way" the argument that stresses those discriminations (for want of clarity about other tests) is a good thing because "it keeps people from saying that since their own cause is just, they need not proceed justly *in bello*. Restraints *in bello* remain valid even for us—if our cause is just—as protection for our opponent's rights—even if their cause is unjust." He seems surprised that the slipperiness of just authority and "just cause" ("comparative justice," the Catholic Bishops might say) drew his attention correctly to stringency at the heart of just-war teaching. Still, Christian moral thought should, as Yoder says, look to those other criteria as well. This point, however, advances us little in any direction.

In the final paragraph (numbered 10), entitled "Metamorality" (pp. 68–70), Yoder understands James Childress to hold that no "substantive" just-war theory which could give concrete guidance is possible in a society with competing theories of justice, that there can never be a clear *no* to an unjust war, yet that a formal theory provides a common language within which to debate! This is the ultimate retreat or rout Yoder has been approaching. Asking for bread, we are given stony silence, or rather, a ridiculous outcome: "It is not perfectly clear what compliance would mean, but at least we have a common vocabulary" in which to discuss the fact that we cannot know what compliance or noncompliance might mean (p. 70). Of course, the truth of that depends on the meaning of "perfectly clear" and "a clear *no*"; and again I am reminded of the wisdom in what the Catholic Bishops said about "comparative justice."

I assume here that Yoder has not written a caricature of Childress's position. It has been clear for some time, in any case, that Childress's uses of *prima facie* and *actual* duties in moral analysis are not *explanatory* of the just-war tradition but instead are *replacement* terms for its fine-tuning. Unfortunately, his proposal is widely used. David Hollenbach—a young Jesuit scholar who should know better—has recently written of the norms of Christian morality generally that "these norms are all of the *prima facie* variety" (*Nuclear Ethics: A Christian Moral Argument* [New York/Ramsey, N.J.: Paulist Press, 1983], p. 87). This includes the Ten Commandments— presumably because "when we try to discern what these commandments call for in concrete decision, however, prudential judgment is always involved." That can, rationally, only mean deciding whether, for example, a particular case of fornication (in the circumstance of not knowing whether one's partner was *married*) was "imperfect adultery" or the "perfect" sort in violation of God's command! Prudence, fairest of virtues, reduced now to the moral philosophy of W. D. Ross! By *prima facie*, Ross, of course, referred to duties in conflict, not to the application of plain commands or the specification of quite clear moral notions. So it may be more than a bit prejudicial for Yoder to understand Childress's position to be the nadir of *just-war* reasoning. Childress's resolution of *prima facie* into actual duties is *his* way of stating the supposed presumption against violence in just-war theory. But this is enough to throw doubt on that presumption.

Hollenbach's book, however, affords us a final opportunity to *explain* the erroneous conviction that pacifism and just war have in common *the same* presumption against violence. Hollenbach's adoption of this mistake seems to trace home to James Turner Johnson's account of "the original just war question" ("On Keeping Faith: The Use of History for Religious Ethics," *Journal of Religious Ethics*, 7/1 [1979], p. 112. Quoted by Hollenbach, p. 14). Hollenbach's language "should be presumed to be morally unacceptable" (p. 14), and especially his expression "places the *burden of proof* on . . ." (p. 48; my italics) suggests a meaning of the word "presumption" that our previous discussion has not acknowledged. Scarcely noticed in the conventional wisdom concerning pacifism and just war is a simple confusion between basic *assumption* (in the sense of "central premise" [*The Challenge of Peace*, par. 82]) and *presumption* (in the sense of burden-of-proof to be borne). The central premise or bottom-line "assumption" of a tradition of moral reasoning (e.g., resistance of injustice for the protection or deliverance of its victims) is entirely consistent with and quite different from a "presumption" against injuring anyone in the pursuit of such a just cause, if such injury is avoidable. I suggest that a quasi-legal burden of proof is what Hollenbach means by "presumption." His error is only the odd choice of language in which to express that thought: "a *prima facie* obligation of non-injury" (p. 42). Perhaps burden of proof also explains the language of "exception" often used to align just-war ethics with pacifism. "Just cause" is the logically prior premise or assumption in just-war ethics. "Last resort" is given logical priority by those who confuse moral premise with burden of proof against doing harm. To identify just war and pacifism in their sources is a mistake. There can be, in a quasi-legal sense, a *presumption* against violence without "nonviolence" being the basic ethico-political *assumption* in just-war traditions. The original just-war "assumption" is that "social charity" comes to the aid of the oppressed, and yet, secondarily, the *burden of proof* should be placed on resort to violent means, or on those who resist evil (Matt. 5:39).

But the point of just-war tradition is that this is a burden of proof that can be borne. Indeed, in this world—and not some other—there are situations of injustices so massive and concentrated and threats so overwhelming that the "presumption" shifts against anyone who continues to believe that nonviolent means are our reasonable service. Then proportion limits just war, and not a commonly held, general obligation to do no harm. Speaking from within just-war perspective, I would be willing to say that no one should ever injure or kill another *unjustly*; but I seriously doubt if a single pacifist would join me in adherence to such an assumption. Even so, to call that assumption or central premise a *prima facie* obligation would contribute little or nothing to the clarification of moral discourse concerning just and unjust wars.

Yet this confusion of fundamental moral assumption with "presumption against" is apt to continue to be voiced so long as contemporary pacifists continue to meld together nonresistance and nonviolent political resistance, or if we are to believe that pacifism leaves these options open in its account of Christian discipleship. At the same time, the enormous destructiveness of modern weapons impels many people who stand within just-war tradition to forget the function of judgments of proportion and thoughtlessly to accept the basic premise falsely ascribed to them. That nonmaleficence is an absolute duty for the pacifist, admitting no exceptions, but that for just-war theorists nonmaleficence is a *prima facie* duty (a duty usually binding, but one that may be overriden in exceptional circumstances), tells us quite clearly that pacifism and just war have little or nothing in common—if the question was their theological and moral *sources* or points of departure in moral reasoning.

Richard B. Miller has been to some extent misled by Childress's replacement of just-war norms. He praises the Catholic Bishops for resisting "exclusive fascination with the dilemmas of war," for relegating such casuistry to the boundary of moral discourse, for creating a "clearing" for more positive and nuanced thought about peace. This was accomplished, he suggests, by "casting just-war ideas in the language of *presumptive* duties" ("Christian Pacifism and Just-War Tenets: How Do They Diverge?", *Theological Studies* 47/3 [September 1986], pp. 448–72, at p. 470; my italics). The combination of "presumptive duties" with burden-of-proof language on the next page qualifies his apparent adoption of Childress-Ross analysis. Miller's excellent article is flawed by both confusions of which I have spoken (assumption/presumption and nonviolent resistance/not violence/nonresistance), and I do not need to go over that ground again. I want mainly to commend note 10 on page 449 for its fine contrast of justice in the pastoral with Childress's "thin" theory of moral obligation.

In my own writings, the defense of justice for the protection of the innocent must be fundamental if there ever is *jus ad bellum*. I do, thereafter and secondarily, appeal to a "presumption" against killing the innocent (in already justified war) to derive the indefeasible *jus in bello* prohibition against deliberately attacking noncombatants.

The Catholic pastoral (as I have argued above) is better than Bryan Hehir thinks if (as he tells me) Ralph Potter's "The Moral Logic of War" (*McCormick Quarterly*, 23 [1970], pp. 202–38) and James Childress's *prima facie* duties authorize his own belief that the justice-premise comes into play only in determining "exceptions" to the presumption against killing. See *The Challenge of Peace*, par. 84, n. 35.

The subtitle, *Being Honest in Just-War Thinking*, of Yoder's *When War Is Unjust* made it imperative that I take this slender book into account at some length. Yoder would be due an apology for what I honestly had to say about it if I did not exhibit a fuller appreciation of his rendering of Christian pacifism. In the mode still of an ecumenical consultation, I propose to take up two additional issues: (1) the question of differing accounts of the person and work of Christ, and (2) whether justified-war Christians presume that by "responsible" political action we can dispose events so as to insure that history comes out right, or must presume that Christian pacifism is irresponsible. On both these topics I mean rather to delineate clear *options* for Christian consciences and churches and to suggest an end to pejorative comparisons (not to mention name-calling).

The crux (the cross, the crossroads) at which Christian pacifists and justifiable-war Christians part company is our respective accounts of the person and work of Jesus Christ as these bear on divergent understandings of discipleship. *Christology* is the heart of the matter. No understanding of Christian discipleship can be more *Christocentric* than that of pacifists such as Yoder and Hauerwas. Without prejudice I change that wording to *Jesus*-centered; this will help abbreviate my pinpointing the basic theological issue. "Jesucentrism" is a neutral term, leaving open the possibility that different Christologies may in different fashions take the life, teachings, and crucifixion of Jesus with *equal* seriousness. It is also a summary term that came to mind from a reading of Yoder's extraordinary chapter on the "Anabaptists in the Continental Reformation."

See John H. Yoder, *Christian Attitudes to War, Peace and Revolution,* pp. 165–200. This volume is a record of Yoder's teaching and a textbook he used in teaching Mennonite seminarians. It has never been issued by a trade publisher and is available only from the Co-Op Bookstore, Goshen Biblical Seminary, 3003 Benham, Elkhart, Indiana 46517. In this chapter Yoder traces the "logic" by which the problem of the sword arose and moved to the center among Anabaptists of the sixteenth century. Two documents are crucial for the emerging pre–Menno Simons church undergoing continuing reform by Scripture: a 1524 letter from Conrad Grebel, a "radical" Zwlingian in Zurich, to Thomas Muntzer; and the 1527 Schleitheim formulation.

Jesus-centered discipleship came first in the reforming church now named the Mennonites. This emerging Christian pacifism did not appeal in *legal* or proof-text fashion to the *teachings* of Jesus. Discipleship came first, and this meant *participation* in his life. Not even the Sermon on the Mount was the center; instead, the "rule of Christ" was Matthew 18:15–20: Here Jesus tells his disciples, his church, what to do. They are to be a community in conversation about the meaning of discipleship, reproving, correcting, and disciplining one another. So, by Yoder's account, the church came to distinguish its way of dealing with conflict (with the "ban" as last resort) in contrast to resort to the sword in civil community. There is no God-*given* order or ordinance outside the perfection of Christ. There is rather a providential process of *ordering* the world, but this claims not those schooled by Jesus. With Jesus at the center of the community's life, Christians are drawn off from "the world." They do not start off programmed as separatists.

Similarly, suffering nonresistance was not obedience to New Testament texts but resulted from being—quite literally—members of Christ's body. Separation from the world came from the unity that happened to these Christians, their community together in unity with Jesus. In Yoder's words, "We are to be a part of what he is, and he is as he was. *We are to be in the world now what he was* according to the New Testament text. . . . It was always the same reasoning process. *Jesus did in the world what we are supposed to be doing in the world*" (my italics). Is this not "eucharistic" language for the church, and for Jesus' suffering presence, that influenced a Methodist from Texas who bears the name of Stanley Hauerwas to urge the people called Methodist to recover the Wesleyan celebration of the eucharist at the center of our worship? Transposed to that context, this living unity with Jesus assumes the cast of a "realized eschatology" to be faithfully lived by a large empirical denomination, without taut tension with the Kingdom not yet a presence to the church.

"The foundation of the call for non-resistance is unity with Jesus." Yoder's usage here warrants my "*Jesu*centrism." For he writes, "You could of course say 'unity with Christ' but the Christ it [the Schleitheim formulation] is talking about is not some cosmic figure, and not some present mystical guide alone, but the continuation in our experience, because we are to be a united body. *We are to be in the world what he was* according to the New Testament text" (my italics).

But, by this account of the normativeness of Jesus for a church completely at peace, *this Jesus* is a Christology among others!

Yoder would not endorse the one account of the mystery of the Incarnation mentioned in this chapter: that Jesus passed through Mary (who acted as a sort of conduit) unsullied by the taint of the sin of her humanity; therefore, we have perfection with us in union with Jesus.

I am not suggesting that Christological dogma comes first. Doubtless the Mennonite vision of discipleship came first, in proper order. But there are other visions of faithfulness to him that correspond dialectically with other Christologies. So when Christian pacifists found their discipleship on the incarnation, life, teachings, death, and resurrection of Jesus—and claim to take with greater seriousness his life and teachings—we need to question the claim and ask for conversation about Christology. Other renderings of membership in Christ's body—one as his community, one in Christ as he is one with the Father (John 17:21)—take the life and teachings and "dying love" of Jesus seriously—*in different fashion* (Jonathan Edwards, for example). The point cannot be argued further here. So as a contribution to ongoing discussion, let me sketch briefly the issues as they appear to me.

The man Christ Jesus himself is the Center. He is the Example; he, the Pattern. Again without prejudice (since Luther and Kierkegaard also spoke of Christ the Pattern), I ask: How are we to distinguish serious Christian pacifism based on the person and politics of Jesus from other "exemplary" theories of the Atonement, of the person and work of Christ, with which modern Christianity is awash? To suggest this comparison is already an insult to the profundity of the Christian pacifism I think worth discussing, but we do need to ask for the Christological vindication even if only to disagree. Until I know this, Hauerwas's pacifism does not cohere in my mind with what I know he believes and what he would have all who are Methodists affirm every Lord's Day, in the liturgy of the eucharist (words and doctrine from more ancient times). To be persuaded by the pacifism of a Yoder or a Hauerwas without the Christology implied or unarticulated in it could be to do the right thing for the wrong reasons. That's no way to speak up for pacifism.

The same point can be put in terms of the "imitation" of Jesus. We are told that the politics of Jesus should be our politics; his nonresistance of evil, our nonresisting love even of enemy-neighbors; his way of doing his Father's reconciliation, our reconciling spirit. The disciple is not greater than his master. This states that Jesus is THE pattern, THE example.

Yet, on other views of the person and work of Jesus Christ, the foregoing does not follow. One thing, at least, we do not imitate in Jesus Christ, namely, the fact that he had no Jesus Christ to imitate. He had no savior made flesh. He prayed that "all may be one; as thou, Father, art in me, and I in thee, that they also may be one in us" (John 17:21). His incarnation, his life as the God-man among us, his suffering, his death, his resurrection were unique, never to be repeated. Certainly not by us. He was THE Pattern, so as at any moment to assume an accusative role of Judge. He is Pattern, yet also Savior. We are neither co-Creators nor co-Saviors. Hence, as the Reformers knew, we are to follow him—*from a distance*. We are not to take up *his* cross, but *our* cross to follow him. This is a sufficient sketch of some possible alternative Christologies—some, I say, and only possible—in which are rooted the different discipleships of Christian pacifists and justified-war Christians.

For Hauerwas's Christology, see "Jesus: The Presence of the Peaceable Kingdom," in his *The Peaceable Kingdom: A Primer of Christian Ethics* (Notre Dame: University of Notre Dame Press, 1983), pp. 72–95. For Yoder's, see "'But We Do See Jesus': The Particularity of Incarnation and the Universality of Truth," in his *The Priestly Kingdom: Social Ethics as Gospel* (Notre Dame: University of Notre Dame Press, 1984), pp. 46–62; and the chapter entitled "Christ as Priest: Atonement," in *Preface to Theology: Christology and Theological Method* (Elkhart, Indiana: Co-Op Bookstore, Goshen Biblical Seminary, n.d.), pp. 207–43, esp. pp. 227–31. Yoder's main objections are directed against certain Eastern notions of incarnation that teach that "we are really saved at Bethlehem" and that the death of Christ, although unavoidable, "did not really matter" (p. 214), and against any *Christus Victor* or *Anselmic* theory of atonement that teaches "something done for us out there" and not also "something done to us and through us" (p. 212). For Anselm, in particular, Christ's death purchases "satisfaction" for sin, expiates juridical guilt. This Christology, however, (1) needs no eschatology, no resurrection, and (2) lacks "being in Christ," participation in the life and death of Jesus. Discipleship and *direction* for discipleship are both lacking. There is also no explanation of how the *life* of Jesus can be called obedience (pp. 223–26). I suspect that Yoder (and Hauerwas) read Luther on justification (forgiveness) in the juridical, "out there" mode, and not in terms of filial acceptance. Luther's dialectic "simultaneously saved and sinful" is also only the underside of the dialectic "Christ the Savior" and "Christ the Pattern." And no Christian account of new life in Christ ever supposed his disciples not to need his forgiveness in this life any longer.

The point is not to open discussion of these topics now, but to stress that other accounts of the person and work of Jesus Christ *take seriously* his incarnation, life, teachings, crucifixion, and resurrection. Pacifists find Jesus' life, teachings, and the cross to be inadequately in the center of nonpacifist attention. But without Jesus' life and teachings, traditional Catholicism had no ground for its "counsels of perfection." Without Jesus' life, teachings, death, and resurrection, traditional Lutheranism had no ground for its distinction between the righteousness of faith and civil righteousness. Without these, the Reform tradition had no understanding of the asymptotic goal of regeneration, which with justification is the "double grace" that comes from being "in Christ"; or Wesleyans, of the holiness or purity of heart without which none of the sons or daughters of Adam shall see God. Without these, Reinhold Niebuhr would have had no appeal beyond the "social gospel." He would have had no hold by which to recover for American Christianity "the strange new world within the Bible." He recovered less than Karl Barth, it is true; but the figure of Jesus as he is there in the text was undeniably in the center of his attention. To avoid acknowledging this, many people today say that Niebuhr's "theological source" was anthropology and politics. This is manifestly false. My point here, however, is simply to say that there is nothing to be gained from adherents of one or another of these actual or possible accounts of the person and work of Christ saying of the others, "We all participate in Jesus; you in your way, I in *his*."

I would not say that in taking up *his* or *her* cross (which cannot be the once-only cross of Jesus Christ or a repetition of it) the pacifist leaves to his brother or sister in Christ a more *or* a less difficult cross to bear in resisting injustice to relieve the oppressed. I say only that both are *our* crosses, and that the difference between these vocations likely stems from different fundamental accounts of Jesus Christ *pro nobis*.

The words of Helmut Gollwitzer at the 1966 Geneva Conference on Church and Society need to be rewritten:

> The answer given by Christian pacifism leaves to non-Christians that very secular task which requires the greatest love and unselfish-ness, namely the use of force; and the answer given by the great churches involves Christians so deeply in the conflicts of the world and in the settlement of these conflicts by the use of lethal force that it is almost impossible for Christians to bear witness to the joyful message of Christ to their adversaries. (Quoted in my *Who Speaks for the Church?*, p. 111)

These words are correct in describing the *tasks* and the temptations of each. They should be rewritten, however, so as to distribute the tasks and the perils *between Christians*, without reference to "non-Christians" or to "secu-lar" tasks.

Another question surfaced again in the foregoing that must be answered by twentieth-century Christians who are pacifists. This is my iterated and reiterated question about where Yoder and Hauerwas stand on "nonviolent resistance." Unless the love of nonresistance is purified of its twentieth-century alloy with "nonviolence," the grounding of pacifism in its account of the person and work of Jesus Christ would have to be corrected back to a sort of *legalism*. If the line pacifists draw falls between nonviolent and violent resistance of evil, then what is said to be outside the perfection of Christ flies the banner "Thou shalt not kill." This introduces a rather unsophisticated reading of the Old Testament commandment, or else it resorts again to proof-texting the teachings of Jesus to find there the core of a new legalism. Ironically, nonpacifist Christians might then have to call attention to the unison of Jesus in word and deed, of his life and death, with his words at Matthew 5:39–48. To the contrary, according to the history of pacifism on Protestant soil just recounted, it was the common search for the meaning of being his disciples (Matt. 18:15–20) that first led the church undergoing reformation by Scripture to note those teachings, and others in the Sermon on the Mount, as *signs* of our unity in him. How do I avoid these conclusions?

The later chapters of Yoder's *Christian Attitudes to War, Peace and Revolution* introduce a degree of unclarity as to where he stands on the distinction between nonresistance and nonviolent resistance. His *positive* notion of "revolutionary subordinationism" in *The Politics of Jesus* consists with the former. Yet I get no clear understanding of his relation to Guy F. Hershberger's *War, Peace and Non-Resistance*, or to more recent affirmations of this distinction, by Don Smucker and others, between a pacifism of the cross of Jesus and political pacifism. It is true that these later chapters continue the story through Quakerism, Enlightenment Humanism, the Nineteenth Century and Liberal Protestant Pacifism, Reinhold Niebuhr's "Realistic" Critique, Mennonites after Niebuhr, Just War Thought Revived, and the Lessons of Nonviolent Experience. The systematic question I am asking was not Yoder's in these teaching materials.

Yet it is precisely the history he traverses that raises the systematic question more urgently. That question is: As the conversation continues into the twentieth century concerning the meaning of discipleship among those who quite literally believe that they are *members* of the suffering service of Jesus, and that they are to do as he was, is there a meaning of "nonviolent resistance" that gains acceptance and embodiment? Is there a nonviolent resistance that is *not* political pacifism, that is *not* an impurity when encompassed in nonresistant love? Can we speak of a "nonviolent cross" without contradiction, in any other than the trivial sense of "*not* violent" as an outlying circumscription of taking up our cross, the cross Jesus bore, which is significantly circumscribed only more narrowly as nonresistance and overcoming evil with good? The importance of these questions is highlighted by the fact that Hershberger's opposition of the pacifism of nonresistance to Quaker and other political pacifisms was drawn from the ethos of his own community, quite independent of Reinhold Niebuhr's coming to the same distinction from his own reading of the life, teachings, and crucifixion of Jesus, and the quite different use he made of this Jesus as Lord and Savior.

My espionage of the *normative* judgments embedded in the rich and complicated story Yoder tells leads me to the following observation— which is an extended question to him and to Hauerwas. Hospitality to the ethics of "nonviolent resistance" is often a reaction to the charge of passivism and irresponsibility. I can cite only a few contexts in which this seems a reasonable explanation. Yoder describes "a basic typology which distinguishes between non-violent direct action which is aggressive and coercive and in one sense impure [!], and on the other hand, non-resistance which is faithful to the model of Christ as crucified Lord *and by that token powerless*"

(p. 314; my italics). This sets faithfulness and effectiveness, "absolutistic nonresistance" and "pragmatic pacifism," in polar opposition (p. 315). In this context Yoder tells his students, "You may go on, if you wish, thinking that 'nonresistance' *when taken in this heightened form*, is an inadequate position, *as I do*" (p. 316; my italics). It wasn't "very churchly" for Smucker et al. to adopt "the verbal expression" of Niebuhr's critique in reverse, by using "nonresistance" for the correct position and "pacifism" for the wrong one (p. 340). So it was Niebuhr who taught some Mennonites to use "the word 'pacifism' for what we don't believe. Guy Hershberger . . . continued to use the word in a good sense" (p. 359). (Earlier, characterizing Niebuhr's view, Yoder writes, "Pacifism (or *nonviolence* in a *broader* sense) was the basic issue. . . . He agrees that Jesus teaches suffering love, the renunciation of all violence, readiness to give without limit your life for your neighbor, even for your enemy" [p. 349].) But, although Yoder describes Niebuhr as reactive, he does not himself jettison Niebuhr's distinction between (1) nonresistance, which is unconcerned for power and effect, and (2) non-violent tactical commitment (p. 358).

At the same time, Yoder wants to rescue younger Mennonites from the "dichotomous" analysis (p. 417) that results from too much Niebuhrian "acculturation" (p. 418). Yoder cites a passage from the second (1953) edition of Hershberger's *War, Peace and Nonresistance* that left open the door for other kinds of action (not designed to *compel* others to do justice, but actions other than those of "nonviolent coercionists"), which would also be nonviolent but would be driven by a spirit of love (p. 416).

The inter-Mennonite tension is best and briefly summarized in Yoder's *Nevertheless: Varieties and Shortcomings of Religious Pacifism* (Scottsdale, Pennsylvania: Herald Press, 1971, 1976). The conservative position is given the title "The Non-Pacifist Nonresistance of the Mennonite 'Second Wind'" (pp. 106–14); the type most expressive of Yoder's view, "The Pacifism of the Messianic Community" (pp. 123–28). The following quotations will suffice. "The question put to us as we follow Jesus is not whether we have successfully refrained from breaking any rules, but whether we have been participants in that human experience, that peculiar way of living for God in the world, of being used as instruments for the living God in the world, which the Bible calls *agape* or *cross*." This is not a matter of an individual's integrity, but of "the human community experiencing in its life a foretaste of God's kingdom. . . . a human community dedicated in common to a new and publicly scandalous enemy-loving way of life." Addressed to all men, "such a life is not cut to the measure of men in general"; but by the same token, Yoder is not concerned to *affirm* or to *deny* minority status. Another advantage of this position is "that it does not promise to work." So the question of effectiveness is decentralized, as it is not when Yoder writes in a more *reactive* (anti-Niebuhrian or anti-dualistic Mennonite) mood.

All this is in line with my concern that Christian pacifists and nonpacifists break out of the accusatory-reactive syndrome that has afflicted us in the past. This cannot happen, of course, so long as the palpably question-begging assertion is made that "*only* this position collapses if Jesus be not Christ and if Jesus be not Lord. . . . Even Christian theologians generally dedicated to making Jesus normative in their thought about deity and the creeds, tend to be startled by the suggestion that He might be indispensible in defining a proper political humanity" (p. 127; my italics). There are, of course, other views of "political humanity" that claim to be "utterly dependent on who Jesus was and the attitude one takes towards him." To say that the crux (the cross, the crossroads) is Christology is the *beginning* of ecumenical conversation, not the end of it.

Yoder does not help me much—or Hauerwas much yet—on what to say to our great Methodist cultural church about the systematic equivocation in the use of "nonviolent resistance" and nonresistant love of the enemy that afflicts current Christian discussion of pacifism. Are we to warrant the alloy of "nonviolent resistance" provided only that the Christian places no hope in it, or many times does not? In *Nevertheless* Yoder speaks of the sacrifices of war as "ultimately so much easier to make than those demanded by *nonviolent love*" (p. 76; my italics); "violence is a vice to be avoided; *nonviolence or meekness* is a virtue and to be cultivated" (p. 78; my italics). Should we not clean up the equivocation in our use of the word "nonviolence"?

Nevertheless is a remarkable little book that depicts a baker's dozen, and more, "pacifisms." In each case the type is briefly stated first, then objections are brought against it, then (in paragraphs beginning with the word *Nevertheless*, roughly equivalent to Aquinas's *I answer that*) replies are given to those objections. Finally each chapter closes with a paragraph beginning with the words *After all*, which affirms that *military ethics* (notably *not* just-war ethics) is equally open to the same objections.

The many "pacifisms" have in common that they are anti-war. That's "okay" for the intellectual exercise the author sets himself in this volume. Jenny Teichman also finds that the single thing pacifisms have in common is "antiwarism," in her *Pacifism and Just War: A Study in Applied Philosophy* (Oxford: Basil Blackwell, 1986). "Antiwarism" would be enough to support slogans like "We renounce war." But there is need for a more limited range of meanings, and clarity in distinguishing one from the other, in significant debates about *Christian* pacifism. So—without supposing an affirmative reply—I ask: Do uncertainty about the meaning or meanings of Christian pacifism and persistent equivocal use of the word "nonviolence" feed one another?

We come now in Yoder's textbook to his comment on his own *The Politics of Jesus*: "We shall not ask, 'does Jesus teach pacifism?' Niebuhr takes that for granted. . . . We shall ask whether Jesus' pacifism was political" (p. 424). In that question (to pursue my word study) "pacifism" can only mean "nonresistance" to evil, plus possible "nonviolence" that is by design "noncoercive." In all this Yoder's effort is to overcome "the duality between *guilty responsibility* and *irrelevant purity*, which . . . dominates recent debate" (pp. 427). "The whole key to [Jesus'] new order is non-coerciveness" (p. 428). The way Jesus lived it was to die for it. If noncoerciveness is the kingdom, his disciples must be a voluntary, gathered, minority community. Yoder goes so far as to say that "it would be linguistically honest to say, that Jesus was a *nonviolent Zealot*, except that there wasn't any other nonviolent Zealots. . . . He was crucially different from the Zealots at the point of violence. . . . He was not ready to kill for God's righteousness. . . . But he was like them willing to die for it" (p. 432; my italics).

The foregoing review has done little to remove the equivocal use of both "pacifism" and "nonviolence." But is there not an underlying drive to break free from the dichotomy between *irrelevant purity* and *guilty responsibility*? Therefore I wonder, if this charge from the legacy of Reinhold Niebuhr were withdrawn, could it be that pacifist and nonpacifist Christians would begin to use our normative words with one meaning? Then also—whether we espouse it or not—might we also learn that "nonviolent resistance" means to *compel* us to do justice but cannot compel us to love mercy? Martin Luther King told us that much!

A strange thing happens when we come to the chapter on "The Lessons of Nonviolent Experience." Here the reaction against the charge of "ineffectiveness" is most powerful; and I ask myself even more urgently, Why let one's account of following Jesus be caught on the horns of the dilemma "You must either commit yourself to active effectiveness (and then sometimes you are going to have to cheat on your nonresistance) or you commit yourself to faithfulness (and then sometimes you are going to give up effectiveness)"? The dialectic of the chapter moves between William Robert Miller's position (which accepts those Niebuhrian options and finds in "nonviolence" a tactic that can "succeed") and that of James Douglass (who "trusts the truth to change the adversary"; "the cross is a power, suffering is a way to move history"). Yoder is troubled by Miller's "clean dichotomy," which is "kept alive, as we have seen, by some socially conservative Mennonites." On the other hand, if we say with Douglass "that nonviolence works, we need to ask next whether we would drop it if it did not." "Jesus was not successful. . . . The non-coerciveness of *agape* (i.e. uncalculating Christian love) includes renouncing the promise of power. . . . It rather means a promise of victory whose paradigm is the resurrection" (p. 493).

Notice the ambiguity in the meaning of the word "nonviolence," taken over by Yoder in his critique of these two positions. This continues to be the case in the resolution Yoder proposes: "that we do not try to prove our hope." It doesn't help to clear up the equivocation remaining in the kind of "pacifism" Yoder espouses for him to continue to "use language like that of Douglass in order to proclaim the hope which I cannot prove" and to engage with Miller in trying to prove that "nonviolence" is as effective as any other tactic.

The latter course is undertaken because the way of violence is also a trust and a hope. "Nonviolence" has not been proved any more ineffective than violence. "If we hear it argued that organized military force will achieve certain desirable goals, the alternative against which we should test it is not doing nothing, or some improvised nonviolent gesture, but rather what could be done if the same amount of creativity, the same funds, the same advanced institutional planning, the same strategy thinking, etc., were invested in the nonviolent reaction as are currently being invested in preparations for war" (p. 495).

So it seems to me that Yoder and both the Catholic and the Methodist Bishops give currency to a systematic equivocation concerning the meaning of "nonviolence"; and that in Yoder this may be because he is overly reactive to the charge of political "ineffectiveness." Where is the "noncoerciveness" in nonviolence? Indeed, I might interpose here the suggestion that any commander-in-chief will need to have in preparation a gradation of options: nonviolent troops such as Yoder describes and troops equipped and trained to use violent resistance, with "command" able to move from the first to the second level of "force" and "control" able to draw back from the second to the first. This is entailed if the point is simply that "nonviolent tactics must always be tried first and tried harder than they have been in the past" (p. 497). So, amid the obfuscation of our language concerning "nonviolence," I keep searching for the Christian pacifism our Methodist Bishops might speak up for. And I suggest that Yoder might be more helpful to me if he were not so reactive to the charge that "whoever renounces effectiveness for the sake of faithfulness is doing an unsocial minority purist thing" (p. 500). Does or does not Yoder mean to draw the line between violent resistance and nonviolent resistance? Would this not be a legalism of "Thou shalt not kill" versus Matthew 6:39–48, far distant from the church's participation in Jesus' participation in his Father's way of dealing with conflict, as in Matthew 18:15–20, where we began?

On the other hand, the charge of "irresponsibility" or "ineffectiveness" needs to be withdrawn by those of us in the tradition of Niebuhr and just war. Absent the condescending tribute to the "witness" of the "peace churches," there need be nothing off-putting in affirming that authentic Christian pacifism is not a doctrine *addressed to states*. It is, is it not, a doctrine addressed *to the church*?

The final point I want to make is, I hope, an irenic one. It is sometimes alleged that Christians of the justifiable-war persuasion err in that they "try to make history turn out right." Thus at the very heart of Yoder's account of the politics of Jesus—that is, Jesus' politics in fulfilling the hopes of his people in their oppression—he locates Jesus' choice between "effectiveness" and "obedience":

> The choice that he made in rejecting the crown and accepting the cross was the commitment to such a degree of faithfulness to the character of divine love that he was willing for its sake to sacrifice "effectiveness." Usually it can be argued that from some other perspective or in some long view this renunciation of effectiveness *was a very effective thing to do.* "If a man will lose his . . . life he shall find it." But this paradoxical possibility does not change the initially solid fact that Jesus thereby excluded any *normative concern for any capacity to make sure that things would turn out right.* (*The Politics of Jesus* [Grand Rapids: Eerdmans, 1972], p. 240; my italics)

Jesus was God's way of dealing with evil. The Christ event, thus understood, is determinative for Yoder's theme, "revolutionary subordination," which would seem to entail a clear choice *against* revolutionary violent *or* nonviolent (would-be effective) resistance. We can also say of such obedient discipleship: It could be argued from many a perspective or in some long view that *that* was a very effective thing to do. But this paradoxical possibility does not change the fact that a disciple of Christ has no normative concern for the effectiveness that may follow upon obedience.

Either of these appeals to the future should be rejected. This is the only way to take hold of the charges and countercharges that roil the debates between pacifists and just warriors. The first party says the other is trying to make history turn out right; in the extreme, the charge is that we are "survivalist" for some of the world's political systems or states of affairs. Then just warriors "reply" that the "peace churches" provide a very important "witness" to a higher (but politically irresponsible) way of discipleship. The latter, condescending acceptance of an authentic role in the divine economy for Christian pacifists enforces once again the charge of pacifists that "responsibilists" think they have anticipatory disposition of history's outcome.

The distinction between responsible and witnessing action, as well as the distinction between effectiveness and obedience, needs to be withdrawn. A Mennonite family I know, now living in Lesotho (one of the enclave "nations" carved out within South Africa), is teaching black people there how to live better with the simplest economy. I would call that both witnessing action and effective action. Nor should those Mennonites be charged with trying to insure that history turns out right, if, as they believe, the more rapid depletion of earth's *unreplenishable* resources can be the only result of "modernization." Even if they conceive of themselves as contributing to an inhabitable planet, their present activities are in no way dependent on that outcome. They do not pretend to hold the future in their hands.

In my view the spirit of charity that impels *jus ad bellum* and *jus in bello* judgments in conscience, on the part of nonpacifist Christians who cannot pass by on the other side of threatening tyranny or actual oppression, is not essentially different from that of the Mennonites I have just described. Whatever Reinhold Niebuhr may have thought he was doing in rallying the religious resources of the nation against the Nazi menace, this likely was not making sure *history* turns out right. "Things," yes, in Yoder words; some things, and for a time, time in which all things pass away. Surely he did not believe we could control the future. The recessional hymn usually sung after Niebuhr preached thrust the hearts of his hearers away from trust in a world in which *nothing abides.*

> Age after age their tragic Empires rise,
> Built while they dream, and in their dreaming weep.
> Would Man but wake from out his haunted sleep . . .

The climactic hope expressed was eschatological: "earth might be fair and all men glad and wise"; in "that hour shall God's whole will be done." Surely Niebuhr was not surprised by the massive shifts of the continental plates in the wake of Hitler's defeat, the unpredictable outcomes of that "just and necessary" war in weakening Great Britain's colonial power over the Indian subcontinent, in decolonializing Africa, in casting up on the crust of the earth's surface new nations (India and Pakistan), already with their histories and animosities. He would have been saddened but not surprised by the consequence for Great Britain herself of going to meet her vocational hour of responsibility as a great power. Surely he would not be surprised by the massive shifts now taking place in the continental plates of the political world (NATO and the Soviet Block).

After all, Hitler could promise only a *thousand*-year Reich. And a thousand years is but as a day. Niebuhr's sense of the transiency of every human achievement of a somewhat more just order, or the prevention of a worse one, suggests that effective action and witnessing action are not greatly different from one another. *The future is radically unpredictable*, for pacifist and just warrior alike. We need to withdraw Niebuhr's somewhat condescending tribute to the peace churches. We need to affirm the coeval, equally worthy, irreducible parting of the ways of Christian pacifists and justified-war Christians. Neither is able to *depend* on the consequences in the whole of their activities, or discount the effectiveness of the other's witness. All this can be said, I believe, while holding that in the divine economy for this world just war is the meaning of statecraft, and that pacifism cannot be addressed to states. Still, these are equally Christian discipleships. And the *freedom* of state action trammels up but little that *destiny* has in store.

The intermingling of the Two Cities is through the heart of every just-war Christian. We live in the midst of a people—whose history and future are ours also—who cannot vividly imagine that democracy, freedom as we know it, America, the Constitution, are among those tragic empires, built and upheld while we dreaming weep, haunted by a future when all these things, too, shall have passed away. We belong to this temporal city and are engaged in the continuance of it, yet our citizenship is also in another City, not made with hands, whose builder and maker is God and his Christ.

5

Speaking on Particulars for the Church to the Church and World

I NEVER cease to wonder why there are so many "post-Constantinians" in our so-called "liberal" churches who (1) proclaim with joy the end of that era, yet (2) never hesitate to issue advice to states as if they were Christian kingdoms, and (3) continue to applaud the destruction of the remaining "social space" that sustains the independence of educational and other church institutions—which will be needed if the church is to be even an effective *sect* in today's world, capable of conveying Christian ethos, faith, and practice to our children's children. Such people would reduce the church to the freedom of inner faith and preaching (which only Lutherans were supposed to think enough) while continuing to preach the gospel of reconciliation to states. All the while there is (4) much talk about "discerning the signs of the times," as if these were "theological sources" from which to gather the message the church is to return to the world whence the message came.

The expression "the signs of the times" did not mean an additional theological source when first introduced in the literature. The Second Vatican Council urged us to discern "the signs of the times," yes; but then to "interpret them in the light of the gospel" (*Gaudium et Spes*, par. 6). Subsequently, various historicisms and relativisms in Christian morality have appropriated the slogan.

The foregoing paragraph is *not* about *In Defense of Creation* alone. It is meant rather to introduce the most vexing problem of all concerning the church in the modern world. The question is how the church can be *the church* and at the same time speak *to the point* on military policy and other public questions. And one thing we need to learn from Hauerwas is whether, how, and by what authority a pacifist church should do this.

Monasteries aspired to be colonies of heaven on earth, embodying a higher righteousness, but they still depended on the great medieval cultural church in making their witness to the world. The "sects" of the left wing of the Reformation followed Christ's call to discipleship in coming out of a Catholicism, a Lutheranism, and a Calvinism that, they believed, were like Noah's Ark, into which went both the clean and the unclean. Still, these sixteenth- and seventeenth-century Protestant sects depended upon the existence of the surrounding general Christian culture even in their "withdrawal" from it. Mainline Protestant churches in America are no longer "denominations" (compare Troeltsch's "church"-type and "sect"-type). "Denominations" once rightly supposed they were relevant, and they were generally acknowledged by others to be relevant, on public questions. The Constantinian era died hard. Those days are gone forever, all of them. Some of us were at the bedside when God culturally died; he passed away so slowly it was hardly noticed. Many now say they have no regrets over his passing, only freedom at last. Some of us may have helped to kill that god. And a few (formerly the most faithful) continue to stab at Christ's cultural embodiments here and there, attempting desperately to render humankind *better* than in the Christian ages. Those days also are almost gone, except in the minds of some who make themselves ridiculous by continuing to punish a corpse. Not even *atheism* is *Christian* any longer. What now?

Aspiring to more perfect discipleship, contemporary churches wander between the "sectarian" temptation (possibility) and the "church" temptation (possibility) remembered to have been there once upon a time in our legacy. *We speak like sectarians speaking like churches.* Or, in order to speak like churches having still a direct or at least an important cultural role, we speak more and more against today's world, like sects. The possibilities of "tooling up" to become a genuine, going sectarian community *or* of becoming culturally influential again (like "church"-types or "denominations") in the world of today are *both* unlikely. Still, that world, its ethos, institutions, and practices, is too much with us, within us; the churches speak with the voice of partisan positions already heard in the public forum. We echo. *Therefore* some think that the more we speak like sectarians the more we might become "churches" or "denominations" again. *Therefore* Christian "directions" that are specific "directives" continue to be issued to people who are no longer Christian princes or Christian "lesser magistrates" (citizens), in an indifferent or hostile culture.

This is the context as I see it in which I raise my most vexing question. I am one who believes that the church (here I cease to use the word with Troeltsch's meaning) has more to witness to, more to say, than to itself or by cultivating its own inner life for Christ's sake or for witness. The church should not *of itself* cease to influence public policy having grave moral import for its own members and for the community at large. It ought not to *seek* to have such influence no longer, nor should it *avoid* what little it may still have or *void* what it may yet regain in God's afflictive and overruling providence.

My "speaking to the world," I am told, is only a relic of early twentieth-century "liberalism" in my soul (which even Reinhold Niebuhr, the charge is, continued to share with the "social gospel"). This account is not true, if what is meant is a liberal view of political society. Those who voice such objections themselves often hold a soft or hard neo-Marxist view of political society together with a variety of new winds of doctrine or pictures of Christ. Perhaps this is why they label as "liberal" the perennial impulse of Christian faith and love to refine, transform, and elevate whatever justice is to be found in the common life. This will never cease to be an authentic voice of the church.

It is also an authentic voice of the church to be *willing* to become a sect. The perplexity is that the world of today does not invite either option.

Those who search for "the signs of the times," and talk of great numbers of "anonymous" Christians, are exceedingly apt—whether intending to or not—to turn those "signs" into "theological sources." Such "signs" are only one term of the church speaking *to the point* in the world of today. If this is not understood, the *first* term—the church's authentic *voice*—will be muted or turned into something else, something really relevant (as they say). Moral perspectives emergent from the Gospel will be replaced by what's "preachable" or can gain a hearing today. This way lies apostasy, new versions of "culture Christianity," and, instead of the church, a web of organizations still called "churches" and "Christian" that bear no resemblance to past visible communities having the same names.

The expression in Matthew 16:3, "You know how to interpret the face of the heaven, but you cannot interpret the signs of the times," is laden with threatening eschatological significance. Surely it is not mean-spirited or anti-clerical for me to suggest that many people, both in and outside the churches in this secular age, do not understand "the signs of the times" in context with the sense of approaching Presence it has in Scripture. Thus, *only* when interpreted in the light of the Gospel do the signs of the times give grounds for hope. Here, too, fundamental differences among theological traditions surface, according to the degree of light and darkness thrown by that Light of the world.

So why try to be pertinent? The sectarian option—always an option in seasons of great and long-enduring evil—seems a possibility to be welcomed. That understanding of the contemporary church's fidelity to its Lord is, indeed, an attractive possibility until one tries *to think it through practically*. It is a fine, fine thing that the Mennonites, for example, are still alive and well today, their *traditioning* of the Christian life ongoing and vital. But those traditions were formed within Constantinian Christendom, though in opposition to its principal ecclesiastical formations. Their book of martyrs and their habits of heart and life are from before the assaults of modernity that readily penetrated and have all but overwhelmed mainline denominations. It boggles my mind, at least, to try to think steadily about the extraordinary changes that the spiritual leaders of the Methodist Church would have to stimulate and bring to pass if—in fidelity to the *Christian* side of the church-world tension—we were resolved to become *sectarians* worthy of that name.

But these are the options: hence the title of this volume, *Speak Up for Just War or Pacifism*.

Why do I continue to say "Not yet" to the sectarian possibility? Not, I judge, primarily because of the *practicalities* just mentioned, or the exodus of great multitudes from the United Methodist Church if we were seriously bent on witnessing to Christ to and against the present age. My father once reported to his Bishop at Annual Conference a great revival in his churches. When asked how many accessions to church membership, he replied there were none. What? Didn't you "open the doors" of the church? Nope, he replied; opened the back door and turned out twenty! I'm not predisposed therefore to dislike the sectarian option. My reason is rather the force of that other authentic voice of the church: to be the church speaking some healing word to the world.

So I say we need to continue to try to design the ecclesial procedures that will release that voice, drill again for the substance of Christian practice that can be the church (and not other voices) speaking to itself and to the world concerning justice and the common life. This search of mine for the authentic voice of the church speaking *for* the church *to* the church *and to the world* of today on public questions comes, as I said, not from any particular view of political society, but from within my understanding of the Christian community on pilgrimage through many ages, times, and political systems.

The just-war tests, for example, bespeak *justice* most sensitive to the neighbor's needs. Those criteria are *of* the church; they are its understanding of the imperatives of government. They should be addressed to authoritarian no less than to liberal democratic societies. While these norms show the way only to an "alien" work of love in a conflicted, fallen world, nevertheless this Christian ethico-political tradition is also our understanding of *the truth to be done* in earthly cities not only by Christians, not only by liberal democratic governments, but by any government of any human community. When importuned for their meaning today, these criteria yield political wisdom. That is the claim made in their behalf. Although these norms are not the "absolute natural law" of Paradise politics, they are the "relative natural law" governing power-encounters (violent or nonviolent), that is, the justice "relative" to the vocation of states in a fallen world. Christians are supposed to know something about God's preservative ordinances.

See the use of "absolute natural law" and "relative natural law" in Emil Brunner's *The Divine Imperative* (London: Letterworth Press, 1937), especially in his learned footnotes.

So I remain convinced that, if the church has anything authentic to say on issues of war and peace in the nuclear age, we must not omit any of the heights and depths of the Christian gospel: This is our only distinctive source of moral discernment or claim to anyone's attention. At the same time, we need to do our homework in order for that discernment to be at all relevant *to the point* of urgent public questions. So I urged our Bishops and their staff to "do some close-order work in parsing the morality of nuclear war and deterrence in a nuclear age by the tests of discrimination and proportion [other tests as well], and say what then seemeth good to say."

Two preceding chapters were appraisals of the adequacy of Christian sources of discernment (Ch. 1) and the adequacy of the moral argument (Ch. 3) in *In Defense of Creation*. Continuing now our quest for the church's authentic but pertinent voice, this final chapter stresses the question of *procedures* by which speaking *for* the church may be truly *of* the church *to* the church and (so far as Christian warrants go) *to the point* of public questions—in this case, justice and the common life in war and peace.

So it was that in my written "testimony" at the "hearing" held by the drafting committee I urged that our Bishops attend to the light and shadows thrown upon human pathways in this and every age by the cross of Christ; that they test all other enlightenment by Creation, Fall, and Last Things

(Ultimate Things); and that they *then* say everything they were impelled to say from as close a grasp and depth of understanding of the conditions of this world's peace as are forthcoming—*and say no more*. I urged them to fix a great gulf between their pastoral letter and specific solutions to grave political and military problems on which there may be (and is) legitimate *Christian* disagreement on the part of some or many members of the body of Christ.

In sum, I distinguished between anyone's "competence" or expertise on this or any other public question and their "competent authority" as pastors and teachers of the church when speaking *for* the church in whatever they say *to* the church and to *the world* we live in. By midafternoon I knew that this elementary distinction was not understood, from the manner and words with which one member of the panel asked Ambassador Gerald Smith what degree of "competence" the committee needed in order to address themselves to issues of arms control. He replied that they needed very little, or at least no more than the ordinary informed citizen. My point, of course, was that *no degree* of that sort of competence bestows "competent moral authority" on a Council of Bishops, *acting as such*, to say anything without clear Christian warrants. This is true of those who do Christian ethics—that is, church ethics—as well. The church as such has no mandate to say anything at all about public questions, unless this be from the point of view of the transcendental elements and doctrines of the Christian faith.

"It is quite easy to produce a 'competent' document," I reminded the panel at the July 1985 hearing in Washington—continuing with some irony to press the point: "You simply pick your experts; issue your own thorough exposition of the analysis and foreign policy they advocate, with some variation and added Christian language; go lightly on what can be said against your chosen solution or in favor of some other; stress what seems problematic or *realpolitik* about any opposing position, and imply that, while there may also be experts favoring it, it is attracting the Christian 'right.' This is easier done in opposition to current administration policy." There is also no scarcity of "experts" on one side or another of controverted public questions who would like to co-opt the church's voice.

How far to go in church pronouncements is a difficult line to draw and an easy one to overstep. How shall a pastoral letter fix a gulf between things properly said in pursuit of earthly peace and *specific* answers to urgent questions of policy for which bishops, ministers, and church people *as such* have no "competent authority" or continuing responsibility? How can we grapple earnestly enough with the issues of war and peace in a nuclear age, and yet stop short of excluding positions that may legitimately be held by others on equally Christian grounds? The more urgent the question, the more difficult it is to refrain from introducing division and a partisan spirit.

So I proposed to our Bishops a "Model for Specific Political Pronouncements" from my *Who Speaks for the Church?* (Nashville: Abingdon, 1967; pp. 118–24), with a significant amendment of that model. My model unamended was the statement of the Archbishop of Canterbury concerning Great Britain's choices in face of the "rebellion" of Ian Smith's Rhodesia against the British empire: "If the Prime Minister and the government find it necessary to use force for the perpetuation of our existing obligations in Rhodesia, then a great body of Christian opinion in this country will support him in so doing."

After presenting that model for (only) *stating* clearly the options on which Christians may legitimately disagree and between which statesmanship or the political process must decide, I suggested that two of my previous formulations were still relevant and responsible episcopal or Christian ethical statements today:

> If in order to secure an international treaty pledging "no *first* use" of nuclear weapons the Administration should find it necessary to increase greatly the standing army and other, possibly more costly, conventional forces, the government would not fail to be supported by Christian opinion.

> If in order to secure an international treaty pledging "*no use of nuclear weapons*" the Administration found it necessary to go to universal peace-time military service, the government would not be forsaken by Christian opinion.

For my "testimony" submitted in writing to the Washington hearing, I composed two additional illustrations:

> If, in order to abandon the vulnerable MX missile system, and keep from breaching the Salt II treaty by large additions to our submarine capability, the administration should find it necessary to accelerate the development and deployment of Midgetman, it will not fail to find strong support among Christian opinion-makers in this country.

> If, in order to escape our present "shoot 'em or lose 'em" predicament in case of massive tank attack upon NATO's forward position in the European theater, with the terrible danger that entails of

nuclear war nobody wants, the administration should decide it is feasible and choiceworthy to form a "foreign legion" consisting of Arafat's unemployed juveniles (with their shoulder grenade launchers) for use as NATO's anti-tank "weapon," such an innovation in defense of the West, we believe, would clearly pass the tests of greater discrimination and greater economy of force (proportion) which determine the *justice* of military means.

This was, I think, a rather clever design for *self-enforcing line-drawing* at points where Christians are no longer able to appeal to faith-warrants backing their diverging political positions, and thereafter must proceed at their own risk along different pathways upon Christian *inspiration* alone.

Concerning an earlier debate over weapon systems (now past, for good or for ill) on which the decisions of church people in politics have no Christian warrants *either way*, I remarked in my testimony: "We can well do without churchmen telling us, for example, that the neutron bomb is peculiarly immoral because it destroys 'people,' spares 'property,' when that high intensity weapon was proposed as a battlefield defense against a massive tank attack less lethal and more discriminating than the defense the West now has in place."

The foregoing was also among my recommendations to the U.S. Catholic Bishops in the hour-long consultation I was invited to have with their drafting committee. They didn't believe me either. Theirs, too, was the problem of how to provide church members with help needed in "forming their consciences" without going into detail way beyond the church's teaching authority. More than *principles* (or, I would prefer to say, *sources*) of moral decision-making in this area seemed to be needed in church education, and also in succinctly addressing our fellow citizens on public questions.

Why was that in need of amendment? Because it was too *restrictive*. My proposal was too restrictive upon the teaching function of Bishops. It only *pointed out* the way or ways Christian citizens may help decide our nation should go. This required the suppression of legitimate *pedagogical* concerns on the part of the moral and spiritual leaders of Christian communities—indeed, more restraint upon their impulse to teach than upon the writers of books on Christian ethics. Of course, persons who have served too many years on boards of church and society and in church councils (including, I suppose, Methodist Bishops) are tempted to regard the unwashed laity as especially in need of their instruction. But that is only their temptation, which in no way proves that teaching—even teaching concerning divergent ways of Christian action in our complex and conflict-filled world—is not a vocation for which they are set apart as chief pastors in the church. So my model was too *restrictive*, as the illustrations showed.

Therefore, I looked for less restrictive ways in which our spiritual and moral leaders might encourage and foster a higher level of Christian discourse both in the church and in the public arena. Such encouragement can extend to matters where church people are not bound to a single position by Christian "distinctives." More than *principles* of moral and political decision-making seem to be needed in church education, and also in succinctly addressing our fellow citizens on public questions. But then how can we avoid political partisanship and "unchurching" many? How can we provide church members with the help needed in "forming their conscience" without going into detail way beyond the church's teaching authority?

Thus I went in quest of some workable, *practical* Protestant analogue (not theoretical equivalent) to the claim in Roman Catholic social encyclicals that the church's divine mission and mandate are to *teach the entire moral law*: both divine guidance for the Christian life distinctive to the faith community and the moral and political wisdom for Christian living that is also accessible and may be shared by all other reasonable creatures.

Paragraphs 16–20 of *The Challenge of Peace* express the *inclusiveness* of the church's teaching mission in terms of "two purposes," "two complementary but distinct styles," "two distinct but overlapping audiences," "two modes of address."

Throughout, the U.S. Catholic Bishops' pastoral letter on war and peace gave one answer to my questions. There is in Catholic teaching a standard distinction between Christian social *principles* that can be enunciated and *prudence* in their application. Even with greater Catholic claims to teaching authority, this distinction enabled the Roman Catholic pastoral to *not intrude* on the scope of prudence in specific political and military decision-making and thus to protect freedom and legitimate disagreement from priestly scolding. Concerning the application of principles to specific cases and recommendations, they "wish readers to recognize . . . that *prudential judgments* are involved . . . which can be differently interpreted by people of good will." Only "serious attention and consideration" were asked for such verdicts *beyond* principle. "We shall do our best to indicate . . . whenever we make such applications." Then, almost as a warning, they quote the Vatican Council's *Pastoral Constitution on the Church in the Modern World*: ". . . [N]o one is allowed in the aforementioned situation to *appropriate the church's authority for his opinion*" (par. 9–11; my italics). High time we Methodists did the same, or as well.

Granting that the *pedagogical* goal of specificity was worthy, the question I asked myself was whether the attempted procedure of marking off from one another these very different sorts of judgments, while including both in the same document, *worked*. My impression is it did not. The fury and frustration of many Catholics who disagreed with the episcopal *prudential* elements show that *they* didn't recognize the distinction. Naturally, the media homed in on the specifics as if having unequivocal moral authority for Catholics. My further impression is that those charged with directing the use of the pastoral in educational settings do not stress the levels of authority it contains. These may be abuses and misunderstandings; but the point is they have widespread currency. Indeed, the distinction between principle and prudential application is *far from clear* in the pastoral letter itself, despite the iteration and reiteration of it, until one realizes that there are only *two* controlling moral principles in the entire document, namely, discrimination and proportion. I have no doubt the U.S. Catholic Bishops "did their best to indicate whenever they made such prudential applications"; but their best was not sufficient to prevent many, many people— including some among the Bishops themselves—from appropriating the church's authority for their own opinions. So I was convinced that the attempted resolution of the problem of authoritative moral principle and prudential applications, while undertaking to expound both in the same document, cannot succeed.

Nevertheless, my testimony was that the reiterated Catholic distinction between principle and *prudent* particulars in the same document was a good way to go, if a better could not be found. That way, our Bishops might both raise the level of Christian discourse in our church and raise the level of the political discourse Methodists bring to public questions. It now seems doubtful that this model could prove helpful when taken out of the context of a church whose traditional "language of morals" has foci in "universal moral principles" and "prudence" in application. My reasons for saying this are not the usual "liberal" ones, or the late Methodist ones of trammelling the use of reason in morals. There should be a greater gulf, I believe, between Methodist and Catholic social outlooks because in Roman Catholicism there is less distinction between the Two Cities, and more confidence in common "natural" capacity for justice, than is shared by post-Reformation churches or the Wesleyan tradition. Moreover, *it is understandable, if not entirely fitting*, for the Catholic Bishops, with their claim to hierarchical teaching authority, *not to distinguish clearly* the levels of authority in a pastoral letter.

Why have I taken time out for so much discussion of the Catholic pastoral on this point? Do I really think that our United Methodist Bishops are in danger of being *believed*? Accorded too much deference by the "faithful"? Misunderstood by the media to be intervening with claims to *real* religious and moral authority when only venturing to formulate prudential judgments that are, among others, only "differing evaluations"? That would be NEWS!

The reason is that the notice that our Bishops were planning to issue a pastoral letter raised something approximating *hope* for our church in my breast. In earlier days our Bishops were more than administrators. They were, I believe, also chief pastors and teachers. Individually and to some degree collectively, they exercised moral and spiritual leadership. A pastoral letter on *any* grave current problem would be to move beyond the episcopal address every four years at General Conferences. This opportunity to seize the high ground and to act more often as pastors and teachers of the whole church must not be muffed. Our Bishops' leadership is defined in the *Discipline* (sec. 514) as both "spiritual and temporal": "*To lead and oversee* the spiritual and temporal affairs of The United Methodist Church, which confesses Jesus Christ as Lord and Savior, and particularly to lead the Church in its mission of witness and service to the world" (my italics).

Albert Outler once wrote an article showing that this mandated a much larger role for the Council of Bishops than is even now envisioned. If memory does not fail me, there was a vigorous response from the Board of Church and Society over his challenge to their turf.

The following happening in my life may have some relevance here. Some years ago Emory University awarded me an honorary degree. On that occasion members of the faculty of the Candler School of Theology extended to me splendid hospitality, which naturally I relished. On the last evening I was there, old and new faculty friends gathered at one of their homes. Pausing on the front steps late that night, reluctant to depart, I learned that a committee was meeting the next morning to plan a part of their program for "minister's week." The idea was to rehearse some of the issues soon to come up at General Conference. Never hesitant to put my foot in my mouth by offering unsolicited advice, I said, "Why don't you get your pastor-alumni to put their minds on a *procedural* reform our church needs, such as promoting the teaching authority and leadership of Bishops and weakening those of the Board of Church and Society, which keeps bringing in statements, for example, on homosexuality, that the Holy Spirit has vetoed three times already?" To which my host replied, "Then we'd be worse off than we are now!" I have often thought of that exchange. I confess I do not know *how* any contemporary Protestant denomination should move to regain the authentic voice of *a church speaking* to itself and to the world of today. How shall we correct the politicization of the social-concerns decisions of every Protestant denomination today? The world is too much with us, too much within the churches. Readers of my analysis of our Bishops' recent episcopal initiative may, at the end of the day, want to reread my account of the Social Principles Commission's deliberations and ponder for themselves whether we are better off, or worse, or about the same.

Since we have bishops, I said to myself, there's *better* to be done with them. Anything I possibly might do to help moral authority to *accrue* to their guidance and teachings, beginning with this pastoral, was, therefore, imperative upon me because I am, first and last, a churchman. This was the source and intention of my advice to the drafting committee. Therefore, my recommendation was an *improvement* of my 1967 Model Proposal for Specific Political Pronouncements.

My *amended* recommendation was that far more can be said, if this is done correctly, whenever Christian moral reasoning about "The Nuclear Crisis and a Just Peace" comes to a true fork in the road, beyond which differing practical wisdoms may and must take either road. Or whenever our Bishops locate three or more paths ahead at such a juncture. Whether in the pastoral, or in a separate study document, *both* paths, or three, could be followed to their hoped-for ends. Let the argument for each be fully made, along with the reasons believed to be telling against the other(s). Let all the facts and the predictions be marshaled on each side, by each side's chosen school of experts, or by someone who has made the one or the other "practically wise" choice his or her own.

The example I gave was taken from the Catholic pastoral's *support* (under its *prudential* judgment endorsing a strictly conditional moral acceptance of nuclear deterrence) of "immediate, bilateral, verifiable agreements to halt the testing, production and deployment of new nuclear weapons systems." That was prudential application within prudential application. It sounds right, so long as one thinks only of massive strategic weapons. But what that endorsement *says* is quite wrong, at least arguably so. So my suggestion was that the *arguments* pro and con *be made.* It very well may be that to move this sad, threatened world away from reliance on massive strategic weapons aimed at populations will require the development of some new nuclear-weapons systems. At least, that is arguable—which should be a warning that *church* guidance may be coming to the end of its line. So let both sides be heard, if either, from the Bishops by the churches; and let congregations be enabled and encouraged to listen to both. That was an illustration only.

The significance of my amended proposal is even greater today, for suddenly the administration has dropped the Scrowcroft Report's recommendation that the Midgetman missile be developed to replace the huge MX system. What about submarine-based Cruise missiles or fighter aircraft equipped with Stealth technology, which at the moment seem to have the edge over Midgetman? Or what about the greater reliance on conventional forces that may be required if we are to rid the world of nuclears? Let both sides of some of these ways ahead be fully argued for the political instruction of our church people on choices facing them as citizens with only Christian inspiration to move them in the debate. These, too, are illustrations only, of particular options that could be used *to teach* concretely the moral criteria to be used in assessing them. Indeed, one *must* get into specifics in order to *teach* political principles. How to impart skill in moral reasoning—skill in Christian casuistry—without partiality for outcomes was the issue.

The pity is that our Methodist Bishops did not accept this proposal, there where it is most needed. For, as we have seen, there are *two* gaping holes, thinly covered over by question-begging, in their argument over specifics. The gaps are made evident by the Bishops' expressed abandonment of *moral reasoning* at these places and their resort instead to nonmoral appeals. The first of these holes was their appeal to "responsible" maintenance of nuclear deterrence after having uttered their categorical No and withdrawn the church's blessing from it. The other gaping hole was their assumption that staged nuclear disarmament can be harmoniously coupled with staged conventional disarmament until the lion and the lamb lie down together. How vastly more *instructive* "workshops" and conference and discussion sessions launched throughout the church would be if *both sides* of these two questions had been argued out in the Foundation Document, or some other. Instead we have a lengthy document which even a moderately critical reader must say marshals statistics and military, political, and ethical argument for one side only of many a specific question on which Christians may and should disagree.

Indeed, our Bishops suggest they do so, as is appropriate in a church that does not claim hierarchical "teaching authority." "We invite reflection, amendment and enrichment" (FD, p. 36). Concerning Strategic Defense, the Bishops say that, "on this as on many technical issues, we cannot as bishops claim to have the expertise to make an authoritative judgment" (FD, pp. 49–50). The most complete disavowal introduces, quite appropriately, the most particular policy suggestions (which still are called "best"): "Here we set forth those policy alternatives which may best express our own principles of peacemaking. We do so knowing that our knowledge is incomplete, that some Christians will conscientiously hold contrary positions, and that fuller understanding and changing historical circumstances may soon cause us to revise our own recommendations" (FD, pp. 64–65).

Pondering such reservations raises interesting questions that I shall not pursue here. Are our Bishops double-minded about episcopal initiatives on which they have ventured? Do they want to be "*equal* among equals" or "*first* among equals"? Do they want both to be chief pastors and teachers and *not* to be such? Are they speaking *in* the church to the church or also *for* the church? These are nice issues of church polity.

Taking these sincere disavowals at face value, understanding them to qualify the claim to *moral worth* or attention with which these documents are sent forth into the world, my question is: Why was not a better education for disagreement or agreement prepared for the churches? Otherwise, how are we to make sense of the final words of the following passage from the pastoral letter itself, stating the Bishops' intention and hopes: The pastoral "is not given to the church with any feeling that it should be the final word on this issue or with the hope that it will silence all contrary opinions; but rather, we are sending this statement to the church seeking the fullest and fairest possible discussion of our understanding and convictions, *together with an honest consideration of different and critical opinions*" (FD, p. 93; my italics). Why then was not some selection of those "different and critical opinions" fully presented and given to the church, to enable the fullest and fairest consideration of issues that arguably remain open for Christian conscience?

In a thrice one can identify not only practical but some theoretical issues on which thoughtful discussion could have been facilitated by drawing out the contrary arguments. Are justice and peace never incompatible? If they are, which should be given priority? Which is more horrible, breaches of the peace or violations of justice? How *rank* must injustice be for there to be just cause to breach the peace? Is Methodist peacemaking "world order" peacemaking, as is modern Roman Catholic teaching? Which of the following is key to the just-war theory: that war is sometimes justified to *defend* against aggression? *to correct* injustice? *to defend the innocent* who are oppressed? *to rescue* the perishing? in *retribution* for past grave injustice? Does Christian pacifism endorse nonviolent resistance? Just as surely as the Bishops are right in saying that the idolatry of nuclear weapons and of armaments in general makes for grave consequent social injustice all over the globe, would not world authority capable of insuring world peace be an idolatry reaching, like the tower of Babel, to high heaven, with consequent injustice throughout the world?

See #11 of the "Guiding Principles" for "A Theology of a Just Peace" (FD, p. 37) on a new world order as "the only practical hope." This is the place to indicate a significant contrast between the Roman Catholic and the Methodist episcopal initiatives on envisioned "solutions." The U.S. Catholic Bishops' pastoral (par. 334) speaks of "a global body realistically fashioned . . . to keep constant surveillance on the entire earth . . . [investigative] authority, freely conferred upon it . . . empowered by all nations to enforce its commands on every nation . . . so constituted as to pose no threat to any nation's sovereignty." The creation of such a "sophisticated instrumentality" is, indeed, a "gigantic task"; with "boldness" we are urged to make a "beginning" in that direction! But Catholics know how to do "world order" warlessness better than Methodists do. One can sense a flavor of *realism* in their Bishops' statement of that vision which I do not find in the analogous prospect of "common security for the world community" (FD, pp. 78–79) in the Methodist pastoral: "This vision of the common security of a peaceable world community, grounded in Scriptures and made vivid by prophets and poets through the centuries, was given legal form in the Charter of the United Nations. . . . The UN foundation must be strengthened by more effective means of sharing sovereignty under supranational authority. . . . We support the imaginative evolution of the United Nations into global systems of governance with effective authority to assure common security regarding environmental perils, scarce resources, financial instability, trade inequities, food and hunger, and flagrant abuses of human rights." What? The scriptural vision of the peaceable kingdom made vivid by the prophets given legal form and foundation in the UN Charter? Our Bishops seek a "sharing of sovereignty," which may be a contradiction in terms similar to the Catholic goal of a far-flung *global* war-preventing, threat-removing power that poses no threat to any nation's sovereignty. If in this the two "world order" warless worlds approach identity, it is in *power* terms that they do so. The final sentence quoted above, however, shows, by its use of the plural, that "global *systems* of governance with effective authority" means merely a web of bureaucratic international regulatory agencies; and the *non-political* list of perils, defining the "common security" to be assured, shows that *conflict of powers* is expected to end in a whimper of economic and other needs. All the great evils that war causes (the *consequent* social-injustice issues), if and when eradicated, are expected to be *solvants* of national-security questions formerly believed to be (in main part) a matter of encountering powers. War causes the evils that when cured eliminate the threat of war. Nice work, if history consents to run in such a circle!

Our Methodist Bishops, who place such confidence in the United Nations—and who do not distinguish as much as the Catholic Bishops do between Old and New Testament visions of peace—might well ponder the Lord's instruction to Isaiah in prophecy against such trust: "Say ye not, A confederacy, to all them to whom this people shall say, A confederacy; neither fear ye their fear, nor be afraid. Sanctify the Lord of hosts himself; and let him be your fear, and let him be your dread. And he shall be your sanctuary" (Is. 8:12–14).

I did not suggest that our Bishops write a book on the issues before us. *All* books are more particular in advocacy than the chief pastors and teachers of the church should be (or than I, an ethicist, ought to be if representing the church on some board or committee). Nor did I mean they should arrive at no consensus, no closure, concerning their understanding of the meaning of Christ for this hour. Let the Light of the world shine upon our pathways ahead until He no longer illumines particular political choices. Let the light shine and let the shadows be thrown by Creation, Fall, and Last Things upon our common human futures until Christian "distinctives" guide no more. I called for no premature closure upon getting as close a grasp as Christian warrants afford of the world of move and countermove, where there is no resting place for statesmen and citizens alike. Nor do I say it is easy to draw a line between principle and practice.

But surely it is possible at some point to locate a few forks in the road, selectively singled out because of their cruciality, beyond which Christians and non-Christians alike are on their own, so to speak, and must rely on their own discernments, inspired by the Gospel and instructed by close engagement in public discussion. The way or ways ahead beyond these junctures could have been traversed as far as anyone sees, if not in the pastoral, then in a separate study document.

Some will claim they proceed along one way with full Christian authority behind them; others traversing that same way will say they go from *Christian inspiration* only, informed by prudence. This shows that the forks in the road need not be exactly or infallibly located. Among Methodists there is not likely to be much name-calling or priestly scolding; we are, after all, nice people. But surely a unidirectional pastoral and *Foundational Document* (with a *Guide to Study and Action* simultaneously published) will tempt many advocates of special causes, including Bishops themselves, to appropriate the church's authority for their own opinions and to gain additional leverage upon church teaching. Far better than this would have been the "Some say . . ." "Others say . . ." of many a National Council of Churches and World Council of Churches ecumenical document. That produces blandness. Better my amended proposal. I can think of no better procedure by which our Methodist Bishops could *deserve* to be heard, no better procedure that could both raise the level of Christian understanding within our congregations and at the same time contribute to the public discussion of the pursuit of this world's peace.

Let me offer a personal word in conclusion on how the church should speak on public questions. Before discussion of the moral dilemmas of the nuclear age suddenly went out of fashion in the late sixties, my endeavors as an ethicist were directed for a decade or more toward applying the common and traditional Christian standards of discrimination and proportion, especially in a critique and possible radical reformation of the *sort* of deterrence on which the peace of the world still depends. It was a matter of enduring moral sadness that the articulate elites in our nation and in the churches, then as now, were polarized between those who resisted altering our single-minded intention to destroy enemy populations on condition that we are attacked—to prevent that attack—and those who brayed against specific political policies, weapons, postures, and so forth. The greatest betrayal throughout this period, I felt, was that of the churches—who in that polarization, then and now, simply reflected that same polarization of the secular conscience of the modern age. That mentality would rather call all killing in any war "wicked" or "murder" than ever "just," but under provocation intends to do it anyway—all the while hoping to be delivered from that evil-doing by perpetual peace in some age to come. We were given another chance to inculcate, first in our churches and then in the nation at large, sustained attention to principled moral reasoning. We were given another chance to extrude from the mind of the church the eighteenth-century Enlightenment's progressivism toward the heavenly city on earth.

The opportunity was not seized. Nor was there the beginning of a great struggle within the church for the church against the world in the church. Creeds—confessions of the faith of the church—are written in such times of consuming fire (and only then should any be written). And, I have learned, only in such times should social principles or pronouncements concerning urgent public questions be addressed to our members and to the world—at least, not with the expectation that these social teachings rest upon the church's one foundation. It is a fearful thing to approach too closely to that moment when, in the providence of God and guided by the Holy Spirit, his church once again affirms against every foe the saving truth of Christ. Our social teachings cannot hope to manifest a Christian outlook and onlook on problems common to "man and his communities" unless the church is, in all things, *being the church*. No procedure designed to enable the church to be *the church speaking* can succeed if the church, *always reforming* its identity, is not there; almost any procedure will do if the church, always seeking understanding of its faith and life, *is* there. The substance of the church's witness to "doing well" will be forthcoming, and will be "traditioned" to generations to come, so long as confessing the faith and the living liturgy of the church are rightly ordered. Otherwise, we will continue to say, Lo, here! Lo, there!

Since our United Methodist Church is not now in a *status confessionis* (the consuming fires of that struggle), then perhaps we are permitted to speak of a *processus confessionis* (to which the Arminian in me hopes to have contributed). In my written testimony in advance of the Washington hearing, I pleaded with our Bishops *to disprove* my best joke (given me by the church historian Sydney Ahlstrom), about the nineteenth-century British Methodist who said, "Methodism and all her institutions will stand strong and firm long after Christianity has disappeared from the face of the earth!" Did they or didn't they? That question is indifferent only *insofar* as I believe—as we believe—as our Bishops believe—that the Spirit, acting in unison with the Father and the Son, will nevertheless keep a community of discipleship— under whatever name—indefectable to the end of time.

Hauerwas, almost thou persuadest me that speaking up for real pacifism (and other Christian distinctives) is as apt to impress and work its way into the ethos of the United Methodist Church as speaking up for the imperatives and limitations of just war is to impress and work its way into the moral and political ethos of our nation. As you know I believe, there is an enduring tension between loyalty to Christ and our responsibilites in a less than ideal world. There is, therefore, a dialectic between the motif of withdrawal from the evil or the less than perfect structures of the world and the motif of shaping or reshaping society so as to maintain or better the human dwelling place. There is movement toward perfection of discipleship, which entails selective (perhaps radical) withdrawal, and there is movement toward engagement, which entails selective (perhaps deep) involvement. Indeed, we are called to *do both*, to be in the world but not of it.

Still, everything has its season. Perhaps in this time of God's patience we should speak *to* the church *for* the church about *being* the church—no more, let that witness be overheard or not by "the world of today." Perhaps fidelity to Christ would have us, in this time and place, turn in that direction—and therefore away from speaking for the church to the church and to the nation and to one another also as citizens of an armed power in the international system.

So my reference to "church-denomination-sect" typology meant this: American "denominations" were not territorial or established "churches." Yet they exerted powerful *influence* upon society generally, perhaps more so than if they had been church-state establishments. Nor were "denominations" sect-types. They were a distinctive configuration of Jesus-people in America.

Is our United Methodist Church any longer a denomination in that sense? Has not our great cultural denomination become a great *acculturated* church? Is it of the world more than not? Have not the signs of the times become a chief *theological source*, displacing the Quadrilaterals, Scripture, tradition, reason, and the experience of conversion to Jesus? That's my problem, and yours too, Hauerwas, if your Christian ethics is context-relevant, issued from within and to our denomination.

To be the church in your sense would require mutual discipline. We would need to search for agreement concerning the fruits of our life in Christ as specific as were the "rules" John Wesley drew up for the nurture of his "societies" in class meetings. These "General Rules of the Methodist Church" were, within memory, required by the Methodist Episcopal Church, South, to be read by every preacher at least once a year to his congregations.

Wesley's General Rules are still printed in *The Book of Discipline of the United Methodist Church* (Nashville: United Methodist Publishing House, 1984; pp. 69–71), together with the Articles of Religion and Our Theological Task, under the head of "Foundation Documents." They begin with conversion to Christ as the sole "previous requirement," and then *specify* in ways quaint to modern ears the meaning of the "new life" in Christ, regeneration, and being a people going on to perfect holiness.

> There is only one condition previously required of those who desire admission into these societies: "a desire to flee from the wrath to come, and to be saved from their sins." But wherever this is really fixed in the soul it will be shown by its fruits.
>
> *It is therefore expected of all who continue therein that they should continue to evidence their desire of salvation,*
>
> *FIRST: By doing no harm, by avoiding evil of every kind, especially that which is most generally practiced, such as:*
>
> *The taking of the name of God in vain.*
>
> *The profaning the day of the Lord, either by doing ordinary work therein or by buying or selling.*
>
> *Drunkenness: buying or selling spirituous liquors, or drinking them, unless in cases of extreme necessity.*
>
> *The buying or selling of men, women, and children with an intention to enslave them.*
>
> *Fighting, quarreling, brawling, brother going to law with brother; returning evil for evil, or railing for railing; the using many words in buying or selling.*
>
> *The buying or selling goods that have not paid the duty.*
>
> *The giving or taking things on usury—i.e., unlawful interest.*
>
> *Uncharitable or unprofitable conversation; particularly speaking evil of magistrates or of ministers.*
>
> *Doing to others as we would not they should do unto us.*
>
> *Doing what we know is not for the glory of God, as:*
>
> *The putting on of gold and costly apparel.*
>
> *The taking such diversions as cannot be used in the name of the Lord Jesus.*
>
> *The singing those songs, or reading those books, which do not tend to the knowledge or love of God.*
>
> *Softness and needless self-indulgence.*

Laying up treasure upon earth.

Borrowing without a probability of paying; or taking up goods without a probability of paying for them.

It is expected of all who continue in these societies that they should continue to evidence their desire of salvation.

SECONDLY: *By doing good; by being in every kind merciful after their power; as they have opportunity, doing good of every possible sort, and, as far as possible, to all men:*

To their bodies, of the ability which God giveth, by giving food to the hungry, by clothing the naked, by visiting or helping them that are sick or in prison.

To their souls, by instructing, reproving, or exhorting all we have any intercourse with; trampling under foot that enthusiastic doctrine that "we are not to do good unless our hearts be free to it."

By doing good, especially to them that are of the household of faith or groaning so to be; employing them preferably to others; buying one of another, helping each other in business, and so much the more because the world will love its own and them only.

By all possible diligence and frugality, that the gospel be not blamed.

By running with patience the race which is set before them, denying themselves, and taking up their cross daily; submitting to bear the reproach of Christ, to be as the filth and offscouring of the world; and looking that men should say all manner of evil of them falsely, for the Lord's sake.

It is expected of all who desire to continue in these societies that they should continue to evidence their desire of salvation.

THIRDLY: *By attending upon all the ordinances of God; such are:*

> *The public worship of God.*
> *The ministry of the Word, either read or expounded.*
> *The Supper of the Lord.*
> *Family and private prayer.*
> *Searching the Scriptures.*
> *Fasting or abstinence.*

These are the General Rules of our societies; all of which we are taught of God to observe, even in his written Word, which is the only rule, and the sufficient rule, both of our faith and practice. And all these we know his Spirit writes on truly awakened hearts. If there be any among us who observe them not, who habitually break any of them, let it be known unto them who watch over that soul as they who must give an account. We will admonish him of the error of his ways. We will bear with him for a season. But then, if he repent not, he hath no more place among us. We have delivered our own souls.

The concluding words of the standards by which Wesley's class leaders and class members were to admonish one another show that—without exactly exercising "the ban"—church nurture and mutual discipline among early Methodists claimed to be rooted in Matthew 18:15–20 no less than were those of the Mennonites two centuries earlier. So almost thou persuadest me that there are resources in our Wesleyan heritage (including Wesley's sermons that once were our standard) by which our church could become an alternative society to that of the sword—if I was finally convinced that the ethos of modern nations has ceased to be amenable to transformation by just-war traditions.

Of course, I don't believe that every one of those rules was found in Holy Writ. John Wesley himself *promulgated* them. Today we'd have to aim at coming to some analogous church disciplines by agreement, under the leadership of our chief pastors and teachers. That's some advantage, if we are to take Matthew 18:15–20 seriously and develop standards that are not bare legalisms resting on their own bottom. Here my "almost" remains an emphatic qualifier—although I could wish that it might not be so. How does one (even remotely) manage to do only those things, read only those books, and so forth, that are to the glory of God in a television- and sex-saturated age? If we are to nurture our children in Christian faith, and "fruits" in life, will we not be driven to establish Methodist parochial schools for their education? The world is too much *with* us, *in* our church's life. In a period of "withdrawal" for as long as we can see into the future, in order to find our way to *being* the church again, what ought we to do with the Methodist Building, strategically located in Washington, D.C., when we were a "denomination" in the original sense? The hour cometh, and now is, when the practices accepted within Methodist hospitals may require the removal of the name "Methodist" from them—if we are, with our physicians and health-care professionals, resolved to *be* the church of Jesus Christ.

Simply *being* the church in a world such as this will define a variety of "frontiers," draw a number of lines on "the world," in addition to defining the sword or nonviolent resistance (whichever) as outside the Lordship of Christ. I know, Hauerwas, that you believe we are "called" or "drawn off" from (thereby defining) "the world"; we are not propelled by an entitative or substantially existing "world" to withdraw from it. Accepting this meaning of yours, a sort of "sectarianism" is always an option; and often in the church's pilgrimage there are many "frontiers" required to be drawn by our *simply being* the church. Are we at such a time now, in the waning years of the twentieth century? I venture to say that reading Wesley's Rules you are likely to say that many of them are directives about who Christians should *be* and what we should *do*. Then the next question is: Are these (or revised specifications) only wishful "wouldings" of Christian hearts, that is, desirable states of affairs but so palpably foreign to the current ethos of United Methodism that no one can put his *entire will* into them?

I have a dream, for example, that the people called Methodist become a church that never unnecessarily aborts unborn life, and at the same time a people that refuses technological "cures" of infertility that use *donor* sperm or eggs. This means, positively, that I have a dream that we become a church in which couples feel abortion to be a far graver violation of their "parenting" than to give a child, even only for serious reasons of domestic economy, to another couple that desperately wants one. We would no longer be content simply to favor adoption in cases of unacceptable pregnancies, or simply to support adoption agencies to do that job for us. Instead, the dream is that we *as a church* become an extended family of God's people in quite realistic ways that would *separate* us from the world of free-choice abortion and the world that "cures" infertility by putting utterly asunder the communicative and the procreative goods of marriage. We would develop "adoption liturgies" by which couples who cannot provide for the upbringing of another baby would publicly, "in the presence of God and this congregation," give their infant to a couple needing and wanting a child of their own.

My local United Methodist Church would place ads in the *Daily Princetonian* addressed to the thirty-five or forty women students who each year have abortions (where now abortion clinics place notices, and where—note well!—ads for "surrogate mothers" to bear children for infertile couples now appear). These Methodist ads would invite young pregnant women to live with a local Methodist family while continuing their education. Such a woman would not be pressured to make a hurried decision whether to bring up her baby as a single mother or to give it in an adoption-dedication in church. The ads could say that we have a wonderful forty-five- or fifty-year-old couple, whose children are gone from home, who would make wonderful parents-for-a-time and who are willing to care for the woman student's child for a number of years. Perhaps she could be enabled to finish law school without having to give up her child permanently or having to choose abortion at the risk that this may be the only child she will conceive if she later marries. Children would always know their birth mothers and their mothers know them—wherever they are cared for among the Jesus-people.

This is enough to indicate that not only modern warfare but also the insanity of the epidemic of abortion coincident with an increasing infertility rate is a sign of our sin-disordered world. That world is in some sense definable over against the church. Still, you and I, Stanley, face comparable problems; and I face yours as well. The question is whether the horns of the dilemma in our title *Speak Up for Just War or Pacifism* do not presuppose moral substance that modern nations no longer have and that the United Methodist Church no longer has. Is our nation not a "procedural republic" and a faceless bureaucracy lumbering mindlessly ahead? Can Methodism be more than moribund bureaucracy and self-perpetuating committees, or is it indeed an acculturated church out of anybody's control, blown about by the latest winds of alleged relevancies?

In this sense, *only* almost thou persuadest me. Maybe you're right—if we can get by the 1988 General Conference without abolishing Trinitarian language and the Christological formulations in which the faith of the church is expressed and communicated, or without fossilizing the names above every name for God and Christ by reserving them for only occasional use in Methodist worship. And if the General Conference does not downgrade Wesley's sermons as our theological standards, or elevate "contemporary human experience in all its variety" over Scripture as theological source. Mayn't the Holy Spirit be leading our denomination in directions the Holy Ghost would never have approved?

I've said my piece. Now it's your turn.

Epilogue
A Pacifist Response to the Bishops

Stanley Hauerwas
The Divinity School
Duke University

ON BEING A CHURCH CAPABLE OF ADDRESSING
A WORLD AT WAR

"**P**ERHAPS in this time of God's patience we should speak *to* the church *for* the church about *being* the church—no more, let that witness be overheard or not by the 'world of today.'" Without overlooking the "perhaps," this is an extraordinary sentence from Paul Ramsey. I suspect it will surprise many who know of Ramsey's writings on war. It is my own view that what Ramsey has written in his response to the United Methodist Bishops is not surprising given his past work, but my primary task cannot be to place this book within the context of Ramsey's reflection on the morality of war. Rather I must do, in a much shorter space, what Ramsey has tried to do as a just-war advocate—namely, say how I, as a pacifist, think our Bishops should have addressed our church and world.

Yet in doing so I cannot avoid making reference to Ramsey's arguments and specific challenges to me. I am convinced that Ramsey has written a remarkable book about a quite unremarkable statement by the Methodist Bishops. Indeed I almost regret the quality of Ramsey's response, since it may give the Bishops' statement longer life than it deserves. As will be clear from what follows, I am in agreement with almost every criticism Ramsey has to make of *In Defense of Creation*. That is why this epilogue needs to be written; it is to be hoped that our common criticism of the Bishops will help direct attention to the issues that make the continuing debate between pacifists and just-war advocates so important for the life of the church. For it is Ramsey's and my common conviction that—contrary to the Bishops' claim—the nuclear crisis has not posed questions of faith that point beyond just war or pacifism.

I must begin my response where Ramsey ended his. In the sentence quoted above, as well as in his "Almost thou persuadest me," Ramsey suggests that—due to the character of our current cultural and political situation, as well as the accommodated character of the contemporary church—it may be necessary for the church to speak to itself about ethics before it speaks to the world. I am sure Ramsey is right about this, but I need to explain why what is for him a judgment about our current political and ecclesial situation is for me a continual problem for the church in any age. For that is the challenge Ramsey thinks we pacifists have failed to address— namely, how a pacifist church can at once be the church and at the same time speak *to the point* on military questions. My quick response is that a pacifist church is not in principle prevented from so speaking. It just must do so the way porcupines make love—very, very carefully.

Yet Ramsey is right to raise the question, for as he well knows, in my testimony before the Bishops in Washington I urged them to refrain from addressing the wider society, and certainly to refrain from addressing issues of nuclear strategy and/or policy. I did not want our Bishops taking positions on SDI and/or whether we ought or ought not to recommend a zero-option plan for Europe. The reasons I wanted our Bishops to refrain from such recommendations were not only the ones already set forth by Ramsey but because such strategic questions beg the theological issues to which the Bishops should direct our attention. But alas, it was soon clear to me that the Bishops and the drafting team could not hear or understand why I was making such a recommendation, so intent were they on making a "public" impact.

I feared that if our Bishops took as their audience the wider society they would wander into the wasteland of "crisis" language about nuclear war. In other words, I was fearful that the Bishops would give theological legitimacy to the widespread secular assumption that nuclear war must be condemned because it threatens the survival of the human species, if not the earth itself. Thus I (and Ramsey—even though we had written our testimony independent of one another) urged the Bishops to avoid such "survivalist" rhetoric, noting that what we must fear as Christians is not our deaths at the hands of an unjust aggressor but how as Christians we might serve the neighbor without resorting to unjust means. In urging such a strategy, I did not think I was asking our Bishops to take a pacifist stance. At the time I was unaware that in 1972 the Methodist Church had declared war incompatible with the teachings and example of Christ. Rather I was trying to ask the church at least to live up to the standards of a just-war church that might prophetically challenge the nationalist and survivalist assumptions of our society and unfortunately of many in our churches.

For my critique of the Bishops along these lines, see my "A Pacifist Response to In Defense of Creation," *The Asbury Theological Journal* 41, 2 (Fall 1986), pp. 5–14. I had developed this line of argument earlier in my *Against the Nations: War and Survival in a Liberal Society* (San Francisco: Winston-Seabury, 1985), pp. 160–68. In a review of that book soon to be published in *Modern Theology*, John Milbank notes, "All Hauerwas can see in the arguments of 'survivalists' like Jonathan Schell is a utilitarian concern, but it is possible to argue (like John Locke) that ecological well being is, if not an ultimate, at least a basic goal, as the presupposition of other human goods in this life (and *this* life is coterminous with our present responsibility). This does justice to our embodiment, and without this Hauerwas' pacifism still has a spiritualist and deontological flavour. He fails to distinguish between concern for the survival of 'our nation' and a much more ontological basic concern for the future of the planet and of the human race. It is in a way strange that Hauerwas does not take the opportunity to argue here that the state-Prometheus can make us forgetful of our natural being. Perhaps he is somehow suspicious of the 'universal' appeal of the ecological argument. But it is possible to say that Christian ethics, with its rejection of inevitable nemesis and fatality particularly stresses a positive and nurturing attitude towards our finitude. If part of the secular world stresses this also, then well and good—this is a true point of contact, though it is traceable contingently and historically and not founded in any recognized law of nature, or transcendental anthropology."

Milbank is right that at least part of my concern with survivalist arguments is their presumed "universal" appeal. But the issue is more complex. While I would have welcomed a call from the Bishops for us to recover a sense of our stewardship in God's creation, I think that is quite a different theme than the presumption that we must insure the survival of "God's creation." The latter presumes a story in which mankind plays a Promethean role that is quite different from the sense of service in the former. In more philosophical terms, Milbank is quite right to suggest we need, as a species, a "positive and nurturing attitude toward our finitude," but we cannot forget, even as a species, we are finite. Rather than appeal to Locke in these matters, it seems to me that Nicolai Hartmann was closer to being right when he argued in volume 2 of his unfairly ignored *Ethics* (London: George Allen and Unwin, 1932) that life is a basic value but that as such it can never be the value that overrides all others. As he puts it, "Life was not created by man, but it exists, it is real, and it is given to him—it is laid into his hands, as it were, and is entrusted to his care. He can seize hold on it and with love can lead it to its height" (134). The problem with the Bishops' call to "defend creation" is they give the impression that survival is not only a basic good but also the highest value. As a result they fail to adequately remind us that what has gone wrong in our relation to God's creation is we have forgotten it is a gift.

In all candor I must admit I had an ulterior motive informing this strategy. It has long been my suspicion that, if we could force just-war thinkers (and churches) to recognize the disciplined kind of communities necessary to sustain the discourse and practices necessary for just war, it would make it increasingly difficult to accuse pacifists of being hopeless "idealists" and/or "sectarians." Therefore, in calling for our chief pastors to take as their primary audience the Methodist people, I was trying to remind them that the first word we as Christians have to say to the world about war is "church." In other words, as Christians we do not so much have an alternative ethic to the world's way of war—we are the alternative.

I wanted our Bishops to follow the example of the early Quakers who, in speaking against slavery, first spoke to their slave-owning brothers and sisters. I am not convinced that as a church we are ready to speak to the world about war. Thus recently, in the 1986 Duke Divinity School Convocation, I asked a class of seventy-five pastors how many of them had even heard of just war prior to the Bishops' letter. Only a third raised their hands. And at a recent talk on the Bishops' letter at a Methodist church in Durham, I was told by the laity that it was unthinkable to ask Christians to qualify their loyalty to America in terms of Christian convictions. As one man put it with no visible sign of shame, "Just look at us; we obviously do not follow Jesus."

Of course it might be objected that these examples support the Bishops' assumption that they should write something to challenge Christians and non-Christians alike to awaken from their nuclear numbness. Without doubting the goodwill that underlies the Bishops' effort, I cannot help but think the project fundamentally misconceived. For when you have a church where the laity thinks it is legitimate to disavow in public the commitment to follow Jesus, then you do not draft statements about war. Rather what is needed is a much more fundamental challenge to the Methodist people concerning the basic convictions and practices that make us Christians in the first place. Pacifism and just war (at least if Ramsey is right in his account of just war) are only intelligible against the background of faith in Jesus as the Lord's anointed. If that faith is missing, then pacifism and just war alike become hollow abstractions inviting casuistical games at best and ideological perversions at worst.

For this reason I found myself less than enthusiastic about the Bishops' plan to draft a statement on nuclear war. I am not convinced such statements foster the sort of moral discourse necessary for the church to sustain an ongoing witness. Indeed I suspect there is almost an inverse ratio between the undisciplined character of the Methodist people and the radical nature of our social statements. We draft radical statements as a substitute for being a radical people pledged to witness to the world that God's peace is not just some ideal but a present possibility for us.

In the following I will try to indicate how I think a pacifist church can be the church and still speak to the society and state about war policy. But far more important for me is that the church must first be the church. As Ramsey rightly notes, I have no use for distinctions between visible and invisible church. The church can be no less real than he who was crucified. The church cannot be an ideal that is never quite realized. Rather the church must be as real as the nation we confront if we are to be capable of challenging its imperial pretension.

That the contemporary church in America may seem to lack the discipline to be either pacifist or just war should not determine how we argue as theologians or how Bishops should exercise their pastoral duties. Ramsey and I would betray our church if we wrote as if God had abandoned the United Methodist Church. I do not believe that. So we rightfully claim our vocations as theologians, trusting that exposing the disagreements between one another and the Bishops may in some modest way be of service for the upbuilding of God's church and, perhaps, even his kingdom.

I shall begin by examining the Bishops' understanding of pacifism and why they seem to think pacifism is deficient given the threat of nuclear war. In the process I will try to suggest the kind of pacifism I wish the Bishops had espoused and to which they had called the church. Once that is done it will be possible to address more directly the issues between Ramsey and me. Finally I shall conclude by making a few suggestions about where we should go from here.

PEACE WITHOUT CHRISTOLOGY OR ESCHATOLOGY

In Defense of Creation is on the whole a quasi-pacifist document. It certainly seems to be for peace as an alternative to war. Moreover, it espouses a peace that is a present possibility for relations between nations. Thus Bishop Dale White in his "Preface" states that the Bishops' purpose "is to encourage and equip our members to become knowledgeable witnesses to the power of God in Christ to bring peace to the human family" (6). Yet neither Bishop White nor the subsequent document makes clear exactly what is meant by that all-important word "peace."

Ramsey is right that the kind of pacifism the Bishops seem to adopt is one built more on a secular hope than on the eschatological hope made possible by Jesus Christ. The Bishops simply fail to see that genuine Christian pacifism, that is, pacifism that is determined by the reality of Christ's cross, assumes we must be peaceful not because such peace holds out the hope of a world free from war but because as followers of Jesus we cannot be anything other than peaceful in a world inextricably at war.

But I am getting ahead of myself. Before such charges can be sustained I must look more closely at what the Bishops actually say about pacifism. They treat pacifism in two separate sections, both rather brief and un-focused. On pages 30 to 32 a brief overview of the pacifist tradition is provided. They note that the early church, at least through the first three centuries, was pacifist. They suggest this was probably due to "scriptural seriousness" as well as to the "historical proximity to Jesus." The latter is no doubt thought decisive, because in the section just preceding we are told that Jesus never resorted to violence in his own defense and even at his death had the power to forgive his own killers. "The crucifixion is an eternal testimony to the transcendent power of forgiving love and nonviolence" (29). As I shall argue below, this kind of exchange model for the atonement is inextricably individualistic.

The Bishops continue their history by noting that the "pacifist tradition" outlived the Constantinian establishment: It was exemplified in the figure of Francis of Assisi and three centuries later in the "brilliant" Erasmus of Rotterdam. Noting that none of the magisterial reformers could be called pacifist, the Bishops nonetheless noted that the Reformation eventually generated the "historic peace churches." Finally, though Wesley was cer-tainly not a pacifist, the Bishops suggested he had an ambivalent attitude toward the American Revolution and generally saw war as a prime example of sin. Moreover, many prominent Methodists of the twentieth century have been pacifist, which I am sure is a telling point, though I must confess I seem to be missing entirely the power of such an observation. After all, many Methodists of the twentieth century have also been racist.

The Bishops, of course, could not be expected in such a short document to provide a well-documented history of pacifism. But certainly we should have expected better than this. They write as if the "pacifist tradition" was just that—a single coherent set of convictions fairly consistently held over twenty centuries. But even the most cursory reading of church history cannot help but dispel that idea. In fairness to the Bishops, Bainton's typological method in his famous *Christian Attitudes to War and Peace* can tempt one to read history as the Bishops have done. But a closer reading of Bainton and, even better, a reading of Yoder's *Nevertheless* (Scottdale, Pennsylvania: Herald Press, 1971) reveal the extraordinary diversity and incompatibility among different forms of pacifism among Christians.

For example, a particularly glaring example of the distortions caused by the Bishops' lumping all who cry peace into one history is their connecting Francis and Erasmus in one paragraph. The former's understanding of peace was based on the presumption that Christians were as nearly as possible to imitate in their life the teachings and life of Jesus. Therefore, to restrain from using violence had little to do with calculations about the honor and/or stupidity of war. Yet that is exactly the basis of Erasmus's objections to war. For as Michael Howard has shown in his *War and the Liberal Conscience* (New Brunswick: Rutgers University Press, 1978), Erasmus is the beginning of the peculiar modern assumption that war is wrong because it is so destructive and stupid. No particular theological beliefs are required for such a position; nor is it in continuity with past forms of Christian pacifism. Erasmus was not a Christian pacifist; he was a pacifist who happened to be Christian.

Lest it is thought that little hangs on these historical issues, I should point out that the Bishops' failure to denote different kinds of Christian pacifism allows them to underwrite the vague generalization about Christians as a shalom people. Shalom is characterized at such an abstract and ideal level that one never has the sense that it is a way of life that can be lived out in history. We are told that shalom is positive peace, more than the absence of war, denoting harmony, wholeness, health, and well-being in all human relations (24); or that in shalom there is no contradiction between justice and peace, peace and security, love and justice (25). It thus appears that what "pacifism" means throughout Christian history is the Christian's attempt to create a world so just that war is no longer a necessity. But as I have indicated, most Christian pacifism, at least before the Enlightenment, never assumed that the Christian commitment to peace promised a just or war-free world.

The Bishops rightly note that too often Christian discussions of war and peace have lost the breadth and depth of the "scriptural understanding of creation, God's action in history, the world of nations, and human destiny" (24). Though I would have been happier if they had included in their list Jesus' crucifixion and resurrection, they are no doubt right about this; or at least they are right about the kind of pacifism so often espoused by Christians since the Enlightenment. Yet one searches in vain for any account of peace in *In Defense of Creation* that has been informed by those theological realities. Instead peace, or shalom, is simply assumed as a realizable ideal harmony among nature, people, and nations that our theological commitments underwrite but play no decisive role in determining its content.

This interpretation of the Bishops' account of pacifism is only confirmed when we look at the second brief treatment of pacifism in Chapter 2. They note that the production, possession, deployment, and use of nuclear weapons must appear illegitimate and immoral from a pacifist perspective. This seems plain enough if, as they assert, pacifism conscientiously repudiates all warfare and weapons of war (40). If knives and guns are out, I suppose we can regard it as a safe bet that nuclear bombs are also to be forbidden. They go on to observe that fidelity to this tradition points to two fundamental questions of the nuclear age—"Can any major war remain non-nuclear? If not, hasn't rejection of war itself become an imperative for all our churches?"

For the life of me, I cannot follow the Bishops' reasoning at this point. They seem to suggest that, since we have no guarantee that we can keep a war non-nuclear, then war itself is no longer a possibility. What puzzles me is why the Bishops think this has anything to do with pacifism. If war is wrong, then nuclear war is clearly wrong, but no conclusions about how to keep war non-nuclear need to be drawn to reach that conclusion.

One cannot help but think the Bishops are trying to slip in a Jonathan Schell-like argument—namely, since war continues to protect a nation's right to build nuclear weapons, then war (and nations, according to Schell) must go. This is clearly utopianism, but even at that it is not pacifism, much less Christian pacifism. Rather it presupposes that if we could eliminate nuclear weapons then war might again be a viable institution. While I am sure at least some of our Bishops might recoil from such a conclusion, I see no way it can be avoided given the logic of this argument.

The Bishops want to be a little bit pacifist. But it is no easier to be a little bit pacifist than it is to be a little bit pregnant. The peace that is sought is not the peace that has been given by Christ. Instead it is a peace that encourages us to put our faith in the threat of nuclear war, for it is assumed that threat is frightening people to the extent that they may finally come to their senses and realize they stand on the brink of annihilation. Yet a peace so built cannot be the shalom to which the Bishops appeal; it is a peace based on fear rather than on positive faith in God.

I do not want to be unfair to the Bishops, but I simply do not understand what position about war they are willing to defend. I understand they believe the nuclear crisis raises questions of faith that neither the pacifist nor just-war position has "adequately addressed," but I remain unclear what kind of alternative they propose.

For example, they quote the Methodist Social Principles: "We believe war is incompatible with the teachings and example of Christ. We therefore reject war as an instrument of national foreign policy and insist that the first moral duty of all nations is to resolve by peaceful means every dispute that arises between or among them." That seems to be about as straightforward a pacifist position as one would want. Admittedly it is a confused one, in that it assumes that simply because war is incompatible with the "teachings and example of Christ" it is also a workable foreign policy for affairs between nations. Ramsey is quite right to chide the General Conference as well as the Bishops for failing to see that the kind of wars we particularly have to fear are those that are not under the political policy of a government. In the same manner I believe Ramsey is right when he says that to ask states to rid themselves of deterrence is to get rid of nations. Yet the Bishops seem to want it both ways.

Because they want it both ways I find it hard to understand the Bishops' constant appeal for the church to be an alternative community. They note that, because of the Fall, government is not only a legitimate expression of creation's natural order but is also necessary because of human sinfulness. Governments can thus become destroyers of community. Yet "Shalom discloses an alternative community—alternative to the idolatries, oppressions, and violence that mark the ways of many nations" (12). Later we are told it is the church that is to serve as an alternative community in an alienated and fractured world: "a loving and peaceable international company of disciples transcending all governments, races, and ideologies, reaching out to all enemies, ministering to all the victims of poverty and oppression" (20). They tell us we have hardly begun to imagine the church as a transnational community that proclaims "the unsearchable riches of Christ" to the "principalities and powers" (Ephesians 3:8; 10) (82).

I could understand these appeals for the "church to be a redemptive model of peaceable diversity" (11) if the Bishops were consistently pacifist. If Christians are called to be peaceable in a world at war, no doubt such a community is required. But if it is assumed that the relations between nations can mimic that community, then I find it hard to understand why such a community is an "alternative." As Ramsey suggests, the Bishops seem to believe that nations are capable of repentance. While I am never one to limit the power of God's grace, I find such a position as a matter of policy naive in the extreme.

Perhaps the clue to the ambiguity in the Bishops' position resides in their claim that, "in the roundness of shalom, a just-war ethic is never enough. Our churches must nurture a *new theology for a just peace*" (13). The phrase "just peace" is obviously loaded for the Bishops, though I remain unclear about its content and in particular why a "new theology" is called for. I thought a just peace was always what just war was about.

At least part of what the Bishops want to encompass with their use of this phrase is their belief that the nuclear crisis is as much a matter of social justice as it is war prevention (52). This legitimates their bringing into the discussion every social issue confronting the modern world in order to suggest how all injustice can be laid at the door of the nuclear challenge. I have no wish to doubt the Bishops' sincerity in trying to make such a linkage, but without showing actual empirical connections justice becomes a covering word with no content. (For my general disquiet about the current enthusiasm of Christians for justice, see my "Should Christians Talk So Much About Justice," *Books and Religion Review* 14, 5 and 6 [May/June 1986], pp. 5, 14–15.)

Even more disquieting is the suggestion that, now that the threat of nuclear war has made clear that the nations only share one earth, a new vision of a just and peaceable human family imbued with the loving kindness of our Creator is made possible. Thus justice requires that we work for common institutions, shared sovereignty, and supernational authority (73). Again the Bishops seem to assume that the threat of nuclear war—rather than the crucifixion and resurrection of Jesus Christ—is what has made a "just peace" possible. Moreover, they fail to understand how the cross challenges all worldly accounts of justice by God's willingness to submit to injustice so that the world might be justly redeemed.

I have only one other suggestion for trying to understand the Bishops' position. It is quite simply that in spite of their avowed preference for peace they finally do not want to exclude the use of violence as legitimate. They observe that the Old Testament is full of violence and warfare—for example, God's victory over the Pharaoh to liberate Hebrew slaves discloses God's opposition to oppression and injustice (26). Yet we are told that "liberation from oppression is hardly on the same moral plane as the building up of standing armies for nationalistic expansion and oppression of weaker nations" (26–27). Do the Bishops mean to suggest that "liberation movements," which often look very much like standing armies, are in moral perspective different from the war-making of established states? I confess I do not know whether the Bishops mean to hold out for this; but if they do, it helps to explain why they seem to be halfway pacifist.

In summary, the Bishops seem to have wanted to have it both ways—to be a little bit pacifist, yet holding out for the legitimate use of force by states and, possibly, liberation fronts. Yet their pacifism is not derived from any determinative Christological perspective but instead derives from the need to avoid nuclear destruction. In effect, the Bishops want to be Constantinian pacifists—that is, they want to be pacifists who continue to rule because now pacifism has become a viable foreign policy due to the threat of nuclear weapons. Yet such a position cannot but be both theologically and politically incoherent.

WHAT A CHRISTOLOGICAL PACIFISM LOOKS LIKE

What the Bishops fail to appreciate is that the peace that sustains Christian pacifism is an eschatological notion. Christian pacifism is not based on the assumption that Jesus has given us the means to achieve a warless world, but rather, as John Howard Yoder suggests, peace describes the hope, the goal in the light of which the pacifist acts, "the character of his action, the ultimate divine certainty which lets his position make sense; it does not describe the external appearance or the observable results of his behavior. This is what we mean by eschatology: a hope which, defying present frustrations, defines a present position in terms of the yet unseen goal which gives it meaning" (*The Original Revolution* [Scottdale, Pennsylvania: Herald Press, 1971], p. 56).

In his classic essay "Peace Without Eschatology" (*Original Revolution*), John Howard Yoder critiqued the kind of pacifism we find represented in *In Defense of Creation*. For the pacifism of *In Defense of Creation* is not new but is simply an updated version of the liberal assumption (illusion) that church and world can be identified and that peace is imminent. What is new about the pacifism of the Bishops is that they think they have discovered the mechanism that will force that peace on the nation—the threat of nuclear destruction.

Ramsey is quite right to criticize the Bishops' eschatology and to ask me to elaborate my own eschatology. Of course the latter, as Ramsey also rightly notes, is a correlative of Christology. To elaborate it I can do no better than to refer to Yoder's essay mentioned above. Like Ramsey, Yoder argues there is more than a slash between the words "already/not yet"—the slash is (exactly as Ramsey suggests) aeonic. From the perspective of the New Testament, our present age—that is, the age from Pentecost to Parousia—is the time that these aeons overlap.

These aeons, therefore, exist simultaneously: The old points backward to history before Christ; the new points forward to the fulfillment of the kingdom of God made fully present in the life, death, and resurrection of Jesus of Nazareth. Moreover, each aeon has a social manifestation: the former in the "world"; the latter in the church.

The new aeon came into the world through the work of Jesus, who is God's agape—self-giving, nonresistant love. Defensible Christian pacifism, thereby, derives its intelligibility not from any one set of teachings of Jesus but rather from the very form of his life and death. As Yoder says, "At the cross this nonresistance, including the refusal to use political means of self-defense, found its ultimate revelation in the uncomplaining and forgiving death of the innocent at the hands of the guilty. This death reveals how God deals with evil; here is the only valid starting point for Christian pacifism or nonresistance. The cross is the extreme demonstration that agape seeks neither effectiveness nor justice, and is willing to suffer any loss or seeming defeat for the sake of obedience" (59).

Christian nonresistance is a form of discipleship to Jesus not in a legalistic way but rather "as he is, so are we in this world" (I John 4:17). Such discipleship is inherently eschatological, for only in relation to evil is it meaningful. Just as Christ suffered on the cross, so the Christian must suffer in the face of evil. The "new thing" revealed by Christ was this attitude toward the old aeon. "The cross was not in itself a new revelation; Isaiah 53 foresaw already the path which the servant of Yahweh would have to tread. Nor was the resurrection essentially new; God's victory over evil had been affirmed by definition, one might say, from the beginning. Nor was the selection of a new faithful remnant a new idea. What was centrally new about Christ was that these ideas became incarnate. But superficially the greatest novelty and the occasion of stumbling was His willingness to sacrifice, in the interest of nonresistant love, all other forms of human solidarity, including the legitimate national interests of the chosen people" (61).

By being raised from the dead, Christ becomes not only head of the church but Lord of history reigning over the principalities and powers. Even the old aeon is now brought under the reign of Christ. The characteristic of Christ's reign is that evil, which still certainly exists, is now made to serve God's purposes in spite of itself. Thus vengeance, instead of creating chaos, is harnessed through the state to preserve order and to give room for the work of the church. Vengeance is not made good, but it is made subservient to God's purposes as an anticipation of the ultimate defeat of sin. What has changed is not that the state, for example, has changed since the coming of Christ but that now Christ takes primacy over the old order.

Put differently, Christ's victory on the cross sealed the victory of the kingdom over the world. The church's suffering, like that of Jesus, is the measure of her obedience to the new age. Thus nonresistance is right, "not because it works, but because it anticipates the triumph of the Lamb that was slain" (64). That such nonresistance may appear to let evil reign invites the charge of complicity with evil. Yet this attitude of leaving evil free to be evil is part of the nature of agape, as God's goodwill finally leaves sinners free to separate themselves from God. The word for God's involvement with sin through letting his innocent Son be killed is not "complicity" but "patience" (65). Such patience only makes sense eschatologically.

From this eschatological perspective Yoder criticizes those, like the United Methodist Bishops, who would seek peace without eschatology. For such a peace resolves the tension between the two aeons, confusing the providential purpose of the state to achieve a "tolerable balance of egoism" (Reinhold Niebuhr) with the purpose of the church, which is the rejection of all egoism in the commitment to discipleship. "This confusion leads to the paganization of the church and the demonization of the state" (67). Constantinian pacifism is but the other side of a Constantinian crusade mentality. Such a stance must seek to make the peace of Christ an ethic workable for all society, believer and nonbeliever alike.

Yoder, therefore, criticizes those pacifists who confuse eschatological pacifism with the optimistic political pacifism which thought that peace might be achieved through the action of unrepentant states. Neither Kellogg-Briand pacts nor the threat of nuclear annihilation is sufficient to force states to achieve peace. Yoder, like Ramsey, draws on Butterfield, who, as an honest historian, rightly saw that the function of the state is like the task of the architect in building a cathedral. "The force of gravity, like human egoism, is not in itself a constructive force. Yet if art and science combine to shape and properly place each stone, the result is a unity of balanced tensions, combining to give an impression not of gravity but of lightness and buoyancy. This sort of delicate balance of essentially destructive forces is what the political apparatus is to maintain under the lordship of Christ, for the sake not of the cathedral, but of the service going on within it" (77–78).

Thus the church does not ask the state to do more than it was meant to do. When Christians speak to the state, therefore, they use criteria that are intrinsic to the state's purpose—"the good are to be protected, the evildoers are to be restrained, and the fabric of society is to be preserved, both from revolutions and war" (78). On the same grounds the church condemns indiscriminate methods of war because such actions are wrong because of the state's commitment to prohibit murder. But a police action within a society cannot be condemned in principle. Rather the only question is whether there are safeguards to prevent it from becoming something more.

According to Yoder, modern war is to be condemned not on the basis of Jesus' ethic but on a realistic basis of the state's purpose.

From this perspective, Yoder considers the issue of whether the Christian as an individual should turn the other cheek for the neighbor. Does the Christian have responsibility for using societal means to protect his neighbor against his bad neighbor? That is, does not the Christian have responsibility to support the police function of the state? Yoder admits that such a view of the state coincides with the biblical view of the police function of the state. But the problem with the argument is that it is "based on a realistic analysis of the old aeon, knows nothing of the new. It is not specifically Christian and would fit into any honest system of social reality. If Christ had never become incarnate, died, risen, ascended to heaven and sent His Spirit, this view would be just as possible, though its particularly clear and objective expression results partly from certain Christian insights" (81).

Ramsey is right when he says that the difference between advocates of just war and pacifists is Christological. But when compared to the Christology of *In Defense of Creation*, that difference seems small indeed. We both take the life and teachings of Jesus with utmost seriousness, but I suspect the crucial difference between us lies in our understanding of Christ's work. Certainly neither Yoder nor I believe that Jesus simply exemplifies a way of life for us to follow. On the contrary, without the ontological change occasioned through Christ's resurrection, there would be no possibility of living as he did. Ramsey is quite right that there is forever a decisive distance between us and Jesus, insofar as Jesus and Jesus alone is the singular faithful Son that makes God's kingdom present. Our obedience to his life is possible only because of the Father's vindication of Jesus' obedience through the resurrection.

However, crucial to my (and I think Yoder's) views on these matters is a refusal to separate the person and the work of Christ. Attempts to develop theories of the Incarnation separate from doctrines of atonement invariably result in individualistic accounts of salvation that distort Jesus' eschatological mission.

Jesus is not about saving the individual from sin. Rather the salvation wrought in Christ makes present God's eschatological kingdom as a possibility for Jew and Gentile alike. All are called to this salvation as individuals, but the salvation itself is the socially embodied life of a community that knows it lives by forgiveness. Pacifism, therefore, is not some "teaching" about nonviolence but rather is a way of talking about a community that has learned to deal with conflicts through truth rather than violence—and that truth is no general or universal teaching about agape but the concrete presence of a life. Such a truth requires the existence of a community, for it cannot be known separate from embodiment in concrete lives. If such a community does not exist, then I think Christians have little grounds to counter the challenge of unbelief and/or the violence it breeds.

So in response to Ramsey's questions to me about Jesus' work, I must ask him, "What exactly do you take Christ's salvation to be?" I hope I have now made clear how I answer that question. It is an answer that is quite traditional—that is, Jesus saves us from sin and death. Yet sin and death are embodied in a history that requires an alternative history if our salvation is to be anything more than a vague hope. The name we give the social manifestation that makes that history present is *church*. We believe the church's history is the only true history of the world, but there is no way to establish that till God's kingdom comes in its fulfillment. In between the times we must live by faith. But such faithful living means we can live confident that God's victory has been accomplished forever through Jesus of Nazareth.

Ramsey is certainly right that Jesus is no less in the center of nonpacifist accounts of the Christian life. That I do not doubt. What I question, however, is whether such accounts properly describe the social and political character of Christ's work. Certainly Jesus is at the center of Reinhold Niebuhr's work, but the forgiveness Christ offers is primarily to the individual, for according to Niebuhr Jesus was the exemplification of the eternal truth of love as the law of our existence. He was not the irreplaceable Messiah who came to redeem Israel only to be rejected.

At issue here is not only the reality of the redemption wrought in Christ but its continuing reality. Ramsey is quite right to characterize my pacifism as eucharistic, especially if he means by that a sense of how the church in all of its life is used by God as the social manifestation of his kingdom. I do not believe Reinhold Niebuhr thought our redemption is so really present or so embodied in community.

Ramsey may well respond that, given the first section of this epilogue, my position is in deep trouble, because there just are not that many empirical indications that the kind of redemption of which I speak is present among us. Yet God's church is not determined by number or influence. On the contrary, I am amazed at the continuing miracle of the many who live faithful to God's calling. Such witnesses are crucial, but we must finally remember that our affirmation of the church is not an empirical claim but a statement of faith. For just as I believe that God has surely made his kingdom present in Jesus Christ, I no less believe that it continues to be present in the church.

One final issue concerning this account of pacifism needs to be mentioned before I turn to the social and political implications of the position. I have not here attempted to provide the scriptural warrants for this position, partly because it has been done well elsewhere, but also because it is a mistake to assume that "pacifism" is a position to be found in the New Testament. I suspect the first Christians had no idea they were "pacifists." They just thought they were following Jesus. The very abstractions "pacifism" and "just war" tend to encourage an ahistorical reading of Scripture and Christian tradition.

I suspect one of the reasons, therefore, that those of us who count ourselves as "pacifists" have so much difficulty making the position intelligible is the widespread assumption that pacifism can easily be summed up as anti-warism or anti-violence. In the above I have tried to suggest that the kind of pacifism I hold, as well as the kind I wish the Bishops had embraced, is not so much a "position" as a way of life of a community. In Jim McClendon's words, Jesus is a pacifist insofar as he "evokes and guides a program of nonviolent action that transforms human conduct for its sharers. It is inwardly but also outwardly oriented, its theme is the love of enemies; its focus, in light of God's mighty signs and the inbreaking of the end, is the building of a community that can survive the dying of an old age while with its Lord it anticipates the new" (*Systematic Theology: Ethics*, Vol. 1 [Nashville: Abingdon, 1986], p. 308).

Since Constantine it has been difficult to recapture conceptually this sense of pacifism. This is not just because pacifists are now seen as "irresponsible," given the assumption that Christians must take up the reins of power. The real difficulty is that pacifism has to be presented as if it were an alternative to just war—that is, as a principled position that is meant to determine the policy of states. As I have tried to show, that is simply not how Christian pacifism, when it is Christologically and eschatologically determined, works. (I am indebted to Mr. Greg Jones for making this point clear.)

Moreover, when pacifism becomes that kind of "position," we miss some of the most important features of war. For then war is treated entirely in terms of whether it serves or accomplishes certain political ends. The power of war as an occasion for societies to renew themselves through sacrifice is overlooked in our concern to make judgments of whether the war is legitimate or illegitimate. Insofar as Christian pacifism is a genuine alternative to war, it is such because it captures our attention by providing us a truthful community that directs the human desire to sacrifice into service to God.

What we must do is find ways to think "ethically" about war that do not repeat our past formulas. Just war and pacifism have become "positions" that are debated in and of themselves without helping us better to understand the complex phenomenon called war. That is what I was trying to do when I wrote "Should War Be Eliminated" in *Against the Nations*—namely, to suggest that more important than the principles used to judge war are the narratives through which we enact and interpret war. Jean Bethke Elshtain, in her remarkable book *Women and War* (New York: Basic Books, 1987), develops this point in an extraordinary way, noting that "the structure of a particular nation's history and experience will be more salient to political decision makers who enter into debates of moral principles than will be finely honed ethical systems. Similarly, for ordinary men and women caught up in structures of wartime killing and dying and peacetime childbirth and rearing, the experiences of soldiering and mothering have been occasions both for reflection, for constructing narratives that tell 'my story,' and moments of silence when their recognition falls outside the frame of acceptable, articulated meanings" (159). Until we approach war from this perspective—a perspective that is in many ways much more open to eschatological construal—we will have little ability as Christians to understand, much less be an alternative to, war. Again, as Elshtain suggests, to deflect a warlike way of thinking "is impossible so long as we remain enthralled by grand teleologies of historic winners and losers; so long as our reigning narratives are triumphalist accounts of our victories; so long as our identities are laced through with absolutist moralism; so long as we seek, need, or require, *on this earth*, a unifying experience that total war or perpetual peace alone promises. To appreciate the relativity of all antagonisms and friendships, to see in others neither angels nor demons, puts one on a track different from that laid down by those who would organize and systematize reality in a relentlessly total way" (256). It is, of course, war that morally seems to require such systematization as we seek to give sufficient moral rationale for the sacrifices war requires. Elshtain's insistence that part of war's moral power derives from its capacity to elicit sacrifice—that is, what we seek is not so much to kill but to be killed—is particularly important if we are to understand the moral complexity of war. In a morally anarchic world, war may be our most important institution for confirming through sacrifice the significance of our particular moral histories.

Elaine Scarry's interpretation of war in her *The Body in Pain: The Making and Unmaking of the World* (New York: Oxford University Press, 1985) is a brilliant attempt to help us see war essentially as a contest where the goal is to out-injure your opponent. One can easily fail to miss the importance of this point unless, as Scarry argues, it is that only at the end of a war can one even determine the benefit of the injuring (95). The great difficulty, however, is that the two functions of war—to determine a winner and a loser and to substantiate an outcome as the result of the first function—are not necessarily related. Thus the frustration of war, since the victor often lacks the "power of enforcement" to determine what the war has been about.

Pacifists, no less than just-war thinkers, must enter into the kind of reflections about war begun by Elshtain and Scarry. Moreover, if I am right about the kind of eschatological pacifism Christians should hold, we should be able to appropriate these insights in a manner that will help us understand why the church as an alternative community is so necessary.

As Yoder observes, to speak of the pacifism of the messianic community means the focus of attention is shifted from the individual asking about right or wrong "to the human community experiencing in its life a foretaste of God's kingdom. The pacifistic experience is communal in that it is not a life alone for heroic personalities but for a society. It is communal in that it is lived by a brotherhood of men and women who instruct one another, forgive one another, bear one another's burdens, reinforce one another's witness" (*Nevertheless*, 124).

Once this is understood it becomes clear why I regard *In Defense of Creation* so negatively. For the Bishops have acted as if they can write for anyone. To the contrary, any serious Christian pacifist must recognize that such a way of life is possible only by the reorientation of the self through the repentance made possible by Jesus Christ. For those who have not begun that reorientation, we cannot anticipate what it would mean for them to live nonviolently. This is particularly true once nonviolence is understood not simply as the avoidance of violence but as the disciplined undertaking of living in the constructive life of a nonviolent community.

But Ramsey may well note that I do not seem to be talking about any Methodist church he knows and that I am a theologian who is a Methodist. Yet I cannot help but wish my Bishops had turned their attention to the church in the way I indicate—that is, that they had called us to take ourselves seriously as a genuine alternative to the world of violence. For we know as Christians that we also are world. We know we are possessed by the hates and envies that feed the fires of our violence. We know we desire to sacrifice ourselves and others in hope of securing a sense of worth. So we needed our chief pastors to refrain from addressing the world and instead first to address the church, hopefully calling us to be what we are—God's peace.

Moreover, I have the sense that, in spite of the obvious accommodation of the contemporary church to the world, God may well be winnowing us to be able once again to read the Gospel with non-Constantinian eyes. For the increasing irrelevance of the church—an irrelevance that fuels the desperation we feel—may well provide the opportunity for the church to discover again that God has made us an alternative to the world's violence. If only our Bishops had thought it possible to say that word, then they would have genuinely acted as our chief pastors.

HOW A PACIFIST CAN SERVE THE NEIGHBOR
IN A VIOLENT WORLD

In trying to go beyond pacifism and just war, the Methodist Bishops' position concerning Christian social responsibility is a hopeless muddle. For example, in the section "A Theology for a Just Peace: Guiding Principles," the Bishops assert that "government is a natural institution of human community in God's creation as well as a requirement for the restraint of evil" (36). One assumes the Bishops mean to suggest by this that government would have existed if the Fall had never happened, but after the Fall the purpose of government has had to take on the added function of the use of force for the restraint of evil.

These sets of claims are not intrinsically incompatible. But we need to know more if we are to understand their relation to other positions the Bishops take in *In Defense of Creation*. Do the Bishops think it possible to have a state that can or has disavowed all violence? If so, what are we to make of their call for government to pursue justice on behalf of the poor, the weak, and the oppressed? Do the Bishops think that such justice can always be achieved without resort to violence?

It seems they are really of two minds in trying to respond to these questions. In "Guiding Principle" 16 they tell us that "all Christians, pacifists and nonpacifists alike, ought to share a strong moral presumption against violence, killing, and warfare, seeking every possible means of peaceful conflict resolution" (37). Yet in Principle 17 they maintain that "any just resort to coercive force must seek the restoration of peace with justice, refrain from directly attacking noncombatants, and avoid causing more harm than good," but we are never told when and on what grounds we might know such coercive force to be justified.

What the Bishops seem to have failed to understand is that you simply cannot mix just war and pacifism and have a consistent position. In this respect one can only wish that the Bishops had attended to Ramsey's arguments, made as early as *Basic Christian Ethics* (New York: Charles Scribner's Sons, 1950), that just war is not simply a casuistical checklist to determine when violence might be used; it is a theory of statecraft. Thus Ramsey rightly reminds the Bishops that the first presumption of just war is not against violence, nor does it seek "peace"; rather just war seeks the maintenance of ordered justice through which the innocent are protected. (See particularly pp. 157–84 of *BCE*.) Put as starkly as one can, Ramsey rightly notes above that "justified-war Christians *do not believe* that killing is intrinsically wrong" (188).

While I do not wish to go over ground Ramsey has already well covered, I want to fill in some of the background for the position he takes here in order that I might make clear my disagreements not only with the Bishops but also with Ramsey. Ramsey's position hinges on his interpretation of Jesus' ethic as an uncompromising, disinterested love of the neighbor. The crucial test case for such love is love for the enemy-neighbor, for it is only here, where the Christian can expect no good, that we can be sure we are not simply loving ourselves in loving our neighbor (BCE, 98–99). I think it important to emphasize this; otherwise one can miss the radical nature of Ramsey's position.

The problem, however, with Jesus' radical demand of love is how this "non-preferential love" can prefer some persons to others, which it must do in this time between the times. "How can non-resisting love take upon itself any responsibility for public protection or in support of just social reform through the vocation of legislator, judge, sheriff, hangman or soldier?" (BCE, 157). Ramsey's answer is that Christian love remains absolutely nonresistant in one-to-one neighbor relations but may be required to change its tactic to resistance when more than one neighbor is involved. In other words, there may be a "neighbor-centered preferential love" that replaces "self-centered preferential loves" (BCE, 159). Ramsey calls this love "enlightened unselfishness," in contrast to systems of ethics based on enlightened selfishness and/or mutual love of self-realization.

On this basis Ramsey develops a preferential ethics of protection without denying that Jesus, when it came to his own life, showed no preference for his own welfare and did not resist evildoers when evil fell upon him. Yet Ramsey suggests that in his denouncing of those who were evil Jesus manifested a preferential ethic of protection, which, while coupled with his "personal ethic" of nonresistance, suggests the beginning of an ethics of resistance (BCE, 169).

Charity, therefore, remains the basis for a Christian ethic of (violent or nonviolent) resistance to evil. Thus it was a work of charity for the Good Samaritan to help him who had fallen among thieves. It was also the work of charity for the innkeeper to receive the wounded man and to conduct his business well enough that he could extend credit to the Samaritan. Still a further step of charity, not justice alone, would be to maintain and serve in a police patrol on the Jericho road to prevent such things from happening. "By yet another step, it might well be a work of charity to resist, by force of arms, any external aggression against the social order that maintains the police patrol along the road to Jericho. This means that where the enforcement of an ordered community is not effectively present, it may be a work of justice and a work of social charity to resort to other available and effective means of resisting injustices. What do you think Jesus would have made the Samaritan do if he had come upon the scene while the robbers were still at their fell work?" (*BCE*, 142–43). Ramsey thinks this illustrates the problem of how nonresisting, unself-defensive love must determine its responsibility when there is more than one neighbor to serve.

It is against this background that Ramsey argues that the change from pacifism to just war was only a change in tactics. Following Augustine, he continues to maintain that Christians claim no right of self-defense, and thus it is a travesty to base just war on self-defense. Indeed "self-defense is the worst of all possible excuses for war or for any other form of resistance or any sort of preference among other people" (*BCE*, 173). (Ramsey later qualifies this by noting that we may have vocational responsibilities to defend ourselves.) Ramsey is quite critical of "modern pacifists" who reverse the relation between private and public defense and think that they obviously should defend themselves by going to law but doubt or deny that Christians may be called to service on behalf of national defense (*BCE*, 181–82).

In contrast, Ambrose and Augustine argued that "no Christian should save his own life at the expense of another, yet when other persons than himself are involved in the decision, no Christian ought to fail to resist evil by effective means which the state makes available to him" (*BCE*, 172). Thus the primary motive for Christian participation in war was the same love that earlier impelled Christians (out of Christlike love) to reject the use of armed force. "Christians simply came to see that the service of real needs of all the men for whom Christ died required more than personal, witnessing action. It also required them to be involved in maintaining the organized social and political life in which all men live. Non-resisting love had sometimes to resist evil" (*War and the Christian Conscience* [Durham: Duke University Press, 1961], XVII–XVIII).

Unlike those Catholics who continue to base just war on natural-law assumptions of self-defense, Ramsey has from the beginning argued that just war is the disinterested love taught by Christ now institutionalized in the state. Just war is love-transformed justice through which the justice of the earthly city is elevated. Whether this account of the state is compatible with Ramsey's realism about the state (also derived from Augustine) is a question worth exploring. Does this analysis, for example, apply to all states or only the ones that have been formed by people schooled in the Gospels? If the latter, then how would Ramsey counsel Christians to act in states that are not Christian?

This issue is crucial, for it should now be clear that for Ramsey just war is

an attempt to provide Christians with a justification for our secular vocation. Just war is not just about war, but it is an account of politics that is
non-utopian in the interest of keeping the political within humane limits.
Ramsey thus argues, "peace is not the only political good. It is rather that
peace with justice and ordered liberty is a 'process,' a process that sometimes involves resort to non-peaceful means. It is not at all paradoxical that
this should be the nature of international politics. In mankind's endless
struggle for an ordered justice and peace, it is only realistic to expect (even if
no one should hope for this) that 'the fact that there are different ideas of
what constitutes *pacem in terris*' may be 'the final source of human division'" (*The Just War* [New York: Scribner's, 1968], p. 38). Thus Ramsey in
Speak Up rightly notes that there is no "universal view" of justice, only
"views of universal justice" that may mean that both sides in a just war may
be fighting justly.

This should help explain why Ramsey is so disappointed in *In Defense of
Creation*. For it makes the mistake against which he has been arguing for
three decades—namely, it argues in a utopian fashion that war can be
eliminated from our lives, thus leaving us no means to contend against
those who believe that war cannot be subject to or limited by moral
purpose. As a result, we are robbed of the wisdom that has been at the heart
of just-war thinking: We should never fight war for peace but only for more
ordered liberty.

While it is not something on which I wish to dwell, I think it is interesting
how Ramsey has tried through his account of just war to argue for limited
war without losing the realism of Reinhold Niebuhr. Indeed, in many ways
Ramsey's development of just-war thinking can be seen as an extended
commentary on Reinhold Niebuhr's sense of the inevitability of war, while
saving Niebuhr from the consequentialism to which (without "justice more
articulated") his account of violence seemed to commit him. Ramsey may
not want to say with Niebuhr that "society is in a perpetual state of war"
(*Moral Man and Immoral Society* [New York: Scribner's, 1932], p. 19) or to
underwrite Niebuhr's tendency to justify violence primarily in terms of its
effects without an explicit ethics of means, but Ramsey agrees with Niebuhr's claim that "once we have made the fateful concession of ethics to
politics, and accepted coercion as a necessary instrument of social cohesion,
we can make no absolute distinctions between non-violent and violent
types of coercion or between coercion used by government and that which
is used by revolutionaries" (*MMIS*, 179).

Ramsey, who is often his own best interpreter, explicitly says, "All that I have ever written on the morality of war, I have been quite consciously drawing upon a wider theory of statecraft and of political justice to propose an extension within the Christian realism of Reinhold Niebuhr—an added note within responsibility ethics. There is more to be said about justice in war than was articulated in Niebuhr's sense of the ambiguities of politics and his greater/lesser evil doctrine of force. That "more" is the principle of discrimination; and I have tried to trace out the meaning of this as well as the meaning of warfare that Niebuhr never faced. Come to think about it, this may explain why I seem so alone in championing the recovery of the just war doctrine—since Protestant messianists rushed pell-mell to join forces with the new breed of Catholic messianists in jettisoning the elements of Christian political realism from their thinking" (JW, 260–61).

Therefore, like Niebuhr, Ramsey argues that pacifists cannot be involved in this cardinal feature of politics once we recognize that the use of power, and probably the use of force, are the *esse* of politics. "You never have *good* politics without the use of power, possibly armed force" (JW, 5). Armed conflict is an unavoidable feature of the life of nations, so that the attempt to banish force is not only impossible, but more important, if we are to be moral, undesirable (JW, 50). "Genuine sectarian Christian pacifists" therefore prescind from the history of nations insofar as they prescind from the history of warfare. As such they "radically even if still selectively withdraw from politics" (JW, 263). If they are to be consistent, they must cease advising citizens and statesmen concerning what they should do in the restraining function of their offices.

It seems to be a no-win situation for me as a pacifist to be caught between the Methodist Bishops and Ramsey. By arguing against the kind of Constantinian pacifism the Bishops seem to have embraced, I appear to conform to the stereotype that pacifists must withdraw from political engagement. If I argue against Ramsey's characterization, then I seem to have joined up with the Bishops. It thus becomes my task to suggest how badly the Bishops understand the political implications of Christian pacifism as well as to indicate my disagreements with Ramsey.

Both the Bishops and Ramsey remain committed Constantinians. By that I mean they argue presuming that Christians not only still rule but can and should rule. It is therefore their task to show that Christians can develop an ethic sufficient to sustain a civilization. This is a particular temptation for Christians (and even more for Methodists) in America, where the idea has long persisted that there is a close connection between Christianity and democracy. The Bishops clearly assume that if they could simply get the

American people concerned about the nuclear crisis the issue would be resolved, ignoring entirely that our current situation has little to do with the good or evil will of either the American or Russian people as people.

Ramsey is much less susceptible to such a criticism, having little illusion about the capacity of democracies to control their wars. Yet Ramsey's argument that just war is generated and sustained by Christian love would seem to commit him to the view that those civilizations and correlative states that are not formed by Christian presence cannot sustain the ethos necessary to make war an option for Christians; or that those states of modernity that have explicitly rejected their Christian heritage cannot command Christian conscience to fight in their wars since Christians can have no confidence that the wars of such states can be kept limited. Perhaps that is why Ramsey asserts in *The Just War* "that no Christian and no man who loves an ordered liberty should conspire with communism in coming to power. (This is a different question of whether it is possible to serve God in a communist land.)" (*JW*, 449).

It is extremely important that Ramsey not be misunderstood here. He is not uncritically siding with liberal democratic regimes against communism. Ramsey is no cold warrior, or, even if he was or was tempted to be, his moral reflection is better than his political views. Indeed, given Ramsey's criticism about our society's adherence to the "heavenly city of the eighteenth century philosophers," he might well argue as a political judgment that it is increasingly hard to see how Christians can support Western societies' wars since they too cannot be kept limited.

More important than Ramsey's political judgments is his understanding of the role of nations. For while Ramsey maintains that "the nations also are creations of God; and the world would be poorer without any one of these creatures of His," he always insists that it is not nations but "first persons" that the Christian is concerned to serve through the strange work of love called war. As he says, "Christian love, expressed in principles of justice that suit it, does not first of all fashion itself in terms of regard for the fabric of community life, nor does Christian faith, going into political action, take effect primarily in fidelity to the recuperative powers of an enemy nation. Not nations but first persons are elevated to citizenship in another city and to a destiny kept between themselves and God which prohibits any man from reducing them wholly to the status of means useful in attaining some historical goal in the life of the kingdoms of this world. The neighbors and companions God has given us are primarily persons, within the separate national traditions" (*JW*, 163). (I suspect that this is the reason that Ramsey abhors communism, because such societies, as policy, reduce persons to means. Of course, it can be asked if "liberal societies" do not in fact do the same thing in the name of the "protection of the individual.")

Thus Ramsey qualifies Robert Tucker's "initially profoundly true contention that no matter what are the higher values the state serves, and despite the hierarchy of values in human political communities, a 'realistic' statecraft nevertheless holds true if only the state is a *necessary* condition to these higher human goods" (JW, 417). Tucker, as Ramsey notes, does not deny that the state may be only an instrumental value inferior to those it serves. Tucker, nonetheless, maintains that when the chips are down we must recognize or at least act "as if the state were the supreme value" since it is the necessary condition to the higher values it serves (JW, 417). Yet against this, Ramsey argues that not only is the state today an insufficient condition for protecting the values it serves, but "because of the nature of the weapons into the use of which the politics of the nation-state today may extend, 'necessities of state' may quite readily contradict, frustrate, and destroy those very values which the state exists to serve. The state as necessary condition may become destructive of the goals to which it is ordinarily a condition" (JW, 418–19).

Therefore Ramsey's whole program for recovering the authentic function of just-war logic is to remind us that the states *raison d'état* depends on the state's *raison d'être*. Of course the latter, as we saw above, is how the state provides the institutional means to protect the neighbor from unjust attack. Moreover, Ramsey is unafraid to draw the radical conclusion from this: "In an age when the state in seeking its safety can prove positively disfunctional as a condition (and not only insufficient), resort must be made again directly to those unconditional values and finalities which before or ordinarily warrant the exercise of statecraft *as if* the state were the supreme value" (JW, 419).

But one must ask exactly what are the concrete implications of this for our current situation. Even if the broad outlines of Ramsey's defense of the state as the embodiment of love-transformed justice are correct, we must ask if the concrete states we have in fact fit Ramsey's moral condition for sustaining a just war. My judgment is they do not. For example, Michael Quirk, in his "Just War, Theory, Nuclear Deterrence, and Reason of State" (*The International Journal of Applied Philosophy* 3, 2 [Fall 1986], pp. 51–59), observes that even though Robert Tucker has rightly argued that just-war theory and "reasons of state" are at odds with one another (particularly in deterrence, as a logical outcome of "reason of state") this does not in itself mean the pacifist wins the argument by default. Credible deterrence may involve the intention to do evil for the sake of the good, but it does not follow that unilateral disarmament as an alternative to deterrence is thereby morally justified.

To explore this issue Quirk considers David Hollenbach's argument that pacifist and just-war critics of deterrence have a penchant for drawing too "abstract" public-policy implications from their moral theory. Hollenbach agrees that deterrence is incompatible with just-war theory but argues it is a mistake to make moral theory syllogistically dictate policy. A moral policy for nuclear weapons, according to Hollenbach, must forbid their use, recognize the moral presumption against threatening to use them, and take all and only those specific policies that make their use unlikely. Thus Hollenbach provides a conditional warrant for deterrence rather than opting for the Catholic Bishops' strategy of approving nuclear possession without an intent to use as an interim necessity for negotiating their elimination. As Quirk points out, Hollenbach's point is that in a world of suspicious nation-states pursuing a preferable option is only possible under the aegis of deterrence. The nation-state is not going to go away, and a moral deterrence policy cannot ignore this fact (54–55).

Quirk notes that Hollenbach, unlike Tucker, is not prepared to assert the supremacy of "reasons of state" since statecraft is still bound to adopt only those policies which make a moral state of affairs more likely in the end. But Quirk argues further that such a position takes too much for granted, and he stresses that the position of statespersons having to choose between evils is itself an evil one. It may be deterrence is necessary in an evil world, but this "begs the question of how the world *got* to be evil in a specifically nuclear way" (55).

In answering this question Quirk does not, as so often is the case, lay the blame at the door of science and technology, but rather he sees deterrence as a result of moral developments and their political correlatives that are unique to modernity. Drawing on the work of Alasdair MacIntyre, Quirk observes that the eighteenth-century intellectual project of "justifying" the ethical by appeal to universal laws rather than local traditions and the attempt to develop a nomological science of human behavior with the eclipse of small self-governing communities correlate with the rise of the nation-state as we know it. The result was the loss of any teleological framework for evaluating character as well as a destruction of forms of social life in which a pursuit of a good in common was possible. As a result, the role of the state was enhanced; it alone became the effective mediator between citizens and groups now trained to think of politics as a conflict of interests.

Against this background the moral mandate of the modern nation-state is the safeguarding of the interests of its citizens—interests now understood to be the satisfaction of arbitrary desires that require no justification other than that they are "needs" of some people. "The moral legitimacy of the modern state, therefore, is exhausted in preserving 'interests' so defined, aloof as it is from forging a shared vision of the good life. Unless a state can preserve these given interests it does not deserve to be. And in such a state, deterrence is at home. The state in modern society is not, to use Habermas' terms, a forum for *practical* deliberation of the worthiness of ends: it is a *technical* apparatus for preserving as many 'given' interests as possible. But such interests cannot be pursued unless the individuals of the polity are alive to pursue them. The legitimacy of the state, therefore, hinges upon its ability to maintain its individuals' ability to pursue their given interests—to remain alive. The legitimation of the modern nation-state demands this ability, and in a world of hostile nuclear powers, deterrence emerges as the chosen technique for realizing it. Deterrence thus becomes politically attractive. But it is as important as it is depressing to remind oneself that this attraction is characteristic of one sort of historically contingent social arrangement, and that in other possible forms of social life it might only be an unattractive but an unintelligible institution" (56).

The reason I have dwelt on Quirk's analysis is not only because I think his analysis is largely right, but it helps me contrast my views with those of the Bishops and Ramsey. For I simply do not believe that Christians need any theory of the state to inform or guide their witness in whatever society they happen to find themselves. For the Bishops to say that the state is a natural institution as well as required for restraint of evil may be theologically useful, but it does little to help us understand how to negotiate how to live as Christians in America. For Ramsey to develop just war as a theory of statecraft is useful, but again it does not help us know how this or that state may command our loyalties, given the form of order it provides along the Jericho road.

As a pacifist, I—no less than Ramsey—believe I am called to be of service to the neighbor, and in particular the enemy-neighbor. But I do not assume the state as such is a special creature of God provided for that service. In that respect I think I assume a deeper realism than Ramsey (or Niebuhr). Like the Christians who gave us the New Testament, I simply believe that the state—which can take the form of any group that provides order, from Augustine's robber bands to North Carolina to the United States of America—exists. I do not need a theory about its existence or its penchant for making war. Rather what I need is a community schooled with skills provided by a truthful account of the world to give up the power to interpret the perversities and possibilities of the states that come and go.

In his review of *Against the Nations*, Milbank makes a penetrating criticism of my position that is relevant to this argument. He notes that, because of my suspicion of rationalist accounts of natural law, I fail to do justice to contingent "points of contact" between Christian convictions and the world. (I have at least tried to correct that through my book *Suffering Presence: Theological Reflections on Medicine, the Mentally Handicapped, and the Church* [Notre Dame: University of Notre Dame Press, 1986].) Milbank thinks this may explain a "perplexing feature" of my essays. "This is that while, for the most part, Hauerwas rightly insists that secular war and violence persist because they belong to the 'imaginary' of the nation-state, because they are written into the plot of its survival; at other times he seeks to underwrite this narrative ontology with its naturalistic ontology which claims, after Rousseau, that conflict is endemic because of the tension between the short-term perspectives of individuals with regard to need and fulfillment and the long-term collective interests of groups (the same logic then applies to nations). But this claim merely translates the logic of political economy which posits separate individuals with private, non-intended means and public, heterogenous ends. Its universal pretensions are falsified by many 'primitive' societies. By upholding these Hauerwas is, in fact, endorsing a liberal position against the general run of his argument and he is only being 'anti-liberal' in the Niebuhrian sense of 'realism about group behavior'— this despite the fact that Hauerwas, writing about Niebuhr in this book itself, has already excellently divined this sort of anti-liberalism as liberalism of the purest water. One can only explain this anomaly by saying that Hauerwas seeks somehow to lock secular power into its power-character in an 'eternal,' ahistorical way, beyond its narrative contingency. This then seems to negate in an arbitrary, naturalistic fashion the import of certain 'points of contact' between the Christian and the secular. Hence one can conclude that any tendency to an *unnecessary* 'sectarianism' that may be suggested by Hauerwas' nuclear discussion arises not, as one might assume, from his 'narrativism' but rather from a residual Niebuhrianism which inserts a naturalistic schism between 'group-power reality' and the 'love-reality' of the church. Yet this is completely at odds with Hauerwas' innovative thrust, for the Rousseauist considerations would tend to limit *also* the possibility of the ecclesial community achieving anything of its own genuine reality in time and space. To a universal natural tendency it would only be able to counterpose transcendental considerations about the rights of spiritual 'persons' whereas Hauerwas wants to say that the church embodies a different, but equally historical, logic to that of the state." Milbank notes that even though this "residual Niebuhrianism" makes only a brief appearance in my work it may be that this residue is why I fail to make substantive social recommendations.

Even though in an obscure footnote in *Against the Nations* I made the extraordinary claim that pacifists cannot exclude the possibility of God's making possible a nonviolent state (208), I think Milbank's criticism is largely on target. In *Against the Nations* I failed to follow out the implications of my historicist perspective by attributing to something called the "state" the peculiar configuration of power and violence that is characteristic of the liberal state. That is why the analysis offered by Quirk is so important—it reminds us that the peculiar challenges facing us are the working out of historical alternatives that are not forever written in stone. Moreover, this issue helps emphasize the importance of issues I discussed at the end of section 3. For it is now clear why pacifism is not so much an "ethic" for judging war as it is the skilled habits of a community that make it possible to give nuanced interpretations to the changing character of war and the state. Such interpretations are the way the church begins to make "substantive social recommendations," as they provide the means to free the imagination from the idea that war is a necessity. Christian pacifism is true even in a world at war, but Christian pacifists are not committed to believing that war is an inevitable aspect of the human condition.

As Milbank confesses in his call for "substantive social recommendations," little is to be hoped for from the state as the state. But yet we can and should hope that on the edges "of the frontier" between church and world we will find ways to make violence less likely. Of course that is why I stress so strongly the importance of a recovery of the significance of charity-informed virtues. For our only alternative to violence is finally dependent on people formed by the love that moves the sun and stars so they would rather die than do a wrong.

Therefore when I called for the Methodist Bishops to address the church first, I meant for them to remind us of the kind of skills we need to be a people capable of discerning the illusions of a world that has created nuclear weapons. Wesley's rules, of which Ramsey rightly reminds us, are to my mind not a bad place to begin insofar as they ask us to take on those personal disciplines and charitable acts that create the distance necessary for us to recognize the demonic. Only as the church becomes that kind of disciplined community do we have any possibility of discerning those forms of secular life that may provide us the opportunity to be of service to the neighbor.

Because I don't think I need a theory of the state and/or a justification for Christians' assuming secular vocation, I find Ramsey's insistence that I make clear my understanding of the relation of nonviolent or passive resistance to nonresistance less than urgent. I do so first because I do not believe that Ramsey's characterization of Jesus' teaching and life as one of absolute "nonresistance" is correct. Jesus' cross was a confrontation with powers that was meant to defeat those forces that hold us to the presuppositions of the old age. He did not restrain from fighting them—and that includes their embodiment in Rome—but rather refused to fight them on their terms. That is why he was victorious as he submitted to their power, trusting in God to vindicate his faithful service. This, of course, we believe to have happened through the resurrection, thus making it possible for us to fight as he fought in service to the neighbor—that is, nonviolently.

Connected to Ramsey's insistence that "non-resistance is incommensurable with any form of resistance" is his penchant for summarizing Jesus' ethic by the principle of disinterested or impartial love. This kind of monistic characterization fails to do justice to the interrelation of Jesus' life and his teaching. Jesus is not the teacher of love, but rather he is the herald of the Kingdom whose life makes possible a new way of existence. I am certainly not denying that love is an important way to describe that existence, but it cannot be isolated in a way that seems to make necessary our asking how such nonpreferential love can take the form of violence in the name of preserving ordered liberty. When the question is put in that way, it no longer seems necessary that Jesus ever lived or died.

As Ramsey nicely notes, the pacifist avoidance of violence is not correlative with the assumption that violence is the name of a set of actions that are inherently evil. Rather the pacifist avoidance of violence is derived from the positive discovery that God has made possible a new way of resolving disputes through the life of Christ that we find continued in the church. That is why the pacifist feels so strongly the contrast with the state. For the state is where violence is legitimated in the name of good. The Christian does not deny that often the state does some good through its violence; the point is rather that the sword of the state is outside the "perfection of Christ."

So the issue again comes back to eschatology. For as I suggested above, the pacifist and the just warrior theologically understand the aeonic tension differently. For the pacifist, at least the kind I wish to defend, there is no reason we should be forced from the world of the state simply because we disavow violence. There is no reason we should not use just-war claims as a means to try to help the state be as nonviolent as possible. But finally, it must be admitted that the rationale for pacifism is not our ability to make the world less violent, but rather our various assessments of Jesus of Nazareth, who taught us to trust in God's kingdom and not in ourselves.

This does not mean that the pacifist makes nonviolence more important than justice—that is, aid to the neighbor. The pacifist is not forced to disavow a concern for, as well as an involvement in, the attempt to secure justice in this context or that situation. The alternative of violence or acceptance of injustice is as false as the assumption that all state action partakes of or depends on violence. On the contrary, most states do not depend on violence for many of their activities; and even more strongly, when violence is used it tends to be antithetical to the social good being pursued.

So I do not agree with Ramsey that nonviolence as a political strategy is war by another means. That does not mean that I think all forms of political action that take nonviolent form are therefore justified. Rather it means that all genuine politics—that is, politics in the sense of conversation necessary for a people to discover the goods they have in common—are nonviolent. Rather than denying the political, nonviolence requires that we become political by forcing us to listen to the other rather than destroy them.

Let me again illustrate this by drawing on Quirk's article. He borrows an example from the life of Mahatma Gandhi that is often cited by partisans of just-war theory and "reasons of state" alike to indicate the moral bankruptcy of Gandhi's politics of nonviolent resistance. Shortly before his death, Gandhi was asked how he would deal with an atom-bomb attack. He said he would not go into a shelter but would "come out in the open and let the pilot see I have not a trace of evil against him. The pilot will not see our faces from this great height, I know. But the longing in our hearts that he will not come to harm would reach him and his eyes would be opened" (56). Quirk notes that most people think this is no answer at all, thus revealing the fatal theoretical point against pacifism: that it prohibits statespersons from overcoming certain types of unscrupulous and energetic evil without recourse to violence.

Yet this interpretation of Gandhi misses the point because it makes Gandhi's social thought a compendium of tactical advice rather than "a vision of a different sort of political life where the use of violence is so antithetical to the shared identities of citizens that a violent political victory is a contradiction in terms" (56). Gandhi was aware that, given the scenario, nonviolent tactics would be ineffective, but that is irrelevant because he endorses, as Quirk observes, a different criterion of "effective" political action (56). The modern nation-state cannot conceive of an effective political act that dissolves the policy itself, but Gandhi could. He could because he refused to conceive of politics except as the creation of communities whose common good excludes violence. The extinction of such communities is not an unqualified tragedy since such communities do not believe the violent life is worth living.

Finally Quirk observes: "What distinguishes Gandhi's pacifism from most contemporary versions is his wise conviction that pacifism as a political program is effective only in the context of a specific way of life, a community which is in part constituted by a belief that no violence is ever justified. It should be clear that modern states—built as they are around managerial rather than practical rationality—preclude such communities on the national scale" (57). But there is no reason for pacifists and/or just warriors to think such communities cannot therefore exist—we just need to have our imaginations freed to consider alternatives to the nation-state.

We must act, as Yoder describes the early Quakers doing in Pennsylvania, to create processes that make questions of violence irrelevant. As Yoder notes, that the Quakers failed had as much to do with the fact that their charter was from the crown, which insisted on fighting on the western frontier, as it did with their failure to live faithfully (*Christian Attitudes to War, Peace, and Revolution: A Companion to Bainton* [Goshen Biblical Seminar, 1983], p. 274).

Even though I have refused to respond to Ramsey's demand to clarify nonresistance and nonviolent resistance, I (and I think Yoder) am in his debt for noting that pacifist reaction on this matter is often distorted by our responding to the charge of passivism or irresponsibility. In fact, Yoder agrees with him in a passage Ramsey did not quote from *Christian Attitudes to War, Peace, and Revolution* (436–37). Yoder responds to a student's question about effectiveness by saying, "The longer I look at the question of effectiveness, the less I trust that way to put the issue to be of any help. The longer you look, the more you see dimensions of the question that change the definitions of terms, so that it is less clear what you are asking about. Do we mean short range effectiveness or long range effectiveness? Do we mean guaranteeing a certain result, or just contributing to a statistical mix in which the chances of a derived outcome may increase by so much that you might come out with something? The interplay between an ethic which *cares only about faithfulness* regardless of cost, and another that is purely pragmatic is a caricature that nobody really will stay on one end of for long. The person who says, 'You must give up some of your scruples in order to be effective' is still saying that because the goal for the sake of which to be effective is *in principle* a good goal. So the argument which takes the clothing of 'principles versus effectiveness' really means this principle versus that principle. It really means that that goal, for the sake of which I want you to give up other scruples, is so overridingly important that those other things are less important. That's an ethic of principle. It differs only in that the choice of which things you are willing to give up for which other things will change. Likewise, the people who say 'You must simply be true to God' . . . and 'let the heavens fall' . . . really say that because of a conviction about Providence, trusting that if the heavens fall God has another better set of heavens ready, which is part of the process, so even that is not thumbing your nose at results. It's trusting God who gave us the rules to know more about the results than we know. So I am increasingly convinced that the debate between the effectiveness ethic and the principle ethic is a false debate."

In the same way, I think Ramsey is right to call a halt to the charge that those who adhere to just war are trying to make "history come out right." At least he is right given his account of just war, which certainly does not appeal to lesser-evil consequences alone to justify and limit its use of violence. What we must both admit, pacifist and just warrior alike, is that there is no way either of us can avoid the tragic fact that at times there is no alternative than to have other people, who may not share our conviction, suffer for our commitment to nonviolence or to just limits upon the use of force. Speaking for pacifists, we are pledged to serve the neighbor by doing all we can to create contexts and habits that make peaceable communities possible. But we cannot deny that in certain circumstances it may be necessary to watch others die unjustly—which is surely harder even than envisioning our own deaths. The only thing worse would be our failing to witness to our brother and sister that God's love took the form of a cross so that the powers that make our world so violent might be defeated. That our death and the death of others might be required if we are faithful to that cross cannot be denied, but it would only be more tragic if we died in a manner that underwrites the pagan assumption that nothing is more tragic than death itself. Without such an eschatological conviction, how the pacifist serves the neighbor in a violent world cannot help but be unintelligible.

SO WHAT SHOULD THE BISHOPS HAVE SAID?

Having come to the end of my substantive response to the Bishops and Ramsey, I still have to say what I wish the Bishops had done. I wish they had begun with a confession of sin in which they called on the church to ask God's forgiveness for our failure *as a church* over these many years to discipline ourselves so we might be capable of making a witness for peace. I am well aware that by God's grace extraordinary witnesses about war and peace have been raised up from out of Methodism. But they were isolated and heroic rather than what might have normally been asked of Christians.

I would have then wanted our Bishops to address the issue of war rather than nuclear war. The Christological, eschatological, ethical, and political issues raised by the exchange between Ramsey and myself should have been brought to the attention of the Methodist people. Given the lack of discussion in the church about these matters, I think it would have been presumptuous for the Bishops to have taken a position either as pacifist, in spite of the General Conference resolution, or as just war. The time is not ripe for positions. Rather what is called for is for the Bishops to exercise their pastoral office as teachers helping the Methodist people recover the resources of the past that we might better think about today.

To better help the Methodist people explore these issues, it would have been useful for the Bishops to suggest how various policy alternatives would look from the perspective of just war and pacifism. The kind of alternatives suggested by Ramsey would have helped people understand better the costs of taking a just-war stance. In exploring the pacifist alternative, perhaps the Bishops should have spoken not quite so much to the point of military policy, but that in itself is an open question. Once the church is clear that it is a pacifist church, if it is going to be such, there is no reason it cannot urge the government to take what is judged to be the least destructive stand.

Intrinsic to the pacifist tradition, or at least the one I have tried to defend, is the overriding commitment to the process of conversation by which a community discovers its true goals. I should like it if the Methodist church could speak as a peace church, but we are clearly not that. So in this time between the times, we must take the time for that part of the church called Methodist to discover its heart and mind about the issues of war and peace. If we do that, we just might recover a sense of being a people of the new age who believe that even in the face of the threat of nuclear destruction God has given us the time to be a people of peace.

I am indebted to Mr. Michael Cartwright and Mr. Greg Jones for criticism of this and earlier drafts of the epilogue. Of course, my greatest debt is to Paul Ramsey, who not only read and energetically criticized my earlier draft, but who graciously suggested I should write this epilogue. His sense of fairness and colleagueship in this and throughout his life will, I hope, continue to serve as an example for all of us who attempt to be theologians.

Appendix
A Political Ethics Context
for Strategic Thinking

S INCE my assignment is to say something theological on our topic, I
shall do so boldly—by espousing instead the virtues of a *mythopoetic*
understanding of the actors and the interactions going on in the
international system.

First, a rapid sketch of insights into and perspectives upon mankind's
existence in political communities is to be gained from looking at ourselves
through the synoptic "pre-historic" culture myths in the first book of the
Hebrew Bible named "In the Beginning" (*Genesis*, the Greeks called it).
Then, assuming that context, in the latter part of this chapter I shall come to
a closer analysis of the moral ingredient of weapons-policy. In taking this
approach, I am confident that the *furor theologicum* cannot add a single
decibel to the noise of the solemn assemblies of strategic analysts and their
opponents when they are gathered together for any other purpose than
conviviality. Into that noise I wish rather to intervene with the outlook and
onlooks afforded by our common heritage of mythopoetic political wisdom. Then I undertake to *specify* certain norms or limits or guidelines that
should govern the conduct of nations in their ongoing encounters beneath
or, as it were, on the underside of the truth those myths contain.

I need hardly remind you that, according to the Bible, human history
began in an act of distrust and disobedience against the original harmony of

Excerpted, lightly revised, and reprinted with permission from *Strategic Thinking
and Its Moral Implications*, edited by Morton A. Kaplan. Copyright 1973 by The
University of Chicago Center for Policy Study. I continue to receive requests for
copies of this chapter, which was never widely circulated.

life with life. Then came economic and other arts such as hunting, tilling the ground, dwelling in tents, building cities, herding cattle, forging instruments of bronze and iron, making brick with bitumen for mortar, playing the lyre and the pipe. All this under the shadow cast east of Eden by the angel's two flaming swords which suggest that all those human endeavors must be based upon the implacable verdict that there can be No Returning to the original harmony. The great Augustine was later to remark that Cain, the first murderer, founded the earthly city; that the relative justice of all kingdoms, empires, and nations has in it some element of fratricide.

However that may be, the account of mankind's pre-history moves rapidly on from arts and crafts to a story that must mean to say something about the division of mankind into political units.

The story of the Tower of Babel is a myth of the origins of a world of countervailing constellations of political power, which we call the multinational system. There was a time before time and before inter-state politics when "the whole earth was of one language, and of one speech." Then men said to one another: "Go to, let us build us a city, and a tower whose top may reach unto heaven; and let us make us a name, lest we be scattered abroad upon the face of the whole earth." It is sad to report what happened to that original "parliament of mankind," at a time (if we are to believe the tale) more auspicious than any time since, for the unity and just ordering of all who dwell upon the face of the earth in a community of unconflicted purposes. The Lord (so the report reads) confounded their language, that they might not understand one another's speech—"and they left off to build the city" (Genesis 11:1–9).

The political life of mankind goes on perennially under the sign of the verdict at Babel. Each man calls to another, every group or nation calls to the others, as they build in every age the City of Man. Each tries to persuade the other workers to adopt his plan for the entire edifice. They strive for vision of the whole, and for agreement. Excellent plans are these, some better than others. But it turns out that each thinks he is making the plan for the center of the tower. Each man and nation has "a view of the universal," but none has "the universal view" he claims. There is confusion of tongues, confusion of justices. Mankind's project of attaining by his own devices an enduring harmony has been subjected to the divine overruling.

Will not a student of international politics be forced to conclude that his science can give us knowledge of only the life of mankind on the underside of that divine decision; that the interaction of nations and alliances goes on as if the verdict at Babel had not been set aside, nor can ever be set aside by such things as "people to people diplomacy"? It looks as if "systems anal-

ysis" must necessarily be what Wohlstetter calls "opposed-systems analysis."

Albert Wohlstetter explains his choice of this term as a process of eliminating
worse synonyms: "conflict-systems design" appeared to suggest that the goal of
study is to generate conflict; "conflict-worthy systems," after the analogy with "sea-
worthy," was more accurate, but more awkward, while "systems analysis" did not
call attention to the *specific* or peculiar nature of the international system [cf.
Babel!]. "Theory and Opposed-Systems Design," in Morton A. Kaplan, ed., *New
Approaches to International Relations* (New York: St. Martin's Press, 1968), p. 22.

The division of mankind into separate peoples by the confusion of their
language should be combined in one thought with the next episode in
mythopoetic understanding of the pre-historic, perennial ingredients of
mankind's historical existence. The verdict at Babel only suppressed man's
"vertical" aspiration to high heaven; it did nothing to allay the resulting
chaos on the horizontal plane. The confusion of tongues, taken alone,
meant that what happened was bound to happen: that by the time of Noah
every imagination of the thoughts of men's hearts was only evil continually,
and God repented that he had made man on the earth, and it grieved him at
his heart (Genesis 6:5–6). Notwithstanding that grief came the first and
only destruction, save for Noah and his family; and—the *telos* of the entire
story—the covenant God established with Noah, insuring the preservation
of the world ever thereafter, over which the rainbow of God's promise was
set. This was the covenant establishing *government*, and determining its
nature, mission, and means. The imagination of man's heart remains the
same (8:21), but against that was set a power commissioned by words that
are harsh but which, however refined, contain a nugget of truth about
government that is not apt to be expunged: "Whoever sheds man's blood,
by man shall his blood be shed, for in the image of God made he man" (9:6).
That mandate, properly exercised, insures that never shall there be any
more a flood of destruction over the earth. The rainbow in the clouds is a
sign that God will remember his covenant with Noah, and so long as
government carries out its mandate the waters shall no more become a flood
to destroy all flesh (9:15).
   What holds the waters of God's wrath in place is what holds in place the
imaginations of men's hearts: the covenant legitimating government for the
preservation of the world. Enforcement and power are an *alien* work of his
mercy.
   I shall interpolate here a view of the inter-state system that can be
attributed to one branch of Christendom—the Lutheran—and the inter-

pretation of the myth of the covenant with Noah given by one contemporary Lutheran theologian, Helmuth Thielicke (*Theological Ethics, Vol. II: Politics* [Philadelphia: Fortress Press, 1964]).

The Noachian covenant means that, among fallen humanity, "arbitrary and unlimited power is to be restrained and limited by further power" (p. 482). That means that power must be limited by further power, else it is bound to become arbitrary and unlimited. The world now is subjected to the "law of move and countermove," as the only ordinance in which can be preserved on earth a tolerable human dwelling place. By the covenant with Noah, according to Thielicke, "the world between the fall and the judgment is not only empowered to set up states; it is *condemned* to do so" (p. 441). I would rather say, condemned to be able to do no more than govern one another through an opposed-system in which power is restrained by further power.

What are we to say about the dreams that mankind may be able to construct international institutions—a world government, no less—that will put an end to the law of move and countermovement on which since Noah the inter-political systems of mankind have been based? In Lutheran religious language, Thielicke replies that men are not to be saved, the primordial division of mankind is not, cannot, and—for that matter— *ought* not to be overcome by "'good works' in the institutional field."

Such good works in the construction of international institutions are fundamentally misguided, they are to be compared with the project at Babel, if the goal is to nullify or remove the limitation of power by further power which presently preserves the world from, on the one hand, chaos, and on the other hand, tyranny. A world government in any imaginable future would be the world hegemony of a single power or a conspiracy of two, three, or more powers. Its justice would not be the justice other men seek. As Thielicke says:

> Because a world state would have no immanent limits in other sovereignties and state egoisms, because it would not be subject to the necessity of self-restriction known in state pluralism, it would have a tendency towards unbridled upward expansion. The arrogant tendency of man and his institutions to want everything would take a vertical turn once it was satisfied on the horizontal level. (p. 439)

To prevent that vertical turn toward unbridled upward expansion, the law of move and countermove, the limitation of power by further power, was established for the good of mankind always. Opposed-systems analysis has, clearly, good warrant in the mythopoetic interpretation of politics we have been examining.

The behavior of actors in the international system (an "opposed-system," or a scene of at best cooperating adversaries or adversarial cooperators) is subject to the law of move and countermove. Today this is called the "action-reaction syndrome." That is not something one can break out of, or wish away. Move and countermove characterizes disarmament races no less than armament races (unless either is a product of programmatic, inflexible rashness). The law of move and countermove governs quiet diplomacy or summitry; international monetary encounters or positioning a nation's power somewhere in the world where it was not before; taking it to the United Nations or not seeking United Nations' warrant; unilateral reconciling initiatives in the expectation of appropriate response or unilateral challenges over some issue deemed vital in the face of possible unwanted response. All this in the context of the rule that power can finally be limited only by further power. This a religious man—who has not been bemused by one or another of the utopianisms or gradualisms of the modern mentality—will understand to be God's secret way of preserving the world as a human dwelling place until the end-time (whatever that may be).

All action in the action-reaction syndrome is fitted to reciprocal action. The anticipated response affects the action put forth, even if not altogether determining it. The actor takes into account how he is expected to act and, as well, how he expects the other to act. He expects not only a range of responses from the other; he also expects the other to take account of expectations playing upon him and, as well, the response he in turn expects. Each interiorizes the other's expectation or his probable response in the effort to act fittingly. Interaction is, therefore, always based on *interpretation* of the actions coming upon the agents from one another. Without *some* interpretation of the action calling for response, a system of interacting actors would be a field of forces. The interplay would be automatic. We would not call it "action," unless the interacting actors were engaged in reciprocated self-involving interpretations of one another's moves and countermoves.

This is familiar, formal analysis. I want to go further and fill that formal analysis with different contents. We can set side by side two different, contrapuntal interpretations of the actions coming upon us in the international system.

The first is familiar to contemporary strategic theorists. Its elements are game theory, scenarios, and other heuristic attempts to anticipate the subsequent behavior of other actors in the "opposed" international system. Above all, the referents of appropriate response are the moves that are open to an opponent, his capability and not first of all his wishes or intentions. I am most familiar with Thomas C. Schelling's brilliantly abstract analysis of the nature of action in a conflict-system. Each actor, he writes, is guided only by "what he expects the other to do, knowing that the other is similarly guided, so that each is aware that each must try to guess what the second guesses the first will guess the second to guess and so on, in the familiar spiral of reciprocal expectations."

Thomas C. Schelling, *The Strategy of Conflict* (Cambridge: Harvard University Press, 1960), p. 87. This embraces a possible downward spiral of the Methodist Bishops' "invitation to reciprocity" as the nations move—everyone hopes—toward disarmament. So disarmament must always be arms *control*.

Whatever the varieties of detailed calculation or range of particular options, still there is a *generalized interpretation* of all the action going on. One is not altogether at sea when he asks: What would I do if I were he wondering what he would do if he were wondering what I would do if he were I . . . ? One is not in an uncharted sea because he is an actor in an opposed-system. That is our common *interpretation* of the action coming upon us, and which we are called upon to put forth; and it is a correct interpretation of all state-action.

This defines the essential nature of the actions of states in the international system. Such an interpretation of the actions coming upon us may not be the best imaginable, but still the political interaction of groups is far different from the behavior of herds or anthills precisely by virtue of the intervention of our conscious interpretation of the system's interaction in which we are involved.

There is another vision, another interpretation of the ultimate meaning of the responses called for by the interaction in which we find ourselves involved. This generalized interpretation of the meaning of interaction, response and responsibility, was the one espoused by the prophets of Israel. It defines the attitude and action of the "church" in contrast to the "state" as an actor in the opposed inter-state system. (Anyone reluctant to use the concept of the "church" may in the alternative substitute his preferred non-denominational interpretation of the *primary* meaning of the actions coming upon us in the international system when this is supposed *not* to be an opposed-system: he may mitigate or supplant that opposed-system by assigning interpretative primacy, for example, to "the longings of the entire human family" as the meaning that defines the appropriate response and responsibility of states.)

It is, in any case, remarkable how contrapuntal H. Richard Niebuhr's theological analysis of responsibility or of appropriate response is with that of the strategic theorists. The latter are dealing with the action of states; Niebuhr, with the attitude, action, and fitting response of those who interpret all the action coming upon us in terms of something more ultimate than the opposed international system. Those whose referent is primarily to some source or meaning or interpretation of all the circumambient action that is transcendent of conflict constitute what I call the "church." Those whose referent is primarily to a conflicted or opposed source or meaning or interpretation of the action calling for response constitute the "state." I suggest, therefore, that the subtle analyses of appropriate response offered by H. Richard Niebuhr and by, say, Thomas C. Schelling are mirror images of one another.

In a sentence that is almost a paraphrase of the quotation (above) from Schelling, Niebuhr writes of "an agent's action as response to an action upon him in accordance with his interpretation of the latter action and with his expectation of response to his response; and all this in a continuing community of agents" (*The Responsible Self* [New York: Harper and Row, 1963], p. 65). Action is not only response; it is response made "in anticipation of answers to our answers." So, for Niebuhr, responsibility means an agent "staying with" his action, accepting its consequences in the form of reactions, looking forward in a present deed to some replying deed, to continuing interaction (p. 64). Moreover, action is always "response to *interpreted* action upon us" (p. 61; italics added); otherwise, we would not call it *action* but "stimulus-jerk" instead. Systemic action-interaction, therefore, entails some "large pattern of interpretation" (p. 62) which chiefly determines whether the questions and answers, challenges and response, are fitting.

That is Niebuhr's *general* theory of responsible action; and it has remarkable similarities to some theories of action advanced by strategic theorists.

But then Niebuhr writes that the great world religions, and Christianity in particular, "make their impact on us by calling into question our whole conception of what is fitting—that is, of what really fits—by questioning our picture of the context into which we now fit our actions" (p. 107). That is to say, the great world religions call into question our whole conception of what is fitting by calling into question the ultimacy of the opposed-system as the pattern of interpretation into which we now fit our actions. What is the fitting response depends on what is happening, upon the meaning of the action coming upon us to which response must be made.

Niebuhr's general theory of responsibility is activated and given content by an interpretation of God's action as the context in which all finite actors live and move and have their interaction. If, then, we wish here and now to respond appropriately we should so act as in every action to respond also to the action of God. In particular, the Israelites were the people whose calling it was "to see and understand the action of God in everything that happens and to make a fitting reply" (p. 67). This was the prophetic view of action/interaction. "The meet, the fitting response of Israel, must be to the divine intention in the first place, to the finite intention only secondarily. This means that the first response, the fitting action in the critical hour, is to be internal reformation; defense against Assyria is the secondary thing (p. 169). Israel was called upon to respond to the actions coming upon her from Assyria so as in that action to respond also to the action of God.

A classic example of the collision in interpretations between a trust-system (the "church") and an opposed-system (of states) is the meeting between the prophet Isaiah with Ahaz, king of Judah, one day when the latter was inspecting the waterworks of the city of Jerusalem ("the conduit of the upper pool") to see whether the city could withstand the northern kingdom of Israel which had made an alliance with Syria to threaten the city. When King Ahaz refused to believe the prophet's assurances that the attack would not come to pass, or that the threat was no danger because "within three score and five years shall Ephraim [the northern kingdom] be broken, that it be not a people," Isaiah gave him this sign of the trustworthiness of the action in all the action the king was preparing to face: "Behold, a virgin shall conceive and bear a son, and shall call his name Immanuel. . . . For *before the child shall know to refuse the evil, and choose the good,* the land that thou abhorrest shall be forsaken of both her kings" (Isaiah 7:8, 14, 16).

True enough, according to the prophetic account of these long-ago events, the attack did not come. Instead, God called up Assyria as "the rod of my anger . . . the staff in their hand is my indignation" to break the power of the Israelite-Syrian alliance; and then he called up Persia to break the power of Assyria, to "punish the fruit of the stout heart of the king of Assyria and the glory of his high looks," for he meant not to be an agent of the divine mercy but it was "in his heart to destroy and cut off nations not a few" (Isaiah 10:5, 12, 7). Yet, without any stolen Jerusalem Pentagon Papers, we may suppose that—unless for reason of the indolence of a petty official-dom—King Ahaz acted responsibly within an opposed-system and repaired his waterworks. The proof the prophet gave him—itself future—signified a deliverance scores of years later through the providence of the God worshipped in Jerusalem overruling the present threatening actions of states by still-greater powers. Perhaps that was a fitting context of action here and now—for the prophet. Meantime, however, another context determined the fitting response needed here and now by the king. The waterworks of the walled city, of course, were not finally trustworthy. Inherently that system could last for only a few years, unless replaced by second- or third-generation defenses, including alliances (which the prophets counseled was no way to respond in trust to the action of God in all the action coming upon the tribes around Jerusalem). Jerusalem was saved, not by the waterworks but only by a miracle (or by a plague in the besieging army) when under Sennacharib the Assyrians came down like a wolf on the fold, his cohorts gleaming in purple and gold; and its defenses were finally overwhelmed by the Persians.

Niebuhr, of course, was first and foremost a theologian, not an analyst of the international system. As a theologian he was concerned to draw out the implications of a radical monotheism. This meant that whatever happens to us could not, for him, be rightly interpreted as issuing ultimately from animosity, finally from an opposed-system, from a realm of destruction (unless we are careful). However unrighteous may seem the actions coming upon us in a finite system, there is good in whatever is happening; the universal Being, the center and source of all existence and action, is according to His good pleasure working out the good for all beings. Therefore, all our self-defensive ethics, our relative evaluations fitted to seemingly ultimate finite action-systems, should be subjected to "the continuing and great correction." So said the prophets. Or again Niebuhr: "No matter how responsible I may be in my various roles as member of societies and holder of offices, I am not a whole responsible self until I have faced up to this action [the action of God in all the action coming upon me in my office], interpreted it, and given my answer " (p. 125).

As also a theologian, I believe the truth Niebuhr affirms, but not what, simply by omission, he may seem to deny or underrate, namely, the need for independent analysis of action in the opposed international system. I think it is true to say that Niebuhr's entire thought is that of a theologian of the church—of a trust-system. Whether the centered self is characterized by trust (interpreting all the existences that surround it as beings to be relied on, showing confidence in life as one moves about among the living) or by distrust (moving with wariness among the living, interpreting the cirumambient action as possibly inimical) was for him a decision concerning

whether "the inscrutable power by which we are is . . . for us or against us."
Such "faith as trust or distrust is inexpungably personal" (pp. 118–20).
That alternative constitutes the self "as one responding self amidst all the
responses of the roles being played" (p. 123).

I admit that the foregoing seems evidence enough for saying that Niebuhr
contrasted the trust-system and any opposed-system as radical opposites,
or else that he absorbed the political roles and offices being played into the
trustworthiness of the power that constitutes the religious man as one
responding self. It seems to show—to say the same thing in other words—
that the church as the trust-system of a radical monotheism can erode or
displace the distrust international system, or at least radically alter the
interpretation validly to be given to the action-interaction going on in the
inter-state system.

That would be to forget that Niebuhr meant always to be a theologian of
the church, reflecting always upon the action of God in all finite action. He
can perhaps be faulted for *not* having analyzed the peculiar nature of various
other action-systems. He can probably be faulted for failure to analyze the
relation between a Christian's trust and the wariness required by his office,
or between "the church" as a trust-system and "the state" as an actor in an
opposed-system. Still it would not be a mistake to attribute to Niebuhr the
view of the great Augustine, that the *civitas Dei* (founded on the love of God)
and the *civitas terrena* (in which there is ever some of the venom of
fratricide) are inextricably *intermingled* to the end of time. In any historical
period, the Christian is a citizen of *both* Cities. That is, he lives by trust and
he also lives in a system of distrust. He responds, in all action coming upon
him, *also* to the action of God; he moves with confidence among the living.
He responds, in all action coming upon him, *also* to the action and the
anticipated action of a companion in an opposed-system; he—at least in his
official actions—moves with wariness among the living.

Two extremes only are excluded by this understanding of trust-systems
(the City of God) and distrust-systems (the City of Man) as *intermingled*
throughout history and in all politics. One extreme would be the view (born
of a generally Manichaean worldview, or perhaps in recent times the
product of a rigid, crusading anti-communism, or currently a product of an
ideological anti-colonialism or anti-imperialism) that the actions to which
we must respond are wholly inimical, that the opposed-system is entirely a
system of animosity, that actors in it are alone in a wholly hostile world, that
there *are* no discoverable common interests between opponents, that the
system is a scene of illimitable conflict. The other excluded extreme is the
view that a trust-system can replace constellations of an opposed-system in

the political life of mankind. That seems to have been the outlook of Isaiah in his confrontation with Ahaz, and of all the prophets against the kings of Israel—who may have been very bad kings but who nevertheless are much maligned in our religious heritage, which transmitted only the record of those who rightly bore witness to an ultimate referent of trust.

Theologically speaking, in the history of biblical religion, the coming of Christ, universalizing the religious mission of Israel, is supposed consequently to have desacralized politics and depoliticized the sacred, and to have brought about in the minds of western man a *distinction* between the inseparable, intermingled two Cities. The notions of a complete trust-system and a complete distrust-system are, of course, ideal types. The reality of any state-system (and of any actual churches) is closer to the intermingling of those two ideal types. But this means that a second extreme is excluded from a proper perception of the affairs of men, namely, the idea that, historically and politically, opposed-systems can be supplanted by a trust-system, that the kingdoms of this world can *in time* become the kingdom of God and his Christ, that the shape of the offices and the responsibility of statesmen can now be construed in those terms. Such is the power of the prophetic tradition that contemporary Jews and Christians sometimes speak, in their address to politics, as if statesmen should act on the assumption that the existing opposed international system is a disappearing reality. That is an indefensible confusion of categories, of "church" and "state"; and it amounts to a vain attempt again to sacralize politics.

To intervene, as I must, in the dispute between the strategic theorists and their opponents, I must say that the strategic theorists are falsely accused of the first error—of interpreting the opposed international system as a system of illimitable animosity—and this seems plausible to their opponents because they in turn commit the second of the above errors: they suppose it to be possible to replace the inter-state system with one or another secular version of the City of God, a system of trustworthy international actors acting trustingly.

· · · · · · · ·

According to St. Luke's Gospel (14:28–33), Jesus once told a parable in which he distinguished two sorts of worldly wisdom, two sorts of cost-accounting. The first was that of the builder of a tower who had a manageable calculation to make, a problem entirely corrigible to "instrumental reason." He should sit down first and *count the cost*, whether he can complete the tower, lest he be mocked by those who see the incomplete foundation which he is not able to finish. The second sort of worldly wisdom is that of a king "going to encounter another king in war." He sits down first not to count anything quantifiable but to "*take counsel* whether he is able with ten thousand to meet him who comes against him with twenty thousand." The disconcerting fact is that one can succeed even in such a venture, as Cromwell showed in his decisive battle against the forces of King Charles.

The international system may be a Babel, but it is not a tower. In politics there are no completed towers, and therefore no ascendancy of technical reason in cost counting. There are no "solutions," no completed edifices. There are only "outcomes"; and few outcomes conclusively prove that taking counsel was wise. If prudent counsel leads the king to conclude that to go further with the encounter that is in process would not be worth the likely costs, he sends an embassy while the other king is still a great way off to sue for a better outcome from among the available alternatives. *Peace* this is called in a world whose continuing political reality is one of incessantly encountering powers.

Statesmen are simply not tower-builders. Technical reason cannot encompass the encounters in the midst of which statecraft must be fashioned. An arbitrament of arms cannot be compared with completing a tower (or any part of one), nor can military policy be compared with planning a building. Disarmament conferences in this world of move and countermove are kings *taking counsel.*

· · · · · · · ·

Reinhold Niebuhr's assessment of Pope John XXIII's encyclical *Pacem in Terris* was a summary judgment upon dreams of exiting from the world of move and countermove by reforming the United Nations, a new world order, or perpetual peace in some more distant time. "The difficulty with this impressive document," Niebuhr wrote (*Christianity and Crisis*, May 13, 1963, p. 83), "is that the Church absorbs some of the voluntarism of the social contract theory, which underlies modern liberalism, and speaks as if it were a simple matter to construct and reconstruct communities, not by organic processes of history but by an application of 'the sense of justice and mutual love.' . . . Augustine's criticism of Cicero's universalism, by calling attention to the confusion of tongues in the community of mankind, is not heeded. The encyclical is thoroughly modern in many ways, but particularly in breathing a Pelagian, rather than an Augustinian, spirit."

Enlightenment peacemakers in the churches today may be compared to the prophet Isaiah, who finally got around the establishment research institutes in Jerusalem and gained access to King Ahaz outside the city inspecting the waterworks; and who then could only give him this sign: a virgin shall conceive and bear a son; and before he reaches the age of discretion to know good from evil, some other action in the international system will intervene against those actions or alliances coming upon you to render your action now unnecessary. Only contemporary prophets do Isaiah one better: before too many years, they say, and without a miracle, the opposed-system of move and countermove can be supplanted by something else—a trust-system, no less.

Jesus Christ was the expected Messiah, but he was not the Messiah the prophets expected (as Reinhold Niebuhr wrote). He was not the sign Isaiah gave King Ahaz, but he was the unveiled meaning of that sign. The peace of Jerusalem was a walled peace, Jeru-*shalom* its name, *ytshlm*. The root word may be from *Salem*, where Melchizedek was king (Gen. 14:18, typically interpreted in Heb 7:1). The coming of Christ desacralized politics in general and the prophetic-kingly-priestly politics of Israel in particular, calling a people to pilgrimage, thereby creating a *saeculum*, worldly affairs not specifically religious or messianic in nature. The Methodist Bishops' understanding of *shalom* is more Old Testament than New, if indeed it is not mainly Enlightenment messianism without an expected Messiah. The peace of the New Jerusalem, however, will be a peace without walls, and we are reliably informed that the King of Glory does not need to inspect its waterworks or keep them in repair. The peace of Christ is tied to no time or place or nation. We do not yet live in that Kingdom.

THE MORALITY OF WAR AND OF DETERRENCE

However, if it is an error to suppose it to be possible ever to replace the inter-state system with a system of trustworthy international actors acting completely trustingly and trustworthily, it is equally an error to suppose the inter-state system to be a system of illimitable animosity to which there are no inherent systemic norms (except the norm of quantifiable rationality) which are applicable to the actors and that govern the achievement of their purposes.

For one thing, animosity and conflict are not, unqualifiedly, the characteristics of the system or its interactions. I do not understand strategic theorists to mean any such thing when they speak of international relations as an opposed-system. While there exists no collectivity in which Cain, the fratricide who founded the earthly city, exists no longer, there exists no collectivity in which Abel, progenitor of the Founder of the heavenly city, does not also exist. Empirically, this means simply that statesmen are called to action in the midst of the *unpredictabilities* of other collectives and their leaders. The nation-state is surrounded by arbitrariness on all sides. That is to say, by autonomous actors; not everywhere by hostility and by enemies. The other is a stranger and a source of independent action affecting outcomes for oneself. Since identification can pass between man and man, between collective and collective, only through structures that must be based on the organic development over time of common heritage and community, never upon social-contracting wills alone, the other in the international system remains a potential enemy. He is only that, but he is that.

Responding to the *unpredictability* of the other collective's action requires, *among other things*, preparedness, threat, and perhaps an actual use of force. This requirement does not assume universal hostility or the universality of conflict. Let us have an end to mongering about stereotyped anti-communism or cold-war mentality or generalized animosity as errors of which the strategists are accused. Let us have an end to simplistic appeals that they should look out on the world with rosier expectations. One should prepare for *some* of the worst *not* because of jaundiced vision, but because of the unpredictability of action in the inter-state system. That cannot be replaced by choosing a better picture of the world; it does not vary with tinted glasses. Public officials must be prepared for the unpredictabilities. This means they have to attend to the *capabilities* of other actors, and not to their hypothetical intentions or even first of all to actual better intentions they may have. The system is characterized by the unpredictability of autonomous actors and reactors. That defines the minimum morality of responsible action within the inter-state system. It is the unpredictability, and not the generalized animosity, in all the action coming upon us that makes another's capability (or some of "the worst") one ingredient among the anticipations of appropriate response.

For another thing, there are demonstrable political ethical "rules of practice" to which action and interaction must conform, or which set its outer limits. Since the actors are peoples (or their governments) who have purposes—the chief of which is to continue to be a people able to effectuate their (however variable and divergent) purposes as a people—these rules of practice are *systemic* rules. An analysis of the opposed international system which abstracted from that purpose would be an incorrect account of the action going on in that system. There is a substantive interpretation of statecraft and of the purposive interactions of nations exhibited and summarized in the "just-war theory." Formulated as statements of the justifications needed for resorts to conflict, this body of teachings also expresses an understanding of the strivings going on among interacting collectives by other political means. For this reason, I describe the criteria of just war as *systemic* requirements, and *not* an external ethics vainly imposed. If the just-war theory was a product of western ethics, it is nevertheless a proposal concerning the very nature of the international system.

The political ethical limits and determination of justice in war's conduct and in deterrence policy I have elaborated elsewhere. Readers who do not know this literature are my loss. That loss cannot be repaired here. I can only summarize certain theses which I have, I believe, proved elsewhere *in extenso*. The following are conclusions which I believe are demonstrable in any sound ethical reasoning about politics and warfare.

1. There are two principles governing determinations of *jus in bello*, the just conduct of war as an instrument of national policy: (a) the principle of discrimination or the moral immunity of non-combatants from intended direct attack, and (b) the principle of proportion or prudence, or the requirement that costs in destruction accepted and exacted be warranted by benefits there is reasonable expectation of gaining. Always and everywhere, of course, there have been violations of both requirements; and, in past wars, only extensive violation of the second caused political resorts to violence, by under- or over-reactions, to lose their objective. I have shown that, apart from peripheral violations (that is, so far as the central design of war is concerned), the principle of discrimination is today—in the nuclear age—equally important in keeping uses of violence related to choiceworthy political objectives. Both the moral immunity of non-combatants from deliberate direct attack and the test of costs/benefits are today clearly—so far as concerns the central war—inherent laws of war as a possible instrument of national policy. So I call them both systemic requirements of encounters of purposeful uses of power in the international system.

2. Still there are *two* principles determining *jus in bello*; these are related but *separate* principles; both apply, and neither subordinates or absorbs or exhaustively interprets the other. A violation of the moral immunity of non-combatants from direct attack need not be in its consequences disproportionate or imprudent or disoriented from political purpose. This is true only of the central war in a nuclear age; there the two "rules of practice" of *jus in bello* converge; an actual war with our most powerful weapons in violation of the principle of discrimination cannot advance the measured political purposes of any people in the international system. The more common error today, however, is the rhetoric which identifies the principle of discrimination with the principle of proportion, which describes any seeming *or actual* disproportionate destruction as "indiscriminate" destruction. This is loose thinking and loose language. The two principles remain separate ways of assessing *jus in bello*.

3. I have shown that in rightly understanding the "moral immunity of non-combatants from deliberate direct attack" there are at least two terms that must be made clear and kept clear, and which should never be confused, if we are rightly to distinguish discriminate from indiscriminate

acts of war. There is, first, the meaning of combatancy/non-combatancy. There is, second, the meaning of deliberate direct attack. Unless these terms are clarified and kept clear, the simple and not so simple physical destruction of non-combatants (past an unspecified number) will erroneously be taken to mean they have been directly attacked; and the principle of discrimination will be regarded as a test that can be quantitatively violated. I have shown that it is *not* possible to violate the principle of discrimination by numbers or amount of destruction. Only the principle of proportion *could* be so violated; and proportionate defense or *protective* justice always concerns more than the *amount* of the costs.

4. The meaning of "combatancy/non-combatancy" is a function in some measure of military technology in any epoch; it is certainly a function of how the nations and their forces are organized for war. The meaning of "non-combatants," those who are morally immune, is *relative* in the sense that it is *objectively* determined by the manner in which the nations are organized for war, the technology with which they can wage war, the contours of war in any epoch. I omit here proofs that the distinction is one that can validly be made under any organizations for war. Suffice it to say that the problem of distinguishing between combatants and non-combatants, between forces and civil life, is tractable whatever an epoch's military technology or posture—under any other assumption than the politicizing and militarizing of everyone in a society, including the inmates of homes for the retarded, as "fighters" in a nation's cause. Only an absolute totalitarianism such as the world has never known could justify total war, or the obliteration of the combatant/non-combatant distinction, even though the latter is *objectively relative* to how the nations are organized for war.

The meaning of "deliberate direct attack" is another matter. It is a matter of the intention of acts of war, of their direction or thrusts in the world, of their targets and objectives, the planned design of the war to be executed. From the *objective relativity* of the meaning of "non-combatancy" it cannot be concluded that the meaning of "deliberate direct attack" is *subjectively relative*, or a mere function of actual or foreseen destruction. One cannot conclude from destruction wrought to what was intended and directly done. A great part of the deaths and damage may be collateral, though foreseen. That could be a violation of proportion, while not of the moral immunity of non-combatants from direct attack; or it may be neither.

This unpacking of the principle of discrimination can be expressed in the carefully drawn language of the Vatican Council, which said: "Any act of war aimed indiscriminately at the destruction of entire cities and of extensive areas along with their population is a crime against God and man himself. It merits unequivocal and unhesitating condemnation" (*Gaudium et Spes*, par. 80). That statement, as such, does *not* condemn as politically immoral actions which physically destroy cities, areas, populations. It rather condemns acts which "aim indiscriminately at" such destruction. To understand the moral immunity of non-combatants from deliberate direct attack, and the possible acceptability of their collateral destruction, one has only to get to know the difference between "aiming indiscriminately" at populations and "aiming discriminately" at legitimate (combatant or military) targets. Discrimination in acts of war never meant *attacking* only combatants, never *attacking* non-combatants. It certainly never supposed they are or could be *separated*. It means rather to forbid *directly* attacking non-combatants, to forbid aiming indiscriminately at everyone alike. To acknowledge the force of this requirement, and abide by it, one does not need to know *who* are non-combatants or *where* they are. One only needs to know *that* there are non-combatants (even only inmates of homes for the retarded) to know that he should limit his targeting to *known* legitimate military targets while limiting circumambient damage as much as possible. So long as to this measure the distinction between combatant/non-combatant is objectively tractable relative to any organization of the nations for warfare, the meaning of the immutable principle that acts of warfare should be aimed discriminately can be given content. So also the meaning of "collateral destruction," permitted but only if what is at stake in the encounter is great enough.

5. I have shown that the morality of war's conduct and the morality of the deterrence of war cannot be separated. Whatever is wrong to do is wrong also to threaten, if the latter means "mean to do." If aiming indiscriminately in actual acts of war (or in fight-the-war policies) is wrong, so also is threatening indiscriminately aimed action wrong to adopt in deter-the-war policies. While, of course, actually to do an evil deed for the sake of supposed good to come is a different wrong—and, we may allow, a far greater wrong—than simply to threaten seriously to do that action for the sake of good to come (deterrence), still these two things are qualitatively cut from the same cloth. To put the point bluntly, if counter-population warfare is murder, then counter-population deterrent threats are murderous. The question, therefore, of the ethical justification of deterrence depends crucially on a question of fact, or of plannable policy: namely, whether the only *effective* deterrent must be suspended from the meant mutual threat of ultimate indiscriminate destruction. If so, then deterrence is irremediably a political immorality, even though to carry out the threatened indiscriminate destruction would be a different species of murderousness, and of course a far greater wrong *of its kind*.

6. Finally, I have drawn attention to the fact that modern warfare (wheth-

er by this we mean nuclear war or sub-conventional war) becomes disproportionate, that is, disoriented from the capacity to effectuate political
purposes that are worth it, sooner than it becomes indiscriminate (since the
latter is a matter of the aim and direction of acts of war and varies with
military technology and the nations' organization for war). This fact, I
further argue, provides grounds for a radically different analysis of a feasible
deterrence and consequently of the moral justifiability of a possible deterrence, which I call "graduated" deterrence—in contrast to deterrence that is
"suspended" from the ultimate and whose effectiveness is supposed at all
lower levels to be indivisibly connected with a conditional willingness to
involve that final political immorality. Since I deny the necessary depen-
dence of the deterrence we need upon seriously threatening the indiscriminate destruction of populations, I argue for the morality of the deterrent
possession of nuclear weapons. Of this, more later.

In light of the foregoing we may ask what are the imperatives for strategic
thinking for the 1970s. One of the tragic results of our Vietnam agony and
of anti-militarism feeding off of increased awareness of the vast funds
needed to meet our domestic problems has been that the intellectual energy
still needed to subdue the paramount military problems of a nuclear age
was drained off; that political scientists' advice to government became as
confused as the general public; that, today, nuclear posture is expected to
stand unreconstructed until abolished by mutual agreement; and that the
slight beginnings in the 1960s toward putting the immoral, anti-population
use of nuclear weapons in a class by itself as something never to be done in
war or meant for deterrence came to a halt. Instead, graduated and flexible
response, and schemes that might be equally or more costly for further
decentralizing and putting intended indiscriminate destruction out of commission in war and in deterrence, came to be regarded as efforts to "save
war" or to save America's interventionary role in the world. Instead of such
moves, we ought rather—it was said—to conclude strategic agreements to
stop the costly arms race and so release the resources to save our cities.

The result has been that at the beginning of the 1970s the United States
adheres even more firmly to a policy of minimum or finite deterrence. Our
power at all other levels of war and deterrence is more and more challenged
or outstripped, and even the possible vulnerability of our nuclear forces is
tolerated for the sake of strategic disarmament treaties to come. It is difficult
to tell the difference between editorials on strategic questions in *The New
York Times* over the past two or three years and Dulles's "more bang for a
buck" policy. The only significant difference seems to be that, while Dulles
believed that nuclear threats could be used at times and places of his own

choosing to deter war at all lower levels and as an instrument of particular political policies other than the deterrence of nuclear war, the *Times* seems to believe the costs of keeping up to date in nuclear technology can be stopped by treaties at times and places and under conditions of its own choosing without full reckoning, public acknowledgment, or advocacy of the need for and cost of battle- and deterrence-needs of other sorts at other levels. That Dulles also omitted.

The upshot seems clearly to be a return (if that is the word for it) to the most politically immoral nuclear posture imaginable, namely, Mutual Assured Destruction. That is to say, we are further away than ever before from the abandonment of the intentional anti-population use of nuclear weapons at the heart of deterrence, their likely use at the planned end of the scale of nuclear war, or from the "first use" of nuclears against massive conventional attack. (There is no way to renounce the latter except by conventional sufficiency.) I would say that the major imperative for the 1970s is that these issues must again be addressed with the maximum concern of strategic, moral, and political reasoning, so that—if at all possible—we may reverse the devastating effects of the Vietnam interlude in confirming our policy commitments to total counter-people war and deterrence at the nuclear level. The Vietnam war, plus domestic tumult and the native aversion of the American mind to the steady acceptance and use of political power and the need for strategic thinking, have caused us to become committed to, morally, the most unacceptable defense and deterrence policies.

It seems to me that in the ABM debates a good many strategic analysts have performed well in calling the attention of citizens and government to the necessity of protecting the non-lethal end of our nuclear missiles: the invulnerability of bases and systems. I state this as an opinion, without any particular competence or right to hold it *in my capacity as a moralist.* In that role-function, I do not make technical proposals or *particular* war-designs—neither war-making nor war-stopping judgments (a self-denying ordinance I wish many of my fellow churchmen would impose upon themselves in their offices, whatever be their views as citizens). Still I have about as much personal certitude concerning the need for ABM defense as I am certain that a small group of Britishers were correct when early in the nuclear age they began to worry about the fact that Great Britain's deterrent forces were planes motionless on open airfields, and from that went on to establish what became the Institute for Strategic Analysis at the University of London. (The RAND Corporation's struggle to convince the U.S. Air Force of the same point is a matter of record.) Myself, I am rather proud of the fact that many of the people involved in that first move toward strategic thinking—which has resulted in a center most esteemed for its objectivity and rationality—were Christians who for many years had participated in the international affairs department of the British and the World Council of Churches. That bit of history is, by contrast, evidence of our present plight in which ethical considerations on the one hand and political considerations on the other have come to occupy separate worlds.

Churchmen's abdication of their responsibility for this is not my concern here; the responsibilities of strategistic analysis *are* of present concern. And so I return to the moral and political imperatives upon strategic thinking in the 1970s. This is simply that more attention should be paid to the lethal end of our missiles, to the ethico-political limits governing targeting both in war and for deterrence, and not solely to the question of maintaining the invulnerability of bases.

There is at least as much evidence—I judge there is far more evidence— of a continuing intellectual effort to turn away from indiscriminate warfare and from deterrence founded in principle on the meant targeting of populations among strategic thinkers than there is in public opinion generally, in the press, or among academic or church liberals. The ethico-political imperative I am talking about, therefore, only accents a tendency, a line of thought, that is already there among many who have thought long and hard about the relation of arms and men, between armed forces and a political society, between armaments and the political purposes they are meant to serve.

Thus, Donald G. Brennan of the Hudson Institute points out that the acronym for Mutual Assured Destruction is MAD (*The New York Times*, Op-Ed page, May 24 and 25, 1971). We ought not to regard such a policy (today renamed "strategic sufficiency") as the most peaceful, stable, secure, cheap, and generally desirable arrangement. If that commonly accepted doctrine were true, the cheapest and most efficient way to achieve it would be for the nuclear powers to mine each other's cities. Such a system is technically feasible, and far safer and more likely to work than missile deterrence. Brennan's *reductio ad absurdum* argument is that, "since a mined-city system is clearly the best way to achieve a MAD posture, it follows that a MAD posture as a goal is itself fundamentally absurd—it is, indeed, mad." A rational posture for providing for the common defense cannot be based on deliberately making us all hostages to enemy weapons; by creating "a system in which millions of innocent civilians would, by intention, be exterminated in a failure of the system." The mined-cities "thought experiment" is enough to show that there must be something

wrong with the complete reversal of the relation between arms and the body
politic which happens when we institutionalize mutual assured destruction
as a way of life. In the structure of Brennan's analysis, it seems to me, it
matters little whether "sufficiency" is obtained by few weapons or many; it
is the posture, the targeting, that is wrong. Instead of being "busily engaged
in forging a permanent Sword of Damocles," to hang forever over our heads,
our efforts through SALT talks as well as military systems initiative should
be to hold down (and redirect?) offense, reduce (and redirect?) our threat,
and to make defense as effective as possible. While Brennan allows that we
should be able to do about as badly unto the Soviets as they can do to us,
still the Defense Department should be more concerned with assuring live
Americans than dead Russians.

Now, it seems clear to me that, although the context of Donald Brennan's
argument is the debate over ABM defense, his mind is beginning to follow
the lineaments of a sound political ethics in regard to the lethal end of our
missiles as well.

Arthur Lee Burns's Adelphi Paper "Ethics and Deterrence: A Nuclear
Balance Without Hostage Cities?" (No. 69. London: Institute for Strategic
Studies, July 1970) is an explicit and stalwart effort to meld together
security considerations and the political ethical norms of the just war. My
plea is simply that strategic thinking has upon it the imperative to address
for the next decade the question of how what is morally right in war and
deterrence can be made feasible. This requires rejection of utilitarianism, a
rejection of "the old liberalism" which "has extemporized itself into contending unambiguously for peace by nuclear terror" (pp. 1, 2).

Burns, as I understand him, believes shared calculations of "unacceptable
damage" to be largely "chimerical" and "mere rationalizations for a policy
that, once adopted, came to be valued for its own sake" (p. 24). He proposes
instead the rule that military capability must be sufficient to "wreak such
destruction on the attacker *that neither its government nor any successor at all
acceptable to that government would continue to rule*" (p. 3, italics added).

That already begins to "lower the bid," and to suggest that present
deterrence postures may not be beyond human amendment. Even if they
should prove—or for the meanwhile prove—to be "beyond human
amendment," Burns wants it clearly understood that that fact would not
make terrorizing kidnapped hostages "any less evil" (p. 6). Even if *for the
present* there is only a choice between different immoralities, we ought not
to say that the "least immoral course" now available is "for that reason really
moral after all." One ought not "to devalue the moral currency" despite the
fact that there may be nothing as yet to spend it on (p. 7). In particular, the

meaning of *jus in bello* and in deterrence should not be degraded. "The traditional ethic," Burns writes, "of sparing non-combatants as a *prima facie* obligation is not reconcilable with making them hostages, and unlike utilitarianism it takes account of the intention and the intrinsic quality of an act of a policy, not *only* of the probable consequences" (p. 12); and he concludes: "I cannot see how a city-targeting strategy can possibly be reconciled with principles of the just employment of armed force, even though the threatened destruction of millions of non-combatants is by no means as evil as would be their actual destruction, and though the threat may deter war" (p. 13).

Burns espouses a policy of threatening to retaliate against armed forces only, including the most vital and vulnerable parts of nuclear forces. He contends that totalitarian regimes would regard the loss of whole armies (supposing they could be reached by the strike forces) as a graver threat to the continued existence of the regime than the destruction of a few cities, and to that state's security against conventional challenges by third powers; "the Soviet Union and China would be prepared to sacrifice some cities and industrial areas in order to preserve their conventional forces in effective strength" (p. 17). What objectives of policy (except, of course, the prevention of nuclear attack itself) could be worth the loss of the larger part of a nation's conventional power?

The same point was recently made by Professor Bruce M. Russett of Yale University, who wrote in defense of the feasibility of a "countercombatant" deterrent: "The Soviet Union's ability to defend itself from its neighbors, even the small and now much weaker states of Eastern Europe, would be destroyed. To make this particularly painful the United States might strike, with particular loving care, Russian bases and armed forces along the Chinese border. In effect, the penalty for a Soviet attack on the West would be Soviet impotence vis-à-vis their Asian neighbor."

Bruce M. Russett, "A Countercombatant Deterrent?: Feasibility, Morality and Arms Control," Conference on the Political Sociology of Arms Control, University of Chicago, Dec. 4, 1971; published under the title "Short of Nuclear Madness," *Worldview*, April 1972, p. 34.

I believe, however, that Burns is wrong in seeming to suggest that only totalitarian regimes might be deterred by threats to destroy the greater part of their armed forces, and in perhaps seeming to suggest callousness in a government that would value defense forces higher than a few cities. Nor, earlier, should we interpret Burns's replacing definition of "unacceptable

destruction" as "such destruction on the attacker that neither its government *nor any successor at all acceptable to that government* would continue to
rule" (p. 3, italics added) to imply a regime's unconscionable desire to
preserve itself in power. A perception of national values and an entire order
of a society's life would be at stake. Such a government would be serving a
people's resolve to be a people continuous through time in the international
system. If deterred by a real and grave threat to its armed forces, that
government would be preserving a cardinal condition on which the political society depends for its independence and continuous life in the world of
move and countermove.

There is good reason for any nation to regard the destruction of a great
part of its armed forces as a more serious threat to the political society as a
whole than the destruction of some part of the population. There is reason
to believe that speculation about an adversary's estimation of unacceptable
damage to its armed forces would be less chimerical than speculation about
the various estimations different societies and cultures would have of
unacceptable damage in cities exchanged. A real threat to an essential
ingredient in a nation's capacity for further independent action is a threat to
its life in the international system. Even so, John Locke argued for the
inalienable right of liberty on the grounds that a real threat to that is
tantamount to a threat against the life of an individual in a "state of nature."
". . . [H]e who attempts to get another man into his absolute power," wrote
Locke, should be understood to have "a design upon his life. For I have
reason to conclude that he who would get me into his power without my
consent, would use me as he pleased when he got me there . . ." (*Second
Treatise on Civil Government* [1690], Ch. III, par. 17). Similarly, a threat to
take away armed forces which are essential to continued independence is a
vital threat to any actor in the opposed international system. Not only
totalitarian regimes or calloused political leaders would so view it. Supposing enough of a nation's forces could be reached by the strike forces to
render it deeply vulnerable to less than nuclear attacks, that *would be* a
threat as serious to the integrity of a nation's life as, or more serious than,
the technical taking of certain hostage cities.

This was in fact the first of several elements in the analysis of a moral,
graduated deterrent which I proposed in the 1960s. I called it deterrence
from anticipated "counter*force* target destruction," plus additional elements
of a composite graduated deterrence system to be mentioned in a moment
(*The Just War*, pp. 248–58, 285–366; originally published in separate
pamphlets by the Council on Religion and International Affairs in 1963 and
1965). If Burns is correct in some of his suggestions, and especially Russett

in speaking rather of a "counter*combatant* deterrent," my expression was too loosely drawn—suggesting as it does a threatening posture *concentrating* on nuclear forces. But then I am a moralist whose business it is to try to indicate the *outer* limits of a possible moral deterrent if one has to go that far to find a feasible way effectively to limit war in a nuclear age. Just as positive law and civil rights provide closer definitions than natural law or natural rights, so it may be that a countercombatant deterrent (if we will but explore it and mount it) can provide a closer definition of an effective moral deterrent than a counter- nuclear-force deterrent. The latter might still remain "not unlawful" when measured by the principles of justice in war and in deterrence. It is my view that a counter*force* deterrent remains just according to the principle of discrimination; a counter*combatant* deterrent—if that is a feasible alternative or stress—may be required by the principle of proportion, or because it further minimizes destruction and risks.

I'd be happy, also, if strategic thinkers could come up with models or arrangements that do not need the other elements of my scheme of graduated deterrent: deterrence from a shared anticipation of collateral civil damage that is unavoidable, unintended, in no measure enlarged; deterrence from the ambiguity inherent in weapons that *could* be used against populations indiscriminately, or ambiguity in how an opponent *perceives* these weapons may be used; and, finally, deterrence from a "bluffing" manner in which these weapons are possessed. I now think that an input of deliberate ambiguity about the counter-people use of nuclear weapons is not possible unless it is (immorally) meant, and not a very good idea in the first place. But, again, I was marking off the outer limits of justice in deterrence, if this final ingredient were needed in crisis to prevent holocaust. But I gather that few experts today think it is a feasible "performance."

On June 14, 1982, *Newsweek* magazine published a feature entitled "What Is a 'Just War' Today?", by Walter Goodman. Relevant to the foregoing list of elements of a graduated and possibly moral deterrent is the following letter to the editor (shorter version published by *Newsweek*, July 5, 1982):

I am honored to have my name linked with that of Reinhold Niebuhr, America's greatest twentieth-century political analyst. Permit me, however, to make one important correction in Walter Goodman's account of my views ("What Is a 'Just War' Today?", June 14, 1982).

I did once argue (1965) that it is morally permissible for a statesman to go so far as to "bluff" about his intention to use modern weapons deliberately aimed at an adversary's society, if but only if that was judged necessary to deter the maximum war possible today. My reasoning was that (1) a military commander need not publicize his intention not-to-use weapons with this aim. *It is no violation of justice for him to keep military secrets (Thomas Aquinas). And (2) deceitfulness in any case is a lesser wrong than a murderous threat to destroy whole populations indiscriminately.*

Those arguments were insufficient, indeed disturbingly insufficient, within the year. The "bluff" was withdrawn from my analysis of a possibly moral deterrence. Again, my reasons were two: (1) one's real intentions (not to go to such use) will be found out; the "bluff" must fail to deter; and (2) even if our top political and military leaders were pure in heart, they must count on thousands of men in missile silos, planes and submarines to be conditionally willing, under some circumstances, to become murderers. One should never occasion mortal sin in another, tempt them to it, or enlist them for it.

The latter was the more important reason. It is never right to do evil, or to intend to do evil, that good may come. Moreover, the fact that an adversary did the wrong first by an indiscriminate attack, or may intend to do so, does not justify our doing the same wrong in the second place. These have been my unvarying beliefs about justice in the conduct of war or in deterrence.

Proportion is a different and a less basic principle than discrimination in the moral governance of the use of violence. A judgment of proportion (or of disproportion) is always a matter of political and military prudence. It was in this connection that I observed, "A threat of something disproportionate is not necessarily a disproportionate threat." No way does that suspend the prohibition of threats, seriously meant, aimed at entire populations.

As Luther remarked, war is like fishing with a golden net: you run the risk of losing a net worth more than the fish. This is true of disarmament as well. Statesmanship has no place to hide from the risks of disproportionate moves and countermoves. Our leaders are always about to have been right in their calculations—or wrong—as they go about preparing for defense or for disarmament. This is the essential thing to be said about political prudence (proportion). Nevertheless, a seemingly disproportionate venture in the direction of new structures to insure world peace may not be disproportionate—as I said of threats that deter.

But neither this statement nor the one quoted in your article weakens the prohibition of indiscriminate attacks and of counter-people deterrence. We ought never to do, or seriously threaten, or (by indiscriminately aiming at peace or disarmament) invite or occasion another power to "any act of war deliberately aimed at the destruction of whole areas and their populations" (Vatican Council II), or at their subjugation.

Paul Ramsey
Professor of Religion, Emeritus
Princeton University

I take it that Burns would not disagree with me that none of these elements of a possible deterrent—and I believe an effective one—would violate the laws of just war by *directly* threatening populations as such. Espousing "an assured second strike counter-resource reprisal only, " Burns says of it that "no threats to population need be explicitly uttered, no hostages explicitly taken"; and he concludes that "since, though you have the means, you have no intention of striking at his people, you appear to avoid the ethical dilemma of nuclear weapons" (p. 14).

Burns is modest enough in the claims he makes for what he attempts to demonstrate. A "policy of military-targeting only," he urges, "appears feasible for deterring *less-than-ultimate* attacks and attempted coercion" (p. 18). Repeating what I believe to be an exaggerated distinction between totalitarian regimes and *any* regime responsible for the safety of an entire nation, Burns writes: "If there is anything in my view that totalitarian regimes depend upon their conventional forces and value them no less than some cities, etc.; or if the loss of strategic facilities would threaten their power-political positions *without greatly increasing the risk of major nuclear war* [italics added]: then against a *less-than-ultimate* threat a nuclear response against military targets only may both promise to be effective and also escape the central moral dilemma" (p. 18).

But we must come at last to the question of deterring *ultimate* attacks, which Burns excludes from the effectiveness of his scheme. Here, on the matter of practicality, Burns rightly shifts from the principle of discrimination (non-combatant immunity from direct intended attack and from direct intended threats of direct attack) to the other principle of the just war: the principle of proportion, or the expectation of success, success measured— of course—by the preservation of societal values. ". . . One of the criteria of the justice of an employment of force is that there will be a strong expectation that the employment will *succeed*" (p. 19); there must be "a rational expectation that the means employed would achieve the proposed end" (p. 18). While altering *past* applications of that to say that against threats of *ultimate* attack a people today should be resolved still to resist by just means only, even though they perish (p. 19), Burns states his conviction that "no universal theory of global deterrence can pass the test" of final success in preserving societal values (p. 12). One "may not acquiesce in the committing of the certain evil of hostage-taking if it no more than probably averts a greater evil" (p. 25), namely, the destruction of both sets of hostages.

Here Burns incorrectly puts together in a supposedly quantifiable calculus of probability two separate, incommensurable criteria: the evil of hostage-taking and averting a "greater" evil of actual destruction. He seems to give primacy to the first prohibition only because averting the latter is uncertain. This contradicts his earlier statement that such threats can never be moral "though the threat may deter war" (p. 13). Shall we absolutize the prohibition of deterrent violations of non-combatant immunity? Or should we say that the violation of populations by deterrent threats is wrong only because saving them is not apt to result from that? Today the two principles governing a rational resort to political violence have in actuality (and in experience rehearsed in scenarios) converged on the same point. That is to say, while in past ages we morally should have known that it was never right to do wrong that good might come of it (although undoubtedly sometimes good consequences came of it), at the higher levels of violence in the nuclear age we now know that *no good can finally come* from doing, in the central war, or planning to do wrong that good may come.

He asks for calculations, if such are possible, and that the public in Deterrent States be informed in a rational manner "*by how much* the deterrent effect of our reasonably assured retaliatory nuclear force would be *reduced* if we were to commit it to avoidance of non-combatants," etc. (p. 25, italics added).

I think, by not much; or not demonstrably any at all, in view of the greater incredibility of threats the more destructive they become, given that the destruction is mutual. For these reasons, when first exploring the possible *feasibility* (which does not fall within my competence) of a moral, graduated deterrence (which does), I called attention to and took full advantage of a basic fact about modern warfare, namely, that war today becomes a *disproportionate* means to any substantive political purpose long before it need be judged to have become *indiscriminate* (if non-combatant immunity from direct attack is properly understood). This being so, if one starts from the bottom and moves upward in the scale, there would seem to be sufficiently powerful ways to persuade an opponent by the deterring effects mentioned above that do *not* give and take hostage populations or reverse the relation between arms and society.

To repeat: deterrence from (1) the perceived likelihood of unacceptable combatant or military target or nuclear force destruction, (2) the perceived likelihood of unacceptable collateral damage from quite discriminate acts of war in a nuclear age, (3) from the ambiguous possible uses of nuclear weapons, or from an irremovable perception as to their possible uses.

This seems to me to follow from an attempt to take seriously the just-war theory as an ethics intrinsic to the nature of politics and to a purposeful use of force, and not as an ethics externally imposed on a neutral and alien realm of behavior.

Many people appear to believe that the concept of just war implies some minimum agreement concerning "the moral order" and symmetrical adherence to it on the part of contending states. I should rather say that just war presupposes minimum agreement as to the purpose of states in a contentious system; an awareness that contention is not an end in itself, and may reach limits beyond which there are no substantive political reasons to go. All the just-war theory requires is acknowledgment that "action and reaction" is designed to serve one or the other common weal, that the common weal of either party ought not to be made subordinate to abstract success in moves and countermoves, and that there are limits of destruction beyond which there is no interest in going. That is to say, the just-war theory is an ethics of the opposed system *as such*; within the system there doubtless are also opposed political ethics.

Given the disproportionality of political resorts to violence sooner than their indiscriminateness, there appears to be a solution to the moral dilemma of nuclear deterrence. One need not suppose that deterrence is necessarily *suspended* deterrence, that all persuasive effects are indivisibly a part of and depend upon one's final willingness to threaten and to use the threat of attacks on whole populations.

Graduate deterrence must, indeed, threaten something disproportionate, since its virtue entails issuing a signal that one is willing to go to a level of destruction which is greater than what the cause is worth, politically, to oneself or to an opponent. If it is said that such an actual violation of the principle of proportionate good, threatened to another and accepted by oneself, would also always be a grave political immorality, three things can still be said in reply, while granting the facts to which the argument appeals. The first is that not every threat of something disproportionate is itself a disproportionate threat, certainly not when the good at stake is shared persuasive limits upon the escalation of war in a nuclear age. The second reply is that the issuance of threats of disproportionate destruction is ever the nature of deterrence under any conditions of warfare. One has to reject deterrence in general or in any war in order to reject this account of justifiable deterrence in a nuclear age. At the same time, it must be granted that herein lies in all ages the tragedy of war, namely, that threats of disproportionate damage, although proportionate to the end of deterrence, may in reality be disproportionately actualized, and on both sides (as in the politically disproportionate countercombatant destruction in World War I). But this is a question of the immorality of warfare that has lost its objective or become disoriented from it. It is not a question of the morality of deterrence oriented upon *its* objective. The third reply is that, of course, there is an obligation never to mean to do and accept damage disproportionate to political goals; but I suppose no military commander would calculate on actually doing any such thing. If these rejoinders have force, then graduated nuclear deterrence, based on the issuance of threats that might do disproportionate damage to an opponent's military forces, can promise to escape the moral dilemmas; and, as well, they promise to be effective in preventing all but the *ultimate* destruction—which cannot certainly be prevented by arrangements of military power that deliberately build exactly that into the scheme of deterrence itself.

Deterrence of the *ultimate* threat or destruction had better be left to the simple philosophic consequence of the possession of nuclear weapons (Kahn), the subjectively unintended consequence of the mere possession of these weapons. This is particularly the case since the attempt to do otherwise inevitably skews the planned use of military power in war or for deterrence at lower, justifiable levels, and sickens political resolution at levels of usable power by the thought of its indivisible connection with unusable power and politically purposeless and therefore largely incredible threats. While ordinary political and military encounters may be a matter of "minimax"-ing the outcome, it needs to be said quite honestly that, when it comes to the ultimate threat or destruction in a nuclear age, one cannot min the max or max the min. This is not only because military encounters often are not "zero-sum" games in which one gains what another loses, but because one can readily traverse the range of violence to which proportion (costs-benefits) applies as a criterion and soon comes to the point where there are only costs, no comparable benefits. After that comes not a "mixed motive game" but only "no motive" games. Continued intellectual effort to devise abstractly rational schemes for preventing the ultimate destruction that is finally unpreventable by any force (should the system fail and have to be used) can only skew needed effort to prevent the preventable. If we are to assume as an opponent—which we must do—a minimally rational decision-maker, we should assume that substantive political purposes inform his reason, and not alone "winning" in an abstract sorites of interaction mounting to a level of destruction well beyond the worth of any objectives he may have and which he properly sought by lesser, possibly deterrable or defeatable means.

One of the most thoughtful comments on the SALT agreements brought up the point about the superpowers' commitment to a MAD policy: "The limits on offensive weapons last only five years, while the treaty limiting defensive weapons is perpetual. Even with withdrawal and review provisions, this probably means the two sides are frozen forever into a system of mutual assured destruction. . . . Mutual assured destruction guarantees the utter devastation of both nations. Mutual assured destruction is probably the best we can do under present technology, though the pact outlaws defensive arrangements that might make it more stable. But if technological advance permits the defense of populations, might not we want to pick up that option? Are we sure enough to foreclose the question in perpetuity?" "Go Slow on SALT, Review and Outlook," *The Wall Street Journal*, May 30, 1972.

Arthur Lee Burns's description of the purposeful interaction going on in the international system is risky enough to any of the purposes of statecraft. ". . . It is necessary to all *political* interaction," he writes, "that those who interact put the ordering of their preferences at risk, endeavor to reorder the others' preferences, and remain in a position at any time to create a new object of preference or to apprehend such a new creation" ("Quantitative Approaches to International Politics," in Morton A. Kaplan, ed., *New Approaches to International Relations*, p. 171). That is an apt account of the world of political move and countermove. But one cannot without systemic violation of the nature of those ongoing interactions imagine that the prefer*ers* (the nations) should put themselves at mutual total risk, and not only the ordering of their preferences. Seriously meant counter-people deterrence can no more be an action within the life of the international system than suicide or meant threats of reciprocal suicide can be an act of life for individual persons. Both can be *done*, of course, as acts or designs; but both are contradictions of the moral terms on which each depends, of the goods such policies were supposed to serve.

Index